EurographicSeminars

Tutorials and Perspectives in Computer Graphics

Edited by W. T. Hewitt, R. Gnatz, and D. A. Duce

K. Bouatouch C. Bouville (Eds.)

Photorealism in Computer Graphics

With 118 Figures, 25 in Color

Springer-Verlag
Berlin Heidelberg New York
London Paris Tokyo
Hong Kong Barcelona
Budapest

EurographicSeminars

Edited by W. T. Hewitt, R. Gnatz, and D. A. Duce
for EUROGRAPHICS -
The European Association for Computer Graphics
P. O. Box 16, CH-1288 Aire-la-Ville, Switzerland

Volume Editors

Kadi Bouatouch
IRISA
Campus de Beaulieu
F-35042 Rennes Cedex, France

Christian Bouville
CCETT
Rue du Clos Courtel
F-35510 Cesson-Sévigné, France

ISBN 3-540-54265-5 Springer-Verlag Berlin Heidelberg New York
ISBN 0-387-54265-5 Springer-Verlag New York Berlin Heidelberg

Library of Congress Cataloging-in-Publication Data
Photorealism in computer graphics / K. Bouatouch, C. Bouville (eds.). p. cm. -
(EurographicSeminars)
Includes bibliographical references.
ISBN 0-387-54265-5
1. Computer graphics - Congresses. I. Bouatouch, K. (Kadi), 1950-. II. Bouville, C. (Christian), 1949-. III. Series: EurographicSeminars. T385.P49 1992 621.39'9-dc20 91-25900 CIP

Typesetting: Camera ready by author

45/3140-543210 - Printed on acid-free paper

Preface

The goal of this book is to present the most advanced research works in realistic computer generated images. It is made up of the papers presented during a Eurographics workshop that has been held in Rennes (France) on June 1990. Although realism in computer graphics has existed for many years, we have considered that two research directions can now clearly be identified. One makes use of empirical methods to efficiently create images that look real. As opposed to this approach, the other orientation makes use of physics to produce images that are exact representations of the real world (at the expense of additional processing time), hence the term photosimulation which indeed was the subject of this book.

The objectives of this workshop were to assemble experts from physics and computer graphics in order to contribute to the introduction of physics-based approaches in the field of computer generated images. The fact that this workshop was the first entirely devoted to this topic was a bet and fortunately it turned out that it was a success.

The contents of this book is organized in five chapters: Efficient Ray Tracing Methods, Theory of Global Illumination Models, Photometric Algorithms, Form-Factor Calculations and Physics-Based Methods.

The book begins with an overview on realistic imagery that discusses the main issues in radiosity and describes the most recent developments. The first chapter (Efficient Ray Tracing Methods) contains two papers that describe improved ray tracing techniques for animated scenes and parametric surfaces. The second chapter (Theory of Global Illumination Models) consists of three papers which develop the theoretical aspects of global illumination models. In the third chapter (Photometric Algorithms), two papers are presented. They both try to combine radiosity and ray tracing to cope with a wide class of photometric problems. The fourth chapter (Form-Factor Calculations) describes techniques aiming at efficient evaluation of form factors. The last chapter (Physics-Based Methods) gives examples showing how physics can be used to solve some rendering problems such as interference, simulation of area light sources, and light propagation through participating media.

Although some subjects have not been approached in this book, we think that it contains information that is helpful for both researchers and developers.

Kadi Bouatouch
Christian Bouville

Table of Contents

Chapter 5. Physics Based Methods

Color Plates

COLOR PLATES (John Wallace)

Plate 1. A steel rolling mill

Plate 2. Chartres Cathedral

Plate 3.
A Dutch interior after Vermeer

Plate 4. A vanity with reflected light

COLOR PLATES (John Wallace)

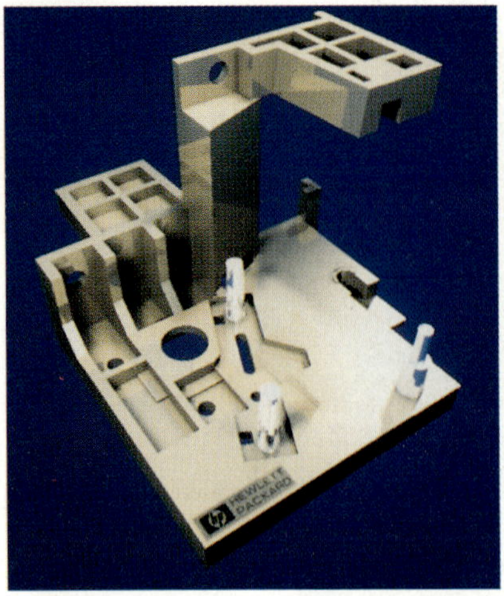

Plate 5. A CAD model

Plate 6. A boiler room

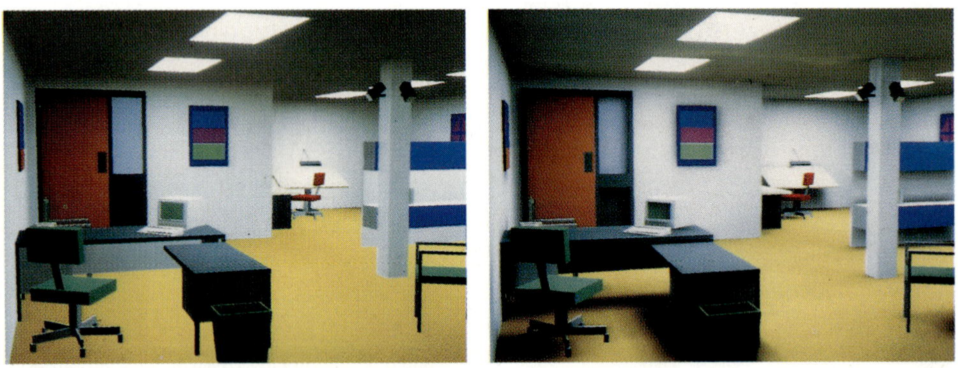

Plate 7. An office after one and 21 solution steps

COLOR PLATES (K. Murakami et al.)

(a) Initial image

(b) One object of one pawn moves

(c) Entire pawn moves

(d) The size of one object of one pawn is changed

(e) The light source moves

(f) The color of entire pawn is changed

Fig. 10. Model "chess" without shadow
The number of objects: 144
The number of the light sources: 3
The average tree size: 2.25

COLOR PLATES (K. Murakami et al.)

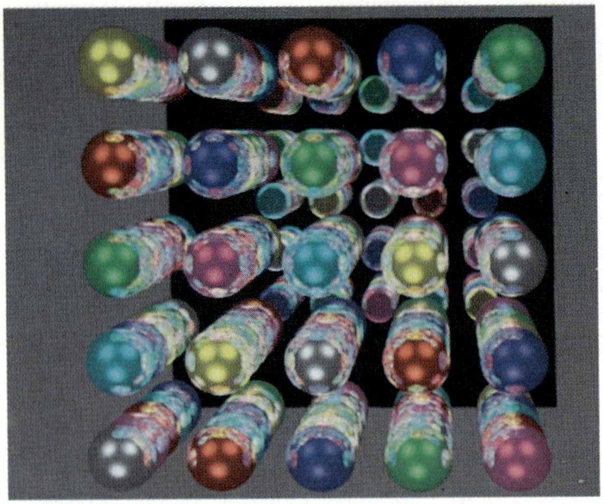

Fig. 11. Model "spheres" without shadow
The number of objects: 126
The number of the light sources: 3
The average tree size: 2.50

COLOR PLATES (A. J. F. Kok et al.)

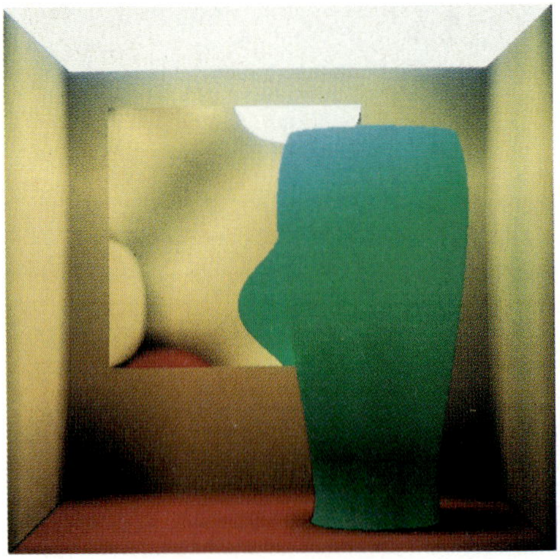

Picture 1

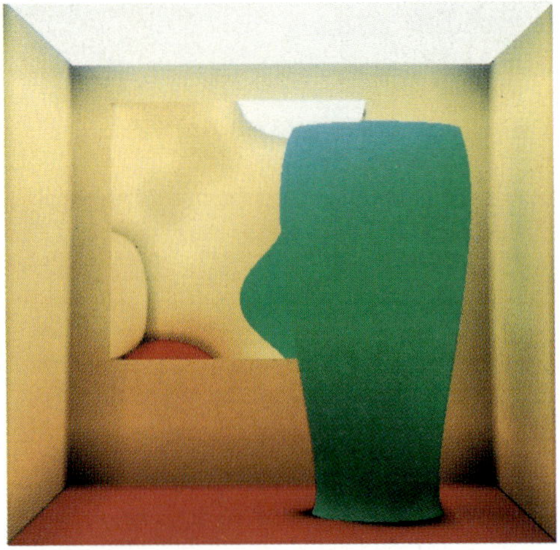

Picture 2

COLOR PLATES (P. Hanrahan and D. Salzman)

Fig. 11. Comparison of Hierarchical and Uniform Solutions

COLOR PLATES (B. E. Smits and G. M. Meyer)

Fig. 4. Result of applying out of gamut color approximation scheme to the spectral colors

Fig. 5. Simulation of the interference colors produced by an oil slick on wet asphalt pavement

Fig. 6. Simulation of the interference colors produced on the surface of a soap bubble

Fig. 7. Simulation of the iridescent blue color found on the wings of the *Morpho* butterfly

Invited Paper

Trends in Radiosity for Image Synthesis

John R. Wallace

1 Introduction

The history of image synthesis has seen a gradual evolution from *ad hoc* shading models to models with a basis in physical reality. By the first half of the last decade physically based reflection models had been applied to computer rendering (Blinn 1977) (Cook and Torrance 1982). Distributed ray tracing provided a common framework within which a large number of previously difficult physical effects could be simulated, including gloss, penumbra, depth of field, and motion blur (Cook et al. 1984). In spite of many successes, however, image synthesis remained unable to simulate one of the most important forms of illumination, the indirect "ambient" illumination provided by light reflected among the many diffuse surfaces that typically make up an environment.

One important consequence of the trend towards physical accuracy was an increase in the attention paid to results available in the fields of physics and engineering. Thus, for example, Blinn (1977) and Cook (1982) each looked to the fields of thermal and illumination engineering for physically accurate reflection models. It was thermal engineering that finally also provided the basis for *radiosity*, the first image synthesis approach to accurately simulate diffuse interreflection.

2 Early Developments in Radiosity

The radiosity method was first introduced to computer graphics by Goral in 1984 (Goral et al. 1984). For the purposes of radiosity, surfaces are assumed to be Lambertian diffuse reflectors, i.e., to reflect light with equal intensity in all directions. Surfaces are subdivided into discrete *patches* for which the *radiosity*, or energy per unit area leaving the surface, is assumed to be constant. A radiosity equation then expresses the patch radiosity as the sum of energy contributions from all other patches:

$$B_i A_i = E_i A_i + \rho_i \sum_{j=1}^{n} B_j A_j F_{ji}$$

where
B_i = radiosity of surface i (energy per unit area)
A_i = area of surface i
E_i = emitted energy per unit area
ρ_i = reflectivity of surface i
B_j = radiosity of surface j
A_j = area of surface j
F_{ji} = form-factor from surface j to surface i

The *form-factor*, F_{ji}, gives the fraction of the energy leaving patch j that arrives at patch i.

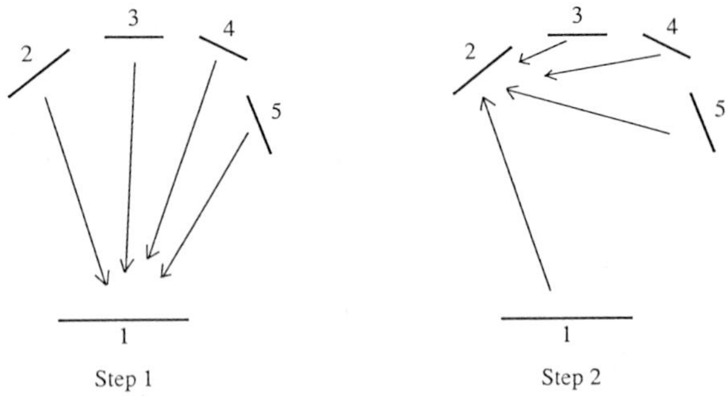

Fig. 1: The conventional "gathering" radiosity approach.

A radiosity equation exists for every patch in the environment. The resulting system of simultaneous equations represents the interchange of energy via interreflection and emission for the environment. Solving the system of equations gives the patch radiosities, which provide a discrete representation of the diffuse shading of the scene.

The radiosity method is unusual in being a view-independent shading algorithm. By definition the shading of Lambertian surfaces does not depend on the view direction. Once the system of equations has been solved, the shading of all surfaces is known and it is possible to view the shaded scene from any eye position without recomputing the illumination. By passing the shaded patches down to a graphics accelerator a shaded scene can be walked through at interactive rates.

Goral's work provided a foundation for the application of radiosity to image synthesis, but it was limited to environments in which the line of sight is never obstructed between any two patches. Thus, shadows were not accounted for.

Nishita and Nakamae removed this restriction with an algorithm in which shadow volumes were used to detect occlusion (Nishita and Nakamae 1985). Form factors were then computed using an analytic form-factor equation valid for arbitrary polygons.

The *hemi-cube* algorithm, an alternative approach to including shadows in radiosity, was described by Cohen and Greenberg (1985). In the hemi-cube algorithm, the form-factors from a given patch are determined by projecting all other patches onto the five faces of a hemi-cube positioned above the given patch. Occlusion is taken into account by scan converting the projected polygons into a z-buffer for each face of the hemi-cube. The form-factor to a given patch can be determined by summing a contribution for each hemi-cube pixel in which the patch is visible.

With the ability to include shadows, images produced using the radiosity method began to take on a startling realism. Since the object was true physically accurate simulation, not just attractive images, attempts were made to quantitatively measure the realism of the resulting images (Meyer et al. 1986). These experiments included comparisons between simulations and physical measurements of actual test environments. Subjective experiments were also performed, in which subjects attempted to distinguish between real and simulated images in a controlled situation.

In spite of the quality of images produced by radiosity, the algorithm as it was first presented had drawbacks that seemed to limit its practicality. In radiosity form-factors must be computed from every patch to every other patch resulting in a time complexity of $O(n^2)$. In addition all form-factors are computed and stored before solving the system of equations, so $O(n^2)$ storage is also required.

These difficulties were addressed by the progressive radiosity approach (Cohen et al. 1987). In the conventional radiosity approach the radiosity equations are solved using Gauss-Siedel iteration. At each step the radiosity of a single patch is updated based on

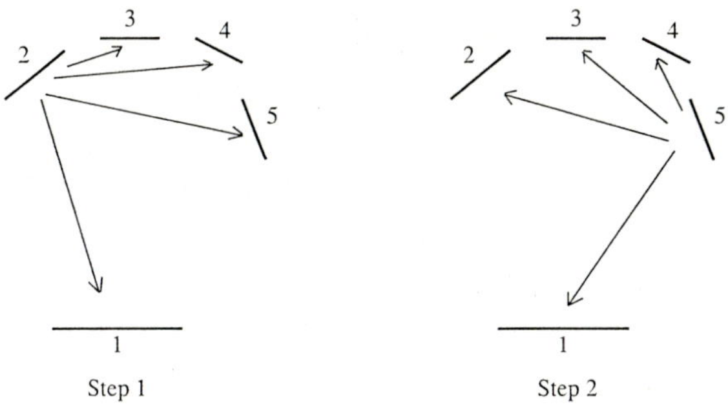

Fig. 2: The progressive "shooting" radiosity approach.

the current radiosities of all other patches. In essence, at each step illumination from all other patches is gathered into a single receiving patch (Figure 1).

In the progressive radiosity approach, on the other hand, the solution proceeds as follows:

do until converged

select patch with greatest reflected and/or emitted energy
compute form-factors from that patch to all other patches
based on form-factors, add contribution from source patch
to radiosity of every other patch

At each step the illumination provided by a single patch is distributed to all other patches in the scene. In effect, the source patch "shoots" its energy out into the scene (Figure 2). In the early steps the source patches chosen will be the light emitters since other surfaces will have as yet received very little illumination. Subsequent steps will select secondary sources, starting with those surfaces that received the most light directly from the light sources, and so on.

Since each solution step updates the radiosity of all surfaces, the increasingly accurate result can be displayed following each step. Useful images can thus be produced very early in the solution process. The simulated steel rolling mill shown in Plate 1 was produced by an early version of the progressive radiosity algorithm. Plate 2 is a rendering of the nave of Chartres Cathedral using progressive radiosity.

3 Extensions of the Radiosity Method

In spite of radiosity's successes, its restriction to diffuse surfaces is a serious limitation for many applications. Aside from the obvious need for specular reflection and refraction in achieving photorealism for its own sake, effects like highlights, for example, can provide a designer with a clearer visual understanding of the shape of a curved surface.

Straightforward extensions of the radiosity method to include specular reflection have proven too expensive to be practical. In an approach described by Immel et al. (1986) the relationship between each patch and every other patch is replaced by a relationship between every (discrete) outgoing direction for every patch and every outgoing direction for every other patch. This increases the size of the problem to be solved dramatically. In addition, it is difficult to precompute directional shading for all possible view directions to the accuracy required for high quality images.

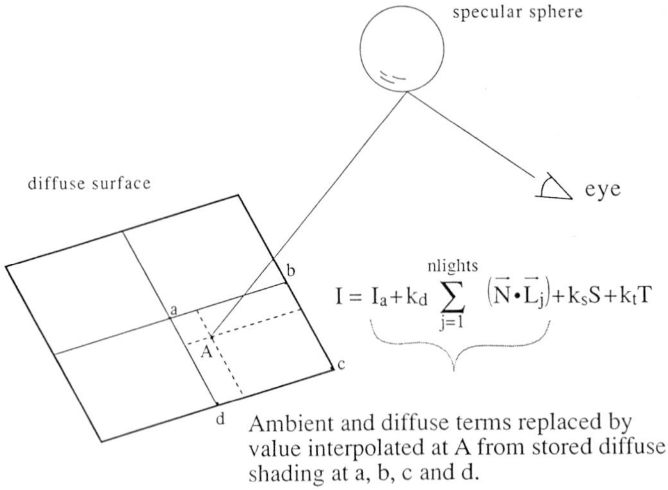

Fig. 3: A simple two-pass approach.

An alternative *two-pass* approach to adding specular reflection to radiosity has been taken by many investigators. Two-pass approaches are based on the observation that view-independent and view-dependent shading methods have complimentary strengths and weaknesses. Radiosity, a view-independent method, is effective for shading diffuse surfaces. Ray tracing, a view-dependent method, has the advantage for shading specular surfaces. In a two-pass algorithm the shading of diffuse surfaces is determined during a view-independent first pass, and the shading of specular surfaces is added during a view-dependent second pass. A two-pass algorithm using radiosity as the first pass was first described by Wallace (Wallace et al. 1987).

A simple example of such an algorithm computes diffuse shading using a standard radiosity solution and adds specular shading during ray tracing of a particular view. Whenever a ray lands on a diffuse patch, the diffuse intensity is determined by interpolating from the precomputed patch radiosities. This value is simply plugged into the ray tracer's shading equation in place of the normal diffuse component (Figure 3). The ray tracing step can be as sophisticated as desired, including distributed ray tracing to achieve gloss, depth-of-field, etc. In Plate 3 a painting by Vermeer has been reproduced using a straightforward two-pass approach.

Although the simple scheme just described can produce dramatic results, it does not completely solve the general shading problem. It ignores the illumination of diffuse surfaces by light reflected or refracted by specular surfaces. For example, it would miss the light focused onto a table by a wine glass. To include this type of effect, the radiosity solution itself must be extended to account for the illumination of diffuse surfaces by light reflected via specular surfaces.

One basic approach, which we will call the *mirror form-factor* method, was first described by Rushmeier (Rushmeier 1986, Rushmeier and Torrance 1990). In the mirror form-factor method specular surfaces are treated as additional routes by which light leaving one diffuse patch may reach another (Figure 4). The form-factor between the two diffuse patches must be increased to take into account the additional energy transfer. The additional contribution to the form-factor can be computed by any method that can determine the path of reflection between the two diffuse patches (Figure 5). Although Rushmeier's implementation was limited to perfect planar mirrors, general implementations

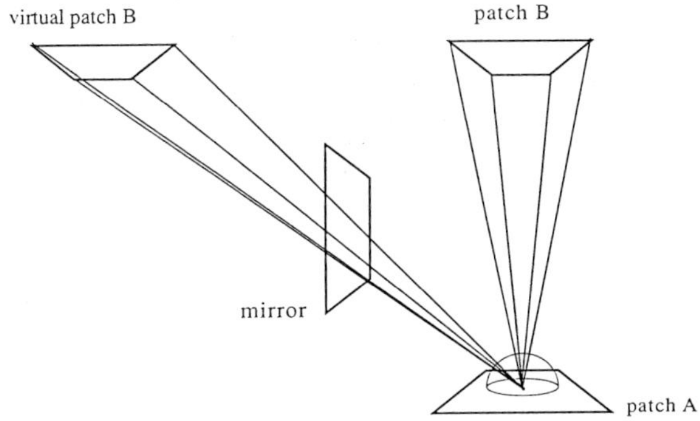

Fig. 4: Mirror form-factors. Light arrives at A directly and via reflection by the mirror.

that use recursive ray tracing to compute form-factors have been described by Malley (1988) and Sillion (1989). In Plate 4 the effect of light reaching the top of the vanity via reflection by the mirror has been computed using the mirror form-factor method.

A different approach to including the effect of specular reflection on the radiosity solution has been presented by Min-Zhi Shao et al. (1988). In this method an initial radiosity computation is performed in which all surfaces are treated as diffuse. Further iterations are then performed in which form-factors from specular patches are determined using a modification of the hemi-cube algorithm. The shading of diffuse surfaces gradually converges to the correct value, including the effect of specular surfaces.

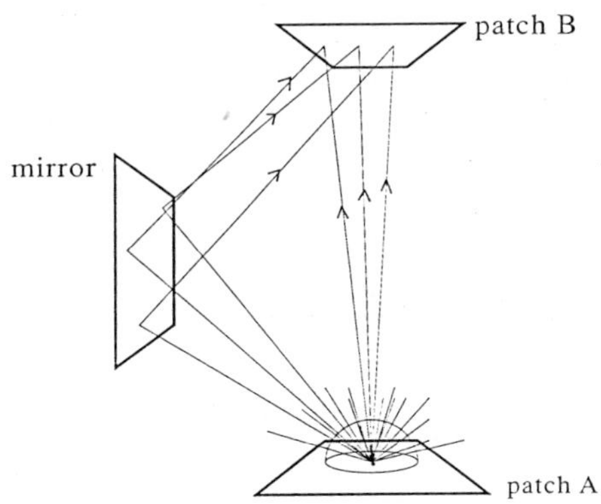

Fig. 5: Use of ray tracing to determine mirror form-factors.

4 The State of the Art

Recent developments in radiosity have been directed towards improving the quality and speed of the algorithm. Improved sampling methods are providing more accurate shading and parallel and hardware implementations are achieving very fast solution times.

4.1 Improved Sampling Methods

The hemi-cube algorithm is a uniform sampling method, since it computes form-factors by testing visibility at the regularly spaced hemi-cube pixels. Thus it can produce aliasing,

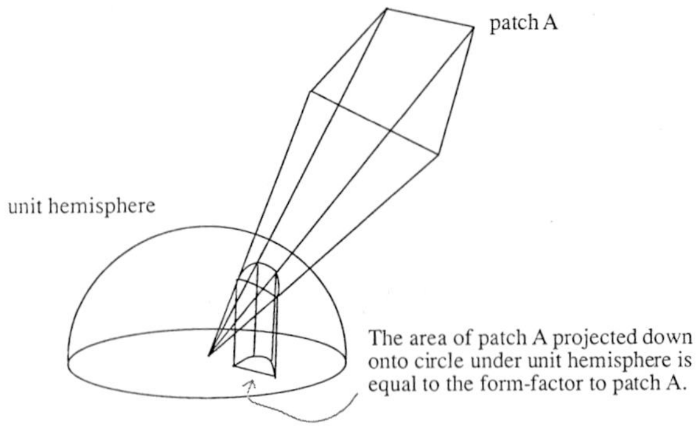

Fig. 6: Nusselt's analog.

particularly where small bright sources of light provide a great deal of illumination. Such aliasing appears as a plaid pattern in the shading. Sampling problems are particularly severe when the hemi-cube is used to determine form-factors in the progressive radiosity approach. (For a full discussion see (Baum et al. 1989) and (Wallace et al. 1989)).

To overcome the aliasing inherent in the hemi-cube algorithm, the z-buffer must be replace by a more flexible method of determining patch visibility. Ray casting is one such a method. Because rays are cast independently they can be shot in any distribution of directions, thus providing a basis for non-uniform, adaptive and stochastic sampling.

Malley describes a stochastic ray casting algorithm for computing form-factors that replaces the hemi-cube. The hemisphere of directions above a patch is sampled using jittered sampling, and the visible patch in each sampled direction determined by casting a ray. Malley's method is based on Nusselt's analog, a geometric representation of the form-factor from a differential area to a patch (Figure 6).

In Nusselt's analog the patch is first projected onto a hemisphere above the differential area. This projection is then projected directly down onto the circle at the base of the hemisphere. The area of this projection divided by the area of the circle equals the form-factor.

Malley first generates a set of jittered samples uniformly distributed in the circle beneath the hemisphere (Figure 7). One of these samples is then projected up to the hemisphere. A ray is shot radially out from the hemisphere through this projected point. After all rays have been shot, the number of rays that hit the patch divided by the total rays shot gives the form-factor. In terms of Nusselt's analog, the total number rays shot is an estimate of the area of the circle and the rays out of that total that hit the patch give the relative area of the projected patch to the area of the circle.

Sillion also describes a ray tracing method for computing form-factors (Sillion and Puech 1989). In Sillion's approach the patches are projected onto a plane above the patch from which form-factors are to be computed. The visibility of the patches is determined using a Warnock algorithm in which the plane is adaptively subdivided into *windows* for which the determination of the visible patch is trivial. Rays are shot through the corners of each window. Since Sillion's algorithm also includes specular surfaces, these rays are traced recursively. If the ray trees generated at the four corners of the window do not match over the first few reflections, the window is subdivided further. This helps to ensure that patches contributing illumination via specular reflection will be adequately sampled.

The ray tracing algorithms of Malley and Sillion are both designed for a conventional, i.e. non-progressive, radiosity approach. In conventional radiosity the form-factors to all patches seen through the hemisphere above a patch are a determined at once. In progressive radiosity the problem is somewhat different. At each step of the progressive

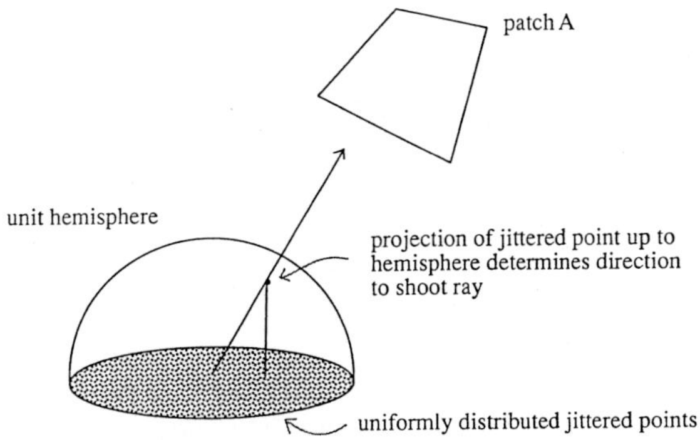

Fig. 7: Malley's method for computing form-factors.

solution the illumination provided by a single source patch is determined. Thus, instead of determining form-factors to patches visible over the entire hemisphere, only the form-factor to the single source patch needs to be determined. A ray casting method for computing form-factors that is designed for progressive radiosity has been described by Wallace et al. (1989).

The form-factor from a differential area (the receiving point) to a finite patch is given by:

$$F_{dA_1-A_2} = \int_{A_2} \frac{\cos\theta_1 \ \cos\theta_2}{\pi r^2} \, dA_2$$

Numerical integration can be accomplished in a straightforward manner by approximating the integral as the sum of form-factors computed for smaller sub-areas of area ΔA_2 (Figure 8).

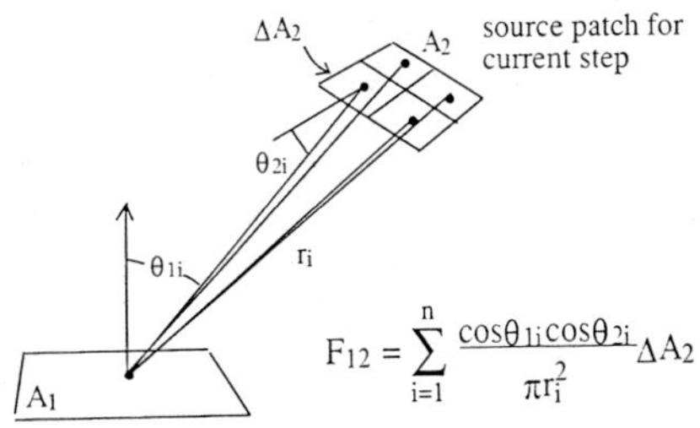

Fig. 8: Numerical integration of differential area to patch form-factor.

A ray is shot from the receiving differential area to the center of each delta area and if no occlusion is detected, the contribution of that sub-area is added to the summation. For accurate results the source must in general be subdivided non-uniformly to ensure that each sub-area is a reasonable approximation to a differential area. A sub-area can be divided recursively into smaller areas until ΔA_2 for each sub-area is much less than the square of the distance to the receiving differential area.

The images in Plates 2, 6 and 7 were all computed using ray casting for progressive radiosity.

A completely different approach to improving the quality of form-factors for progressive radiosity has been taken by Baum et al. (1989). In this scheme most form-factors are computed using the hemi-cube algorithm. For situations where the hemi-cube cannot produce an accurate form-factor, the form-factor is computed using an analytic form-factor equation. This approach thus preserves the speed advantage of the hemi-cube for determining visibility, while overcoming some of its sampling problems.

4.2 Fast Implementations

Current radiosity implementations require that the user wait minutes or even hours for a high quality shaded scene. In some applications such a wait may be acceptable, especially when the shaded scene will then be walked through interactively. In architecture, for example, a radiosity simulation could provide an alternative to expensive physical models for presentation of designs to clients. For example, Plate 7 shows several stages of a progressive rendering of an office interior. Each step of the progressive radiosity solution for this model takes approximately 10 seconds on a Hewlett-Packard Model 835 workstation. A fully converged radiosity solution for this scene would require a wait of several minutes. However, the shaded model can then be redrawn from any viewpoint in under a second using graphics engines available today.

Other applications are more demanding. For example, as a CAD user moves components of a model with respect to one another, shadows and interreflection can give a more immediate and intuitive understanding of changing geometric relationships. To be useful in this way, radiosity would have to produce images at interactive rates and account for constantly changing geometry. The machined part shown in Plate 5 was constructed using Hewlett-Packard's ME30 solid modeler and shaded using a two-pass algorithm. The radiosity solution was run only long enough to compute direct illumination and took approximatedly 10 minutes of a Hewlett-Packard Model 350 workstation. (The ray tracing pass took about three hours.) Clearly, radiosity has some distance to go before it is able to produce this type of image in real time.

But interactive performance is getting closer, as is demonstrated by hardware radiosity implementations and parallel or distributed radiosity algorithms that have been described in the past year.

A number of investigators have taken advantage of the power of currently available hardware graphics engines to perform the expensive hemi-cube computation. The hemi-cube algorithm consists of basic graphics operations like transformation, clipping, scan-conversion and z-buffering, all of which are accelerated in hardware by many graphics workstations. The basic approach is to have the graphics hardware scan convert and z-buffer all patches in the scene for a view originating at the patch for which the hemi-cube is to be performed. At each hemi-cube pixel, a number identifying the visible patch is stored. These numbers are then read back from the frame-buffer and the form-factors determined by summing a contribution for each pixel in the usual manner. This approach has been implemented by Baum et al. (1990) using Silicon Graphics hardware.

A similar approach has been implemented by Recker et al. (1990) using Hewlett-Packard graphics hardware. Recker and George modify the hemi-cube algorithm by projecting the environment onto a single plane parallel to the front face of the normal hemi-cube but with a very wide field-of-view. This increases efficiency since the patches need only be transformed and clipped once rather than the five times required by the five faces of the hemi-cube. Illumination from patches that fall out of the field-of-view (patches close to the plane of the receiving patch) will be missed in this approach, but if the field-of-view is wide enough, the error can be limited to a small percentage.

An interesting hardware alternative to the hemi-cube has been proposed by Fuchs et al. 1989 in which form-factors are computed using Nusselt's analog directly. The hemispherical projection is performed in hardware on the proposed Pixel Planes 5 graphics engine, which is capable of evaluating a quadratic expression at each pixel. The estimated time to compute the equivalent of a hemi-cube for 100,000 patches is one second.

Chapter 1

Efficient Ray Tracing Methods

Incremental Ray Tracing

Koichi Murakami, Katsuhiko Hirota

Abstract

We have developed a method to reduce the ray tracing time that recomputes or updates only the changed parts of the image for a fixed viewpoint for a dynamic sequence of images. This method enables a designer to make small changes in geometry or surface properties of a ray-traced scene without recalculating the entire image. The intersection tree is extended to contain the intersection point, surface normal, and related data that records the path through which the ray propagated using a voxel partition scheme. These descriptions are then used during the update to quickly determine which parts of the image need recomputation and to reduce the number of recomputations. The key idea behind the method is to localize the influence of changed objects using the voxel partition and to minimize the access cost of the data structures. Testing if a ray is changed by the changed objects is done with a hash index, which represents the ray's path. Intersection recalculation to determine a changed ray's new visible point can be reduced with information saved in the intersections. The optimal tree traversal algorithm limits the parts of the data structures to be accessed so that traversal cost is minimized. This method was developed on the *CAP (Cellular Array Processor)* parallel processor. An implementation approach that accounts for data storage and load balancing is also presented. The results demonstrate great performance improvements over calculating an entirely new rendering. With this method ray tracing may become practical for some computer graphics applications, such as CAD and animation which require high-quality images.

Key Words : raytracing, frame coherence, hashing, voxel.

1 Introduction

We wish to employ ray tracing in fields such as industrial CAD and production of high-quality animation sequences where images of excellent quality are required. However, ray tracing suffers from lengthy computation times that limit its practical use.

A number of studies have been proposed to accelerate ray tracing. These studies capitalize on various forms of coherence [Surt74], [Athe83] to reduce the computation, especially for ray-object intersection calculation. Ray coherence, the characteristic that some collections of ray beams tend to behave similarly, is used in beam tracing [Heck84] in which the objects handled are limited to polygonal objects. Speer also uses this form of coherence in a method [Spee85] in which a variety of objects are dealt with. Hierarchical relations between objects [Kay86], [Wegh84], [Rubi80] and space partitioning methods which use voxels [Kapl85], [Fuji86], [Mura86], [Jame87], [John87] or an octree [Mats83], [Glas84] employ space coherence. Space coherence capitalizes on the relative spatial position of objects. Both ray and space coherence are used in order to reduce the number of ray-object intersection calculations.

While these and other techniques have improved the performance, they are still computationally too expensive for interactive use. These studies based on object and ray coherence, were primarily devoted to speeding up the generation of still images. Although the methods from these studies can speed up image generation for dynamic sequences, another approach that capitalizes on frame coherence is more effective for interactive and successive image generation.

We think that the designer improves the model and the images incrementally until he is satisfied with the image. In a succession of incremental modeling phases, the designer refines parts of the image, for instance, he might change a color, and then move an object. When little change is made between frames, overall ray tracing for each frame is unnecessary. For this incremental design process, a partial update method for ray tracing is required that recomputes only the pixels that change between successive frames.

Hubschman [Hubs81] applied frame coherence to the image-space rendering techniques, such as the scan-line algorithm. His algorithm partially updates scenes composed of fixed objects as the viewpoint moves. In image-space algorithms, the relationship between object changes and parts of the image to be recomputed are rather simple. Ray tracing based on global illumination model in the object space must handle reflections and refractions. As the object moves, its image on a reflecting object (for example a mirror) must be changed. Although parameterized ray tracing [Carl89] updates to successive ray traced images using frame coherence, it can not handle changes in the model.

We are presenting a new approach to the problem, which enables ray tracing to generate dynamic sequences of images with little additional computation using the frame description of the previous image. We call the method *incremental ray tracing* since it allows the ray-traced images to be updated by partial recomputations during dynamic sequences. It deals with changes in the model, such as transformation, scaling, and addition or deletion to the database, and changes in surface properties such as color, reflectance, and mapping in a unified manner. Changes in shadows caused by the above changes and the movement of the light source are also included. The intersection tree has been extended to include the intersection point, surface normal, and related data that involves the path through which the ray propagated using voxel partition scheme. Because these description depends on the viewer position, the method works for a fixed viewpoint. In spite of the limitation caused by the view dependent description, the high-speed and high-quality image generation for successive frames that this method provides is useful.

2 Algorithm

2.1 Outline

The method has two stages (Figure 1). In the first stage, standard ray tracing is performed to generate an initial image for the successive frame sequence and to construct the data structures. These descriptions called the history are then used to quickly update the image during the second stage, which involves an interactive updation process. The partial recomputation due to a change of geometry or of the surface properties parameters are performed in the second stage. The frame description is maintained for subsequent frames. As long as the designer does not change the viewing parameters, this loop continues.

Before continuing the discussion, we will provide the terminology used in this paper. A *ray-set* is defined as all the branched rays of a given ray. We say a ray change occurs when the intensity assigned to the ray changes, which is caused by a change of the visible point or of the surface properties. The intensity of each pixel associated with a ray-set must be updated when one of the rays within the ray-set is changed. For clarity we will discuss the method for changes in geometry and changes in surface properties separately, although they are unified later. The flow of the partial update algorithm is described below. First the *tree-traverser* searches for the ray change by traversing the intersection tree in a top-down fashion. During the traversal, the test whether a given ray changes is done by the *detection algorithm*. It examines the change with the *voxel traversal history* and the *hash index* which are described later. The *detection algorithm* must work as

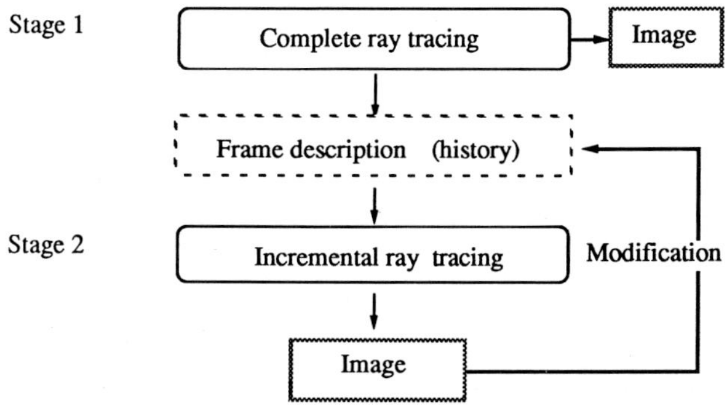

Fig 1: the two stage of image generation

fast as possible to obtain good performance. When a ray is expected to change, its visible point is recomputed. The new visible point can be determined using the history information to limit the intersection recalculation. If the visible point has changed, the shading recalculation is done to determine the new intensity at the surface. Otherwise the saved intensity value in the frame description is retrieved and assigned to the ray. If the change is detected, then the tree-traverser propagates the updated intensity to the pixel value. The full algorithm will be presented in the appendix.

The key idea behind the method is to localized the influence of a changed object with a voxel partition. With the description that contains the path through which a ray propagated in the previous frame and the voxel data structure that contains a flag that indicates whether any object within the voxel has changed, the intersection recalculations can be limited. Testing if the ray is changed by the changed object is done efficiently with a hash index that represents the ray's path. Also, an optimal traversal is required to avoid an exhaustive search and to minimize the access cost of the data structures.

2.2 History Data Structure

Figure 2 illustrates the data structures that contain all of the information necessary to partially update the ray tracing. This section describes these data structures.

2.2.1 Extended Intersection Tree

For each pixel a intersection tree is constructed. The node is extended to include the following information in addition to the intensity value.

(a) ray parameter, such as direction and start point.

(b) information on the visible object, such as its visible point, normal vector at the visible point, and index of the surface properties parameters.

(c) pointer to the voxel traversal history data structure described below.

(d) hash index (described later).

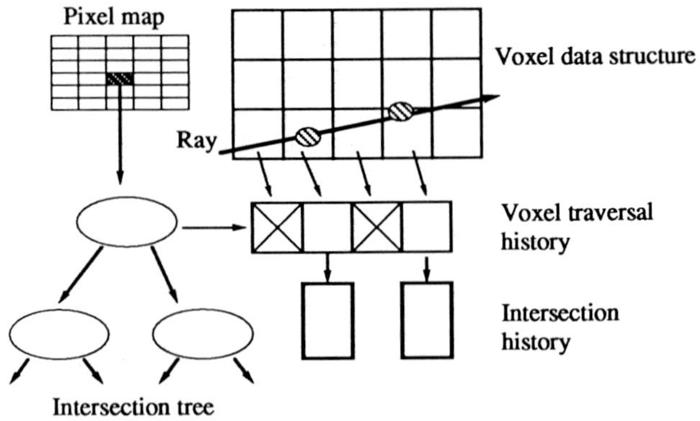

Fig 2: data structure : an extended intersection tree is linked to the pixel map corresponding to each pixel element of the screen. A node of the intersection tree represents a visible object. The voxel traversal history represents the path in the voxel data structures through which a ray reached the visible point in the previous frame. When any intersection exists within the voxel element, the intersection is stored in a corresponding intersection history for the voxel element.

2.2.2 Voxel Traversal History

Our ray tracing system reduces the number of intersection calculations to speed up image generation by partioning the environment with a voxel data structure. The *voxel traversal history* contains the voxel index sequence through which the ray of the node propagated in the previous frame. Loosely speaking, the voxel traversal history is a rough representation of the trajectory of the ray. For each ray this list is constructed and linked to the ray's node of the extended intersection tree.

2.2.3 Intersection History

Intersections with objects within each voxel element are saved in the *intersection history*, which is linked to the corresponding list element in the voxel traversal history. Each record of the intersection history contains an object number and the relative depth of the intersection from the start point of the ray. Intersection recalculation during the partial update can be reduced with this information. Recall that the visible point is the closest point between the intersection points and the ray. The intersection points for unchanged objects are retrieved and used for the candidates of the visible point. In figure 3, suppose the object that was the visible object moves, then the object previously obscured is revealed. In this case, intersection recalculation for the unchanged object is not necessary.

2.2.4 Other Data Structures

- The voxel data structure is constructed in a fashion similar to previous works. The difference is that each voxel element has a flag to represent whether a change has occurred within its volume in addition to the object records.
- The object database contains information on the size, translation matrices, indices of surface properties tables, and change flags of the objects in the environment.

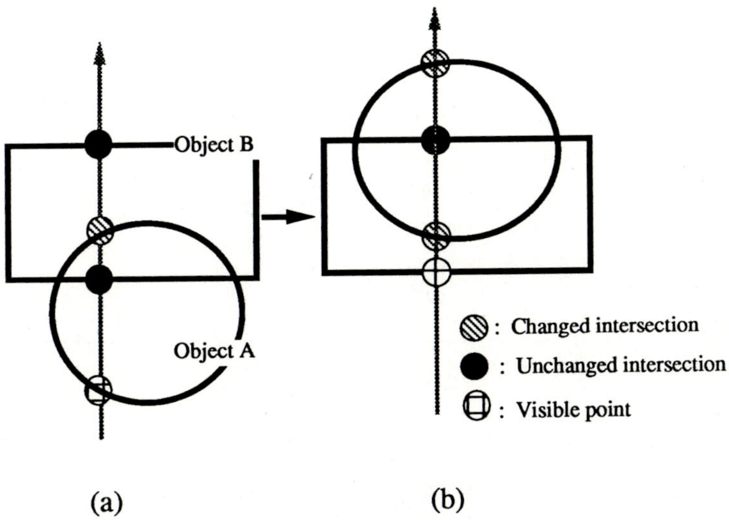

Fig 3: the use of intersection history

2.3 Detection of Changed Rays

One possible choice for recalculating the visible point is a simple algorithm. It computes the intersection between ray and every changing object in an inefficient manner. The computational cost is O(NR) where N and R denote the number of changing objects and rays, respectively. This method would be slow especially for complex scenes because R represents the complexity. Optimally the computational cost should be proportional to the number of the changing objects.

We will present new algorithm which is efficient since the effect of such changes can be localized. Voxel encoding is employed to represent each ray path in the previous frame of the image and to localize the influence of the changes in object geometry. Figure 4 shows a top view of the localized regions with the voxel partitioning scheme.

To begin every second stage (partial update), the voxel elements in which the changed object exist are found and flagged. Also, the object database corresponding to the updated object is flagged. The visible point of a ray may have changed in any of the flagged voxel elements along the ray path that is encoded and saved in voxel traversal history. In figure 5, two sets of voxel elements are shown. The triangles mark the voxel elements through which the ray propagated in the previous frame stored in the voxel traversal history. The stars mark the voxel elements in which an object changed. The conjunction of these two sets of elements may contain visible points that have changed. This voxel element, the conjunction can be found by examining the flag in the voxel data structure while traversing the voxel elements one by one in the voxel traversal history. This traversal is efficient because it only traverses the voxel through which the ray passed in the previous frame. Note that the visible point in the changed voxel element is not always changed because the resolution of voxel partition is rough, currently 32 voxels along each axis. In the example in figure 4, ray *r1* is not affected by the change of the moving object. Since we have assumed that the number of the changed objects is small and changed rays are few, it is inefficient to examine the entire voxel traversal history to detect the changed rays. We will present a more efficient algorithm that exploits a hashing technique to rapidly test whether a given ray changes. Hashing is commonly used as a searching technique for

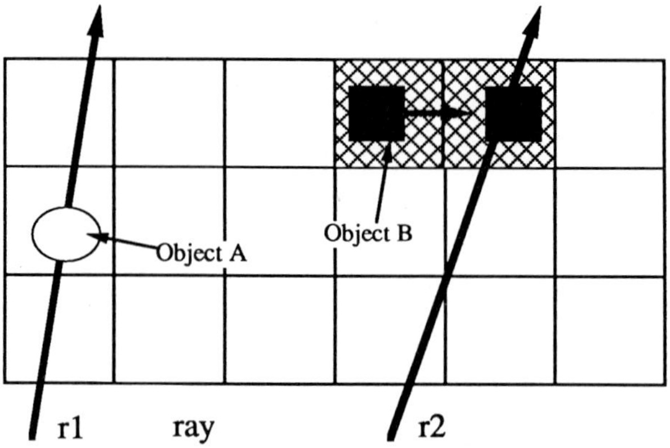

Fig 4: Localization of the influence of change : the ray (r1) is not influenced by the change of object B because this influence is localized in the hatched region.

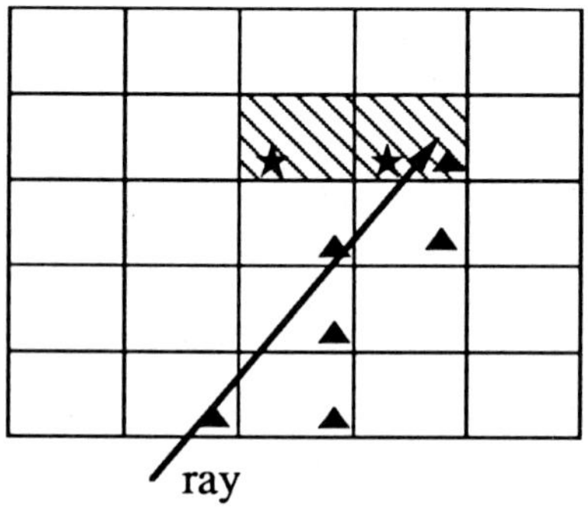

Fig 5: the changed voxel elements : intersections may change in the conjunction region between changed voxel elements marked with stars and triangles.

the symbol table in compilers [Aho79]. A hash function which takes sum for example, is applied to the set of voxel indices. The resultant hash value called the *hash index* is recorded in the node corresponding to each ray. The hash index can be thought of as a concise representation of the path through which the ray propagated. A flag in the hash table is set if the changed voxel index is a member of the voxel index set corresponding to the hash index (figure 6). Each frame is preprocessed to set the flags by scanning the voxel index set of every hash index. During the update, the flag of the hash index of a given ray is accessed to test if the ray changes. Since testing can be made by examing the flag in the hash table, which requires only one comparison, instead of scanning the flag of every voxel element, the hash index reduces the computational cost. An additional merit is that the number of hash indices is much smaller than the number of the total rays because of ray coherence. It allows little amount of data space.

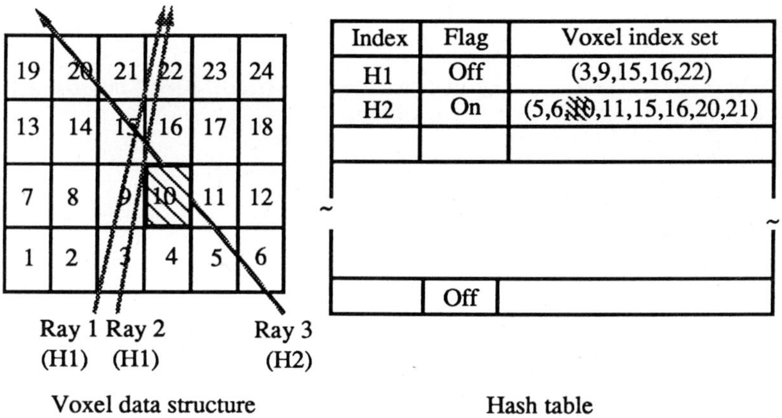

Fig 6: the hash table : the number in each voxel element represents the one-dimensional voxel index. The flag with hash H2 is marked because of a changed voxel element. For example, the changed voxel '10' is a member of the voxel index set of index H2.

Figure 6 illustrates how to construct and use the hash index. The voxel index set of a ray is obtained by sorting the voxel index sequence through which the ray propagated. Sorting is done for two reasons. First, only unique combinations rather than the ordered sequence is needed here. Second, the sorting reduces the size of the hash table, which allows efficient construction and access. Note that the voxel index is converted from a 3D to a 1D representation by an appropriate mapping. In this example, the sorted index set (5 6 10 11 15 16) is obtained from the ordered voxel index sequence (6 5 11 10 16 15). This index set is then recorded in field corresponding to hash index H2 that is sum of the voxel index set. Hash index H2 is assigned to the ray, *ray-3*. If a change occurs within the voxel element indexed 10, then preprocessing will set the flag of hash index H2. During the update, the flag is accessed with hash index H2 to test whether the ray *ray-3* propagated in the voxel element in which the change occurred.

2.4 Recalculation of a Visible Point

The recalculation of a visible point is performed when the algorithm, proceeding along a ray's voxel traversal history, comes to the changed voxel. The new visible point can be determined from the ray's intersections with the unchanged objects and the newly calculated intersections with the changed objects. Intersections for the unchanged objects are retrieved from the intersection history, and become candidates to be the visible point. Also, the recomputed intersections for changed object are added to these candidates. The visible point can be determined by evaluating the distance from the start point of the ray to the candidate points. Since the intersections for the unchanged objects need not be found, this algorithm can reduce the number of ray-object intersection recalculations which is the most computationally intensive part of ray tracing. The following algorithm is used for visible point recalculation.

Algorithm-1 : Recalculation of visible point

```
input:voxel traversal history
output:visible_point

for(i=0; VoxelTraversalHistory is not empty; i++)
   {
   FocusElement = VoxelTraversalHistory[i];
   if(IsThisVoxelElementChange(FocusElement))
      {
      Candidates = getFromUnchangedObject(VoxelTraversalHistory[i].IntersectionHistory);
      while(Object in VoxelElement is not empty)
            {
            if(IsObjectChange(Object))
                 Candidates += GetIntersection(Object);
            }
      VisiblePoint = Closest(Candidates);
      return(VisiblePoint);
      }
   }
return(NoIntersect);
```

2.5 Optimal Tree Traversal Algorithm

Since traversal over the entire frame description will result in very slow updating, an efficient traversal algorithm is required. Our traversal algorithm for searching for a changed ray is achieved using a hash index to select the candidate nodes, which can avoid an exhaustive search.

We define the *global hash index* of a particular node of the extended intersection tree to be the combined hash index of all that nodes children. Global hash index is calculated and assigned to the every node during the first and second stages. If a flag of the global hash index at a given node is unset, then optimal traversal algorithm can reject that nodes entire subtree from further consideration. The flag of a global hash index for the primary ray (the original ray sent from the eye) indicates whether any change occurs that affects that pixel. Similarly, the flag of a global hash index of any given ray indicates the possibility of a change for all the branched rays of the ray. This traversal algorithm using the global hash index reduces the amount of the traversal intersection tree. The global hash index guides the search by selecting the branched rays. The search continues recursively until reaching a terminated ray that has no visible point.

Figure 7 demonstrates how the global hash index is used. Indices *i2*, *i3*, and *i4* correspond to the rays *r2*, *r3* and *r4* and *n1*, *n2*, *n3* and *n4* are the intersection nodes. Suppose only *r4* changes. The change flags of each index are ON, OFF and ON. Recall that the global hash index represents all the branched rays of a given ray, so *i2* reflects the change of *r4*. First the flags of *i2* and *i3* on node *n1* are tested revealing that a traversal the refracted ray *r3* is unnecessary. In this example, the traversal is only done on the marked part of the intersection tree, allowing for an efficient search.

If a visible point changes, then a shading recalculation must be done so that the changed parts can be rendered. The intensity of a given ray is the contribution of all the rays that branched from the ray, which is based ont he *global illumination model.* The global intensity is the sum of the intensity of all the branched rays, and is used for the intensity calculation of each node (equation 1).

$$\text{I\_all} = \text{I\_local} + \text{I\_global\_reflected} + \text{I\_global\_refracted} \quad (1)$$

Equation (1) represents the intensity of a given ray as the sum of the intensity at the visible point and the two global intensities.

These three intensities are recorded at each node. Shading recomputation is performed along with the search for changes, reducing the amount of shading recomputation. The traversal search for changes is done in a top-down fashion, while a shading recomputation is performed on the same nodes and the resultant updated intensities propagate from the bottom up. For example, since *c3* represents the global intensity for *r3*, shading recomputation for node *n3* is unnecessary. Note that the global intensity has to be updated when the intensity of one of the branched rays is updated. Recomputation of intensity *c4* at *n2* causes the recomputation of *c2* at *n1*. The update of the global hash index is done during the traversal similar to the global intensity. A new global hash index is obtained from the hash index of the given ray and the two global hash indices of the branched rays. The voxel index sequences are retrieved with their hash indices and merged to construct a new one.

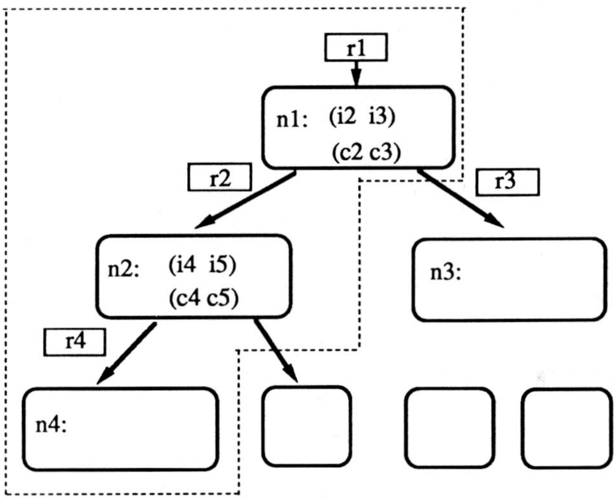

Fig 7: optimal tree traversal : prefix r, n, i, c represent ray, node, global hash idnex, and global intensities, respectively. Traversal is done only on the part enclosed by the dashed line.

Next we consider how the cost of traversing the intersection tree is improved. Suppose that the intersection tree is balanced and only ray has changed. (These assumptions are acceptable in many practical situations). The computational cost for traversal is logarithmic with respect to the number of nodes in the intersection tree. The performance thus increase as the environment becomes more complex.

It is worth noting that in the second stage, standard ray tracing may be performed in somes cases. Since a change of a visible point may cause a change in the direction of the two branched rays and a change of the intersection point, the frame description may not be available any more. Other cases where additional ray tracing is necessary are listed below.

(1) When the normal vector at a visible point changes according to the bump mapping.

(2) when the direction of the refracted ray changes with a change in the index of refraction.

(3) When a new branched ray is fired because of a change of surface properties, such as a change from no reflectance to reflectance.

2.6 Updating Shadows

After the visible point calculation is completed, shadows are determined for the point by firing rays (light ray) toward the light sources. Shadows also must be changed for the following cases during the update.

(1) Objects other than the visible object have changed and may now block the light ray from the intersection.

(2) the light source has moved.

(3) The surface properties of the object that occluded the light rays in the previous frame have changed.

(4) The intensity of the light source has changed.

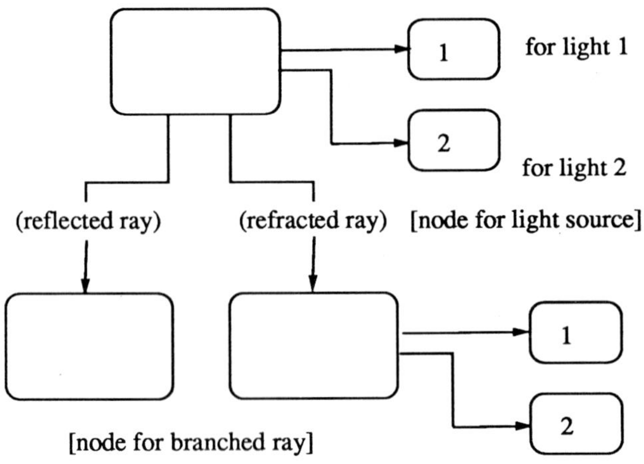

Fig 8: the intersection tree for shadowing : the intersection tree is extended further to contain a description of shadowing. The node for each light source is linked to each intersection node.

Shadow update testing is performed to handle case (1) above for every visible point. This tests if the previous light ray has changed using a technique similar to that used for branched rays. The procedure for this test can be achieved with data structures which are similar to those for branched rays shown in figure 8. However the structure is simpler, containing only a list of hash indices for the light rays to each individual light source from the node's visible point. If a light ray has changed, then intersection recalculation between the light ray and every object must be done. Otherwise, the contribution from the light can be assumed to be the same.

The data structures for shadow recalculation do not include a voxel traversal history or an intersection history for the following reasons. First, since the number of light rays is large equivalent to the product of the number of visible points and the number of the light sources, a large amount of data for shadow recalculation would be required. Second, we have assumed that the designer often changes the position of the light source. When the position of the light source changes the direction of each light ray must be recalculated and thus any history data would be thrown away.

2.7 Changes in Surface Properties

Changes in surface properties can be performed just as for the branched ray. Since only the intensity value and the normal (if a bump mapping is applied) are changed, the structure of the frame description need not be changed. The test of whether the surface properties at a visible point has changed is made by matching the surface properties index of the visible object, with the specified index of the surface properties table. Traversal, recomputation of shading, and the propagation of the intensity is the same except that visible point recalculation is unnecessary. Instead of a hash index, a flag is kept for each surface properties index and is used for the selective search. The position in the list of flags of a surface property index is set to 1 if the index is present in any of the branched rays of the current ray. With both the flag and the hash idnex, the two methods can be unified easily.

3 Implementation

This algorithm is implemented on the parallel processor, *CAP (Cellular Array Processor)* [Sato85], [Ishi87], which we developed. The CAP is a MIMD-type parallel computer currently consisting of 256 processors called cells which are configured in an 16 × 16 two dimensional array. Each cell consists of i80186 MPU, i8087 NDP, and 2M-bytes of local memory.

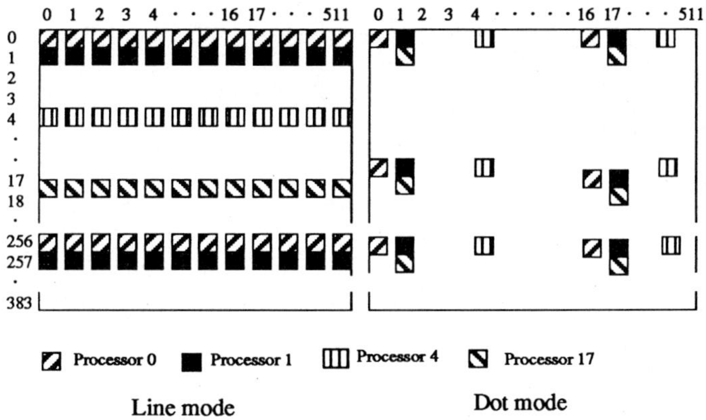

Fig 9: static load distribution method: in the line mode, each cell is assigned to every 256th line on the screen. In the dot mode, each cell is assigned to the corresponding position in each 16 by 16 subregion.

Table 1: load and data balance statistics between the cells.

Model	Processing time min - max (sec) difference (%)	Amount of data storages min - max (KB) difference (%)
Chess without shadow	36.7 - 39.4 6.8%	354.5 - 374.4 5.3%
spheres	27.0 - 29.8 9.4%	294.8 - 319.6 7.7%

(*) difference = (max - min)/max × 100.

3.1 Load Distribution

In the implementation of the ray tracing algorithm on the CAP, screen pixels are partitioned and assigned to cells. the load balance must be considered so that the performance will increase with the number of cells. The dot mode static load distribution presented by us [Mura86] [Mura87] demonstrates good performance. This distribution method divides the screen into small areas, for example 16 × 16 pixel area for the present CAP, before calculation. Each cell performs ray tracing one very eight pixel vertically and horizontally so that the entire pixels are processed by the 256 cells (figure 9). This load distribution scheme statistically averages the amount of processing done in each cell. In order to show the effectiveness of this scheme, we compared it with another type of static load distribution, the line mode, in which each cell is allocated every 256th scan line. Table 1 shows the results obtained from the dot mode distribution schemes. The difference in processing time between the cells is within several percent for the dot mode, while it ranges over more than ten percent for the line mode.

3.2 Data Distribution

The management of the large amount of data used by our method is achieved using the distributed local memory of the CAP system. The total memory size is 128MB. It provides efficient access so that very fast performance is obtained. Data distribution also must be taken into account to prevent huge amount of history data from being assigned to a particular cell, which would exceed the 2MB memory of each cell. We can be assured that this will not happen by the following consideration. The amount of data is proportional to the number of rays, which is also proportional to the processing time. As shown above, the processing time in the dot mode is balanced. Consequently, the amount of data is balanced. Table 1 illustrates the differences between the processing times and the amount of data allocated in each cell. It indicates that both are evenly distributed by the dot mode static load distribution method. Data is maintained for the next frames during the second stages. Since this history data structure may change, during updation, construction, and deletion, this data structure is implemented as a heap.

Although a large data space (approximately 50 MB in total) is required, the amount of actually accessed data can be small. The traversal algorithm and the detection algorithm limit the access cost over the data structure by ignoring rays that are not likely to change using the global hash indices. For example, using the global hash index of the primary ray, traversal of any nodes of the tree is omitted when the global hash indices' flag is unmarked. The nest section shows this effect.

Table 2: timing test

Model	Chess without shadow	Chess with shadow	Spheres without shadow
entire	39.4	93.6	29.8
change-1	1.3 (30.3)	6.0 (15.6)	1.6 (22.9)
change-2	3.7 (10.6)	14.1 (6.6)	2.3 (12.9)
size	1.8 (21.9)	6.1 (15.3)	2.2 (13.5)
light	4.9 (8.0)	32.6 (2.9)	6.2 (4.8)
color	0.5 (78.8)	0.5 (187.2)	0.4 (74.5)

Processing times are listed in seconds.
The relative performance is listed in parenthesis, which indicates the ratio with respect to the entire processing time.

4 Results and Discussion

Figures 10 and 11 (on color plates) show the images used to demonstrate the performance of the partial update. For each ray-traced image, several changes are made. We have provided the processing statistics for the entire ray tracing and the partial updates shown in Table 2. All computing times are listed in seconds. The test images were calculated at a resolution of 512 × 384 pixels. No antialiasing was performed for the tests. Although approximately 40 percent more time is required to construct the frame description in the first stage with respect to standard ray tracing, this method reduces the computation times for changes by a significant amount in comparison with only using standard ray tracing. The relative improvement for a change of color is around 100 times faster, for an object change around 10 times faster, and for shadow changes due to the light source movement around 4 times faster. The reason why the time corresponding to the light source movement is longer than the others can be considered as following. Since the number of the changed light rays is equivalent to the number of branched rays times the number of changed light sources, the amount of processing need is large.

The statistics in Table 3 show the number of processed item in a particular cell for the CHESS model with shadow, including the tree traversal, the new ray generation, intersection calculations, shading recalculations, data management, and preprocessing that involves setting the flag of the hash index. Comparing change-1 and change-2, seven objects moved in change-2 while one object moved in change-1, the processing time is approximately proportional to the number of shading recalculations, which is equivalent to the number of the changed rays. this demonstrates that the localization of the influence of the changed objects works well. Note that the number of actually accessed nodes (81 in size change) is much smaller than the total number of nodes (1433). This also shows that the optimal traversal algorithm using the global hash index is effective. The data management that reflects time spent primarly on bookkeeping due to the small data address space of the i80186 is approximately 2 seconds, which is considerable. A 32-bit CPU will lower this time.

5 Conclusion

We have presented a new method for the partial updating of ray-traced images that is very useful for interactive modeling of geometry and surface properties for a fixed viewpoint. We capitalized on the geometrical properties of the fixed viewpoint and only slightly changing geometry to exploit frame coherence, so that only some of the image needs to be recomputed from frame to frame. Since there is less rendering to be done at each frame, the cost of ray tracing each frame is correspondingly diminished. Ray tracing becomes

Table 3: Detailed statistics (model : CHESS with shadow)

algorithm component	tree traversal	generate new ray	intersection recalculation	shading recalculation	data management	setting change flags
entire	-	23632	220243	12912	10512	939
change-1	2096	80	6704	496	464	21
change-2	3696	432	24288	1552	1536	59
size	1296	448	9920	720	576	33
light move	22928	0	73936	12912	10507	202
color	288	0	0	224	176	0

The number of processed items is listed.

practical for some computer graphics applications, such as CAD and animation which require high-quality images. Although the partial recomputation of the image is limited to a fixed view point, this limitation is irrelevant in practice in both CAD and animation. In CAD, multiwindow is widely employed in the recent CAD systems, where the user views the model without to change the view parameter often. In addition, there are often many frames with the same camera position in an animation sequence.

Although this method is particularly suitable for a parallel machine such as CAP that has a large amount of memory, recent machines have large memories including the virtual memory space so that the method may be implemented. While a large amount of storage space is required for implementation, the actual amount of data to be accessed can be small. The optimal traversal algorithm reduces the traversal cost by selecting the rays that are likely to change with a hash when small changes are made.

The use of a hash index can be extended to other uses. A description of each ray is needed when ray coherence is used. Although the intersection tree can be used for this purpose, matching trees is computationally expensive. One possible solution to the problem is to describe the ray multiple indices, for example by using the ray's path as we did, and the visible object. The set of visible objects that the ray intersects can be represented with a hash in a similar fashion as the ray's path. These indices can be used to identify each ray.

Appendix. Algorithm Overview

Overall algorithm is outlined.

1. Preprocessing

   – Update the object database and set the changed objects' flag to "changed".

   – Find the voxel elements in which the changed objects exists.

   – Set the flags in hash table of the indices that contain changed voxel elements in the voxel index set stored in the hash table.

2. Optimal tree traversal

   – Traverse a node of the intersection tree in a top-down fashion if the current node is expected to be changed.

   – If the ray has changed, then proceed along the ray until reaching the changed voxel element and apply the intersection recomputation algorithm within this voxel element.

- Do shading recomputation for the changed ray.
- Propagates the updated intensity from the bottom-up.
- Update the global intensity and the global hash index along the parts of tree that was traversed.

3. Detection of change
   - Examine the flag with the hash index. If the flag is set to "changed", then a ray within the corresponding ray-set is expected to have changed.

4. Intersection recomputation (algorithm-1)
   - Recompute the intersections for the changed object.
   - Place the obtained intersection above in a candidate list.
   - Place the intersection obtained from the frame description for the unchanged objects in the candidate list.
   - Determine the closest intersection in the candidate list. This is the visible point.

References

[Aho79] V.Aho, and D. Ullman, Principle of Compiler Design, *Addison-Wesley*, April 1979

[Athe83] P. Atheron, A Scan-line Hidden Surface Removal Procedure for Constructive Solid Geometry, *Computer Graphics*, 17(3), July 1983, 73-82

[Carl89] Carlo H. Sequin and Eliot K. Smyrl, Parameterized Ray Tracing, *Computer Graphics*, 23(3), July 1989, 307-314

[Fuji86] A. Fujimoto, T. Tanaka and K. Iwata, ARTS:Accelerated Ray Tracing System, *IEEE Computer Graphics and Applications*, 6(4), April 1996, 16-26

[Glas84] A. Glassner, Space Subdivision for Fast Ray Tracing, *IEEE Computer Graphics and Applications*, 4(10), October 1984, 15-22

[Hanr84] S. Heckbert, and P. Hanrahan, Beam Tracing Polygonal Object, *Computer Graphics*, 18(3), July 1984, 119-127

[Hubs81] H. Hubschman, and S. Zucker, Frame-to-frame Coherence and the Hidden Surface Computation: Constraints for a Convex World, *Computer Graphics*, 15(3), August 1981, 45-54

[Ishi87] H. Ishihata, M. Kakimoto, VLSI for the Cellular Array Processor, *Proc. ICCD*, October 1987, 320-323

[Jame87] James Arvo and David Kirk, Fast Ray Tracing by Ray Classification, *Computer Graphics*, 21(4), July 1987, 55-64

[John87] John M. Snyder and Alan H. Barr, Ray Tracing Complex Models Containing Surface Tessellations, *Computer Graphics*, 21(4), July 1987, 119-128

[Kapl85] M. Kaplan, The Uses of Spatial Coherence in Ray Tracing, *ACM SIGGRAPH'85 Course Notes 11*, Juky 1985, 22-26

[Kay86] T. Kay, and J. Kajiya, Ray Tracing Complex Scenes, *Computer Graphics*, 20(4), August 1986, 269-278

[Mats83] H. Matsumoto, and K. Murakami, Fast Ray Tracing Using the Octree Partitioning, *27th Information Processing Conference Proceedings*, October 1983, 1537-1538, (In Japanese)

[Mura86] K. Murakami, K. Hirota, and H. Sato, Ray Tracing System Using the Voxel Partitioning on a Cellular Array Processor, *Graphics and CAD*, 22(2), July 1986, 1537-1538, (In Japanese)

[Mura87] K. Murakami, K. Hirota, and M. Ishii, Parallel Ray Tracing System on a Cellular Array Processor, *IFIP:System Modelling and Optimization*, August 1987, 74

[Rubi80] S. Rubin, and T. Whitted, A 3-dimensional Representation for Fast Rendering of Complex Scenes, *Computer Graphics*, 6(1), July 1980, 110-116

[Sato85] H. Sato, M.Ishii, et al. , Fast Image Generation of Constructive Solid Geometry Using a Cellular Array Processor, *Computer Graphics*, 22(2), July 1985, 95-102

[Spee85] L. Speer, and B. Barsky, A Theoretical and Empirical Analysis of Coherent Ray Tracing, *Proceedings of Graphics Interface'85* May 1985, 1-8

[Suth74] I. Sutherland, R. Sproull, and R. Schumacker, A Characterization of Ten Hidden Surface Algorithms, *Computer Surveys*, 6(1), March 1974, 1

[Wegh84] H. Weghorst, G. Hopper and D. Greenberg, Improved Computational Methods for Ray Tracing, *ACM Trans. on Graphics*, 3(1), January 1984, 52-69

Parametric Surfaces and Ray Tracing

Luc Biard *

Abstract

A new method for ray tracing polynomial and rational parametric surfaces is presented. The algorithm we describ is based on algebraic tools (implicitization and inversion) and does not proceed by a previous approximation of the surface. Each surface can be associated with numerical matrices in such a way that operations to be done on surfaces can be translated into operations on the corresponding matrices and treated by numerical matrix techniques. These matrices are an implicit version of a given parametric surface and contain all algebraic and topological informations about it.

1 Introduction

In CAGD, curves and surfaces are usually represented in two ways : either by a set of parametric equations or by implicit equations (i.e., algebraic relations between cartesian coordinates x, y and z). Parametric representations are issued from classical techniques of interpolation and smoothing (Coons, Bézier, B-splines) and are particularly suitable for generating points on the surface (resp. the curve), whereas an implicit equation facilitates answering the following points :

- does a given point belong to the surface (resp. the curve) ?
- study and localization of singularities.

So, in many applications, it seems interesting to have both representations in memory, or at least to be able to change from one of them to the other. Parametric representations are widely used in CAD. Modeling of various physical problems by numerical simulation, dynamical study of shapes, minimal surfaces, ... provides solutions in parametric forms, and interpretation of results needs an accurate visualization in the neighborhood of particular points.

Thus, we deal with visualization of parametric surfaces by ray tracing algorithm, and we treat the main problem of intersection for which accuracy is required.

1.1 Parametric Surfaces

In all this paper $I\!R$ represents the real space and x, y, z are the cartesian coordinates of a point of the affine space $I\!R^3$ whereas u, v are surface parameters.

*Laboratoire de Modélisation et de Calcul
LMC-IMAG, BP 53X
F-38041 Grenoble Cedex - France

1.1.1 Definitions

A parametric surface is defined by a set of equations :

$$x = \varphi_1(u,v), \qquad y = \varphi_2(u,v), \qquad z = \varphi_3(u,v),$$

where the φ_i's are any functions of u and v (including algebraic and transcendental functions). However these forms cannot be used directly since they allow non-polynomial equations. So we need another kind of parametrization [6].

DEFINITION 1.1 *A Generalized Polynomial Parametric Surface (abbr. GPPS) is defined by a system of equations of the form :*

$$\begin{cases} P_1(x,u,v) = 0 \\ P_2(y,u,v) = 0 \\ P_3(z,u,v) = 0 \end{cases} \tag{1}$$

where the P_i's are polynomials (i.e., are in $\mathbb{R}[x,y,z,u,v]$).

So we can write :

$$\begin{cases} P_1(x,u,v) = \sum_{i=0}^{n_1}\sum_{j=0}^{m_1} A_{ij}u^iv^j \\ P_2(y,u,v) = \sum_{i=0}^{n_2}\sum_{j=0}^{m_2} B_{ij}u^iv^j \\ P_3(z,u,v) = \sum_{i=0}^{n_3}\sum_{j=0}^{m_3} C_{ij}u^iv^j \end{cases} \tag{2}$$

where the A_{ij}'s, B_{ij}'s and C_{ij}'s are polynomials in x, y and z respectively.

REMARK 1.1 *A such GPPS is said to be of bi-degrees (n_1, m_1), (n_2, m_2), (n_2, m_2) (in u and v). If $n_1 = n_2 = n_3 = n$ and $m_1 = m_2 = m_3 = m$, the GPPS will be said to be of bi-degree (n, m).*

REMARK 1.2 *We may also consider the P_i's as polynomials in u, v of total degree N_1, N_2, N_3 respectively.*

We note that, if (S) is a GPPS defined as above :

$$M\begin{pmatrix} x \\ y \\ z \end{pmatrix} \in (S) \Leftrightarrow \exists (u,v) \in \mathbb{R}^2, \begin{cases} P_1(x,u,v) = 0 \\ P_2(y,u,v) = 0 \\ P_3(z,u,v) = 0 \end{cases}. \tag{3}$$

In the next section, we will establish that many classical parametric surfaces can be described as GPPS's.

1.1.2 Polynomial Parametric Surfaces

Let us consider a polynomial parametric surface (S_P) defined by

$$\begin{cases} x = \varphi_1(u,v) = \sum_{i=0}^{n_1}\sum_{j=0}^{m_1} a_{ij}u^iv^j \\ y = \varphi_2(u,v) = \sum_{i=0}^{n_2}\sum_{j=0}^{m_2} b_{ij}u^iv^j \\ z = \varphi_3(u,v) = \sum_{i=0}^{n_3}\sum_{j=0}^{m_3} c_{ij}u^iv^j \end{cases} \tag{4}$$

where the a_{ij}'s, b_{ij}'s and c_{ij}'s are real scalars.

So, we can consider (S_P) as a GPPS defined as in (2) where :

$$\begin{cases} A_{00} = a_{00} - x \\ B_{00} = b_{00} - y \\ C_{00} = c_{00} - z \end{cases} \text{ and } \begin{cases} A_{ij} = a_{ij} \\ B_{ij} = b_{ij} \\ C_{ij} = c_{ij} \end{cases} for (i,j) \neq (0,0). \tag{5}$$

1.1.3 Rational Parametric Surfaces

Let us consider a rational parametric surface (S_R) defined as follows :

$$x = \frac{p^1(u,v)}{q^1(u,v)} \ , \ y = \frac{p^2(u,v)}{q^2(u,v)} \ , \ z = \frac{p^3(u,v)}{q^3(u,v)} \ , \tag{6}$$

with

$$p^\alpha(u,v) = \sum_{i=0}^{n_\alpha}\sum_{j=0}^{m_\alpha} p^\alpha_{ij} u^i v^j \text{ and } q^\alpha(u,v) = \sum_{i=0}^{n_\alpha}\sum_{j=0}^{m_\alpha} q^\alpha_{ij} u^i v^j \text{ for } \alpha = 1,2,3 \ ,$$

where the p^k_{ij}'s and q^k_{ij}'s are real scalars.

Then, with :

$$\begin{cases} P_1(x,u,v) = x.q^1(u,v) - p^1(u,v) \\ P_2(y,u,v) = y.q^2(u,v) - p^2(u,v) \\ P_3(z,u,v) = z.q^3(u,v) - p^3(u,v) \end{cases}$$

we may consider (S_R) as a GPPS defined as in (2) where :

$$\begin{cases} A_{ij} = x.q^1_{ij} - p^1_{ij} \\ B_{ij} = y.q^2_{ij} - p^2_{ij} \quad \text{for all } (i,j). \\ C_{ij} = z.q^3_{ij} - p^3_{ij} \end{cases} \tag{7}$$

However, in practice, rational parametric surfaces are often expressed in the classical form as in eq. (6) where :

$$q^1(u,v) = q^2(u,v) = q^3(u,v) = q(u,v) = \sum_{i=0}^{n}\sum_{j=0}^{m} q_{ij} u^i v^j \tag{8}$$

which leads to the GPPS defined by

$$\begin{cases} A_{ij} = x.q_{ij} - p^1_{ij} \\ B_{ij} = y.q_{ij} - p^2_{ij} \quad \text{for all } (i,j). \\ C_{ij} = z.q_{ij} - p^3_{ij} \end{cases} \tag{9}$$

We note that in the rational case all the A_{ij}'s, B_{ij}'s and C_{ij}'s are linear functions of x, y and z respectively.

1.1.4 Trigonometric Parametric Surfaces

Let us consider first the circle parametrized by $x = \cos u$ and $y = \sin u$. If we replace $\cos u$ by $\frac{1-t^2}{1+t^2}$ and $\sin u$ by $\frac{2t}{1+t^2}$ we obtain the rational parametrization :

$$\begin{cases} x = \frac{1-t^2}{1+t^2} \\ y = \frac{2t}{1+t^2} \end{cases}$$

But, we remark that the point $(-1,0)$ of the circle cannot be obtained by those equations. Nevertheless, we will see in the following sections that for our purpose we are able in many case to recover the lost points.

We may parametrize such trigonometric surfaces as GPPS by replacing

$\cos\alpha$ by $\frac{1-t^2}{1+t^2}$,
$\sin\alpha$ by $\frac{2t}{1+t^2}$,
$\cosh\alpha$ by $\frac{1+t^2}{1-t^2}$ with $t \in]-1,+1[$,
$\sinh\alpha$ by $\frac{2t}{1-t^2}$ with $t \in]-1,+1[$,

and by applying the ideas of the previous section.

1.2 Intersection with a Ray

1.2.1 Position of the Problem

Let us consider a ray (R) defined by

$$\begin{cases} x = x_0 + t.x_1 \\ y = y_0 + t.y_1 \\ z = z_0 + t.z_1 \end{cases} \quad (t > 0) \tag{10}$$

where $\vec{R}_0(x_0, y_0, z_0)$ and $\vec{R}_1(x_1, y_1, z_1)$ denotes respectively the origin and the direction of the ray and t the ray parameter. We may also define (R) as the intersection of two planes.

We state the general problem (resp. the polynomial problem). Given a GPPS (resp. a polynomial parametric surface) (S) defined by equations (2) (resp. by equations (4)), and given (S_0) the restriction of (S) to the domain $[0,1]^2$ for parameters u and v, we search the first intersection of (R) with (S_0).

1.2.2 The Methods

We first remark that, except in simple examples, this problem is non-linear and does not have explicit solutions. So all methods require necessarily a linearization step. Moreover, we note that every patch of surface has to be tested for intersection with a lot of rays, and so preconditioning will be indispensable. Let us quote the main approaches.

Tessellation. Since it is very easy to obtain points of a parametric surface the first idea is to substitute a collection of facets for the surface. Thus, for each facet, the problem becomes linear but the topology of the surface can be lost.

Numerical Methods. These approaches consist in solving "directly" equations of intersection by iterative methods (such as Newton or Laguerre's methods). After substitution, intersection equations are obtained in the way of two algebraic relations between surface parameters :

$$\begin{cases} \lambda(u,v) = 0 \\ \mu(u,v) = 0 \end{cases} \tag{11}$$

This problem is the one of intersecting two plane algebraic curves, each of them being the section of the surface by a plane including the ray. Clearly the selection of the first intersection cannot be made by inspection of parameters u and v. Furthermore it is well known that iterative methods are strongly dependant on initialization step, so that these approaches require preliminaries in order to localize and select intersections [2,20,22]. In particular, techniques from Interval Analysis provide an initial guess [21,4].

Subdivision Methods. It is always possible to express a polynomial parametric surface as a Bézier or a B-spline surface [14]. Such methods lie on subdivision techniques and convex hull properties of these surfaces. The patch is assimilated to his polyhedron of control which is repeatedly subdivised up to the wanted precision. Subdivision methods are usually used for some initialization step of others methods.

Algebraic Methods. The first example of algebraic approach is due to Kajiya [12] who treats equations (11) by resultant techniques. An other example comes from Sederberg and Anderson [18], who realize implicitisation of Steiner patches. We will describe and generalize this approach in next chapters.

Particular parametric surfaces such as revolution surfaces [5] or extruded surfaces can be treated with appropriate tools.

1.3 Our Approach

We observe first that for curve-surface or surface-surface intersection problems it is better to have one surface defined by an implicit equation $f(x, y, z) = 0$ and the other surface (resp. the curve) defined by a parametric representation $x(u, v), y(u, v), z(u, v)$ (resp. $x(t), y(t), z(t)$), so that after substitution we obtain the intersection equation $g(u, v) = f(x(u, v), y(u, v), z(u, v)) = 0$ (resp. $g(t) = f(x(t), y(t), z(t)) = 0$), which is easier to solve.

We have thus transformed our problem into an implicit one, so that the search for the first intersection leads us to a single variable equation (this variable being the ray parameter), which allows us to select the roots easily. So, we consider the problem of obtaining an implicit representation from a parametric one, which is called **implicitization**. However, the need of surface parameters for checking a ray-patch intersection and for calculating photometric values, leads to the **inversion** problem.

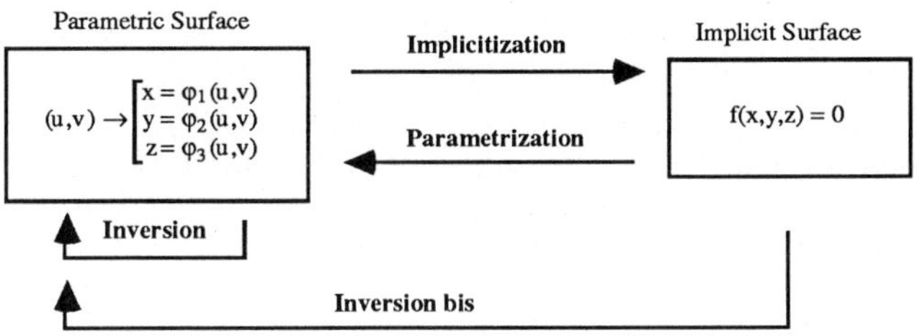

Fig. 1.1

DEFINITION 1.2 *If (S) and (S') are respectively the GPPS and the implicit surface of figure 1.1, we call inversion (resp. inversion bis) the determination of parameters u and v for a given point of (S) (resp. (S')).*

So, the method is described by the following algorithm :

(Conditioning)
For every surface **Do**
  Implicitization
(Treatment)
For every ray **Do**
  (If there is a candidat patch)
  Determination of the intersection equation
    (which leads to a single variable polynomial equation)
  Resolution of this equation in a given interval
  Inversion

2 Implicitization of a GPPS

Our goal is to develop numerical algorithms for geometrical applications in modeling and visualization. We must consider two different aspects : first how to obtain the implicit equation for a GPPS and second, a qualitative aspect which consists in comparing the implicit surface (S') so obtained with the initial parametric one (S). This last point is of crucial importance for our purpose. For example, if a ray intersects the implicit surface (S') on a point I, we must verify that this point belongs to the parametric surface (S), otherwise the inversion step will be impossible.

We do not deal here with this qualitative aspect (see [3]). Nevertheless we give the following ideas :

- For any GPPS (S) we can determine an algebraic implicit equation $f(x, y, z) = 0$ which defines an implicit surface (S') such as $(S) \subset (S')$.
- In algebraic geometry language (S') is the closure of (S) for Zariski's topology. Thus, in most cases, egality between (S) and (S') does not hold.
- In our context of non-projective real geometry, differences between the two surfaces are still more pronounced.
- Implicitization depends on the quality of the parametrization. As an example, here are two following parametrizations of the same surface :

$$\begin{cases} x = 1 + u^2 \\ y = 1 - v^2 \\ z = 1 + u^2 - v^2 - u^2v^2 \end{cases} \quad \text{and} \quad \begin{cases} x = s \\ y = t \quad (s \geq 1, t \leq 1) \\ z = st \end{cases}$$

- A precise approach is given in [6] in a context of computational algebra.

Now, let us consider the technical aspect of obtaining such an implicit equation from a parametric one. Computing various Sylvester's resultants of the parametric equations will eliminate the parameters and give us a multiple of the corresponding implicit equation. In practice, however, this multiple can be of higher degree, making it difficult to factor and determine which factors correspond to our surface [6]. Another way, very interesting for computational algebra, consists in using Gröbner bases [6,7]. However, Gröbner bases do not fit numerical applications. We can still notice that special parametric surfaces such as monoids may be avantageously treated by appropriate techniques (see [17,18] for Steiner Patches).

For the general case, we apply Dixon's approach [10] (as proposed in [19]), which allows us preconditioning and provides a better implicit equation than Sylvester's approach. Some examples are given at the end of this paper and in [3] which compare Sylvester's, Gröbner bases and Dixon's approaches in polynomial and rational cases.

For three quantics in two independant variables, Dixon introduces a tool similar to the one used by Cayley for two quantics in a single variable. We will now present this method for implicitization of GPPS's.

The method is described for a GPPS of bi-degree (n, m) (cf. remark 1.1), i.e., the P_i's are all of degree n in u and degree m in v. In last section, examples show how the method can be extented to the general case (2).

2.1 Notations

Consider a Generalized Polynomial Parametric Surface (S) defined as in (1) by :

$$\begin{cases} P_1(x, u, v) = \sum_{i=0}^{n} \sum_{j=0}^{m} A_{ij}(x) u^i v^j = 0 \\ P_2(y, u, v) = \sum_{i=0}^{n} \sum_{j=0}^{m} B_{ij}(y) u^i v^j = 0 \\ P_3(z, u, v) = \sum_{i=0}^{n} \sum_{j=0}^{m} C_{ij}(z) u^i v^j = 0 \end{cases} . \tag{12}$$

We consider the two dual determinants F_1 and F_2 (where M stands for (x,y,z)) :

$$F_1(u,v,M,a,b) = \begin{vmatrix} P_1(x,u,v) & P_1(x,u,b) & P_1(x,a,b) \\ P_2(y,u,v) & P_2(y,u,b) & P_2(y,a,b) \\ P_3(z,u,v) & P_3(z,u,b) & P_3(z,a,b) \end{vmatrix},$$

$$F_2(u,v,M,a,b) = \begin{vmatrix} P_1(x,u,v) & P_1(x,a,v) & P_1(x,a,b) \\ P_2(y,u,v) & P_2(y,a,v) & P_2(y,a,b) \\ P_3(z,u,v) & P_3(z,a,v) & P_3(z,a,b) \end{vmatrix},$$

where all the concerned variables are real. Then by remarking that F_1 and F_2 factorize by $(u-a)$ and $(v-b)$ we write :

$$\delta_1(u,v,M,a,b) = \frac{F_1(u,v,M,a,b)}{(u-a)(v-b)} \text{ and } \delta_2(u,v,M,a,b) = \frac{F_2(u,v,M,a,b)}{(u-a)(v-b)}$$

and so, for any u,v,M,a,b we have :

$$\begin{array}{l} F_1(a,b,M,u,v) = -F_2(u,v,M,a,b) \\ \delta_1(a,b,M,u,v) = -\delta_2(u,v,M,a,b) \end{array}. \tag{13}$$

Now we consider the *fondamental property* for our purpose. From the definitions of F_1 and F_2 and from (3) we see that if M belongs to (S) there exist parameters u and v such that for any real a and b :

$$\delta_1(u,v,M,a,b) = \delta_2(u,v,M,a,b) = 0. \tag{14}$$

In [3], it is shown thanks to (13) that the method does not depend on the choice of δ_1 or δ_2, so we go on with δ_1 which we note δ.

Note that δ is a polynomial of degree :

$$2n-1 \text{ in } u, \quad m-1 \text{ in } v, \quad n-1 \text{ in } a, \quad 2m-1 \text{ in } b,$$

so we can write :

$$\delta(u,v,M,a,b) = \sum_{i=0}^{2n-1}\sum_{j=0}^{m-1}\sum_{k=0}^{n-1}\sum_{l=0}^{2m-1} T_{ij}^{kl}(M)u^i v^j a^k b^l. \tag{15}$$

2.2 Description

We can consider δ as a polynomial in a and b whose coefficients are polynomials in u, v and $M(x,y,z)$.

$$\delta = \sum_{k=0}^{n-1}\sum_{l=0}^{2m-1} f_{kl}(u,v,M)a^k b^l. \tag{16}$$

This polynomial have **2nm** terms in $a^k b^l$. So, if M belongs to (S) there exist parameters u and v such as :

$$f_{kl}(u,v,M) = 0 \tag{17}$$

$$\text{for } 0 \le k \le n-1 \text{ and } 0 \le l \le 2m-1,$$

which we can write from (15) :

$$\sum_{i=0}^{2n-1}\sum_{j=0}^{m-1} T_{ij}^{kl}(M)u^i v^j = 0 \text{ for } \begin{cases} 0 \le k \le n-1 \\ 0 \le l \le 2m-1 \end{cases}.$$

We then obtain :

$$\begin{bmatrix} T_{00}^{00} & \cdots & T_{ij}^{00} & \cdots & T_{2n-1,m-1}^{00} \\ \cdot & & \cdot & & \cdot \\ T_{00}^{kl} & \cdots & T_{ij}^{kl} & \cdots & T_{2n-1,m-1}^{kl} \\ \cdot & & \cdot & & \cdot \\ T_{00}^{n-1,2m-1} & \cdots & T_{ij}^{n-1,2m-1} & \cdots & T_{2n-1,m-1}^{n-1,2m-1} \end{bmatrix} \begin{bmatrix} u^0v^0 \\ \cdot \\ u^iv^j \\ \cdot \\ u^{2n-1}v^{m-1} \end{bmatrix} = \begin{bmatrix} 0 \\ \cdot \\ 0 \\ \cdot \\ 0 \end{bmatrix},$$

where the T_{ij}^{kl} are polynomials in x, y and z,

$$\Leftrightarrow T.\begin{bmatrix} u \\ v \end{bmatrix}_{(n,m)} = 0, \tag{18}$$

with $T = T(x,y,z) = \left[\left(T_{ij}^{kl}(x,y,z)\right)\right]$ and $\begin{bmatrix} u \\ v \end{bmatrix}_{(n,m)} = \begin{bmatrix} 1 \\ \cdot \\ \cdot \\ u^iv^j \\ \cdot \\ u^{2n-1}v^{m-1} \end{bmatrix}$, where the order of the rows (i.e., of monoms a^kb^l) and of the columns (i.e., of monoms u^iv^j) of matrix T is the one of summations on i, j, k, l defined by (15), i.e., $T_{ij}^{kl} = T[p,q]$ with $\begin{cases} p = 2m.k + l + 1 \\ q = m.i + j + 1 \end{cases}$.

Nevertheless, in practice, we sometimes consider another order for regrouping certain terms (see remark 2.3). Thus, for each $M(x,y,z)$ of the parametric surface (S) there exist parameters u and v so that the homogeneous system (18) has a non-trivial solution (i.e., the vector $\begin{bmatrix} u \\ v \end{bmatrix}_{(n,m)}$). So, the determinant of T must vanish for the corresponding values of x, y, z and this provides the desired implicit equation :

$$det(T) = f(x,y,z) = 0.$$

REMARK 2.1 *If we note T_1 (resp. T_2) the matrix obtained from δ_1 (resp. δ_2), we have $T_2 = -{}^tT_1$, so that $det(T_1) = det(T_2)$.*

In conclusion , if we note (S') the surface defined by the implicit equation $f(x,y,z) = 0$, we have proved that $(S) \subset (S')$.

2.3 Evaluation of Coefficients T_{ij}^{kl}

Every T_{ij}^{kl} of the matrix T is the coefficient of monom $u^iv^ja^kb^l$ in the polynomial δ (cf. (15)).

Let us introduce the following notations :

$$\begin{vmatrix} A_{pq} & A_{rs} & A_{tu} \\ B_{pq} & B_{rs} & B_{tu} \\ C_{pq} & C_{rs} & C_{tu} \end{vmatrix} = (pq, rs, tu) = (\vec{pq}, \vec{rs}, \vec{tu})$$

$$= \begin{bmatrix} p & r & t \\ q & s & u \end{bmatrix} \text{ for composite indices,}$$

where the A_{pq}'s, B_{rs}'s and C_{tu}'s are the GPPS's coefficients and stand for $A_{pq}(x)$, $B_{rs}(y)$ and $C_{tu}(z)$ (cf. (12)).

An expression of coefficients T_{ij}^{kl} can be found in [10], but a simple direct calculation [3] gives the more precise formula :

$$\mathbf{T}_{ij}^{kl} = \sum_{r,r',s,s'} \begin{bmatrix} r & r' & 1+i+k-(r+r') \\ s & 1+j+l-(s+s') & s' \end{bmatrix} \tag{19}$$

with :

$$\begin{cases} 0 \le r \le n \\ 0 \le r' \le n \\ 1+i+k-n \le r+r' \le i \end{cases} \quad \text{and} \quad \begin{cases} 0 \le s \le m \\ 0 \le s' \le m \\ 1+j+l-m \le s+s' \le l \end{cases} .$$

2.4 Degree of the Implicit Equation

2.4.1 Polynomial Case

From (5), remember that every coefficient A_{pq}, B_{rs} and C_{tu} is a real scalar, except for A_{00}, B_{00} and C_{00}, which are linear functions of x, y and z respectively. So, formula (19) shows that :

$$s+s' \le L \text{ and } 0 \le J \Rightarrow s+s' \le J+L \Rightarrow 1+J+L-(s+s') \ge 1$$

$$r+r' \le I \text{ and } 0 \le K \Rightarrow r+r' \le I+K \Rightarrow 1+I+K-(r+r') \ge 1$$

and thus only (r,s) may be equal to $(0,0)$. So, every coefficient of matrix T is at most a linear expression in x, y and z. Matrix T being of order $2nm$, its determinant will be at most of degree **2nm** :

$$f(x,y,z) = det(T) = \sum_{i+j+k \le 2nm} \lambda_{ijk} x^i y^j z^k$$

2.4.2 Rational Case

In this case every coefficient A_{pq}, B_{rs} and C_{tu} is a linear function of x, y, and z respectively. Thus, for a general rational parametric surface defined by (6), every coefficient of the matrix T is of degree 3 in x, y and z, and so its determinant will be at most of degree **6nm** :

$$f(x,y,z) = det(T) = \sum_{i+j+k \le 6nm} \lambda_{ijk} x^i y^j z^k$$

Nevertheless, for a classical rational parametric surface defined by (8) the degree is at most **2nm**, as for a polynomial one [19].

For this purpose, let us consider relation (9). Using multilinearity of the determinant function, each determinant (pq, rs, tu) involved in formula (19) can be written :

$$\begin{aligned}
(pq,rs,tu) &= \begin{vmatrix} xq_{pq}-p_{pq}^1 & xq_{rs}-p_{rs}^1 & xq_{tu}-p_{tu}^1 \\ yq_{pq}-p_{pq}^2 & yq_{rs}-p_{rs}^2 & yq_{tu}-p_{tu}^2 \\ zq_{pq}-p_{pq}^3 & zq_{rs}-p_{rs}^3 & zq_{tu}-p_{tu}^3 \end{vmatrix} \\
&= \begin{vmatrix} xq_{pq} & xq_{rs} & xq_{tu} \\ yq_{pq} & yq_{rs} & yq_{tu} \\ zq_{pq} & zq_{rs} & zq_{tu} \end{vmatrix} + \begin{vmatrix} xq_{pq} & xq_{rs} & -p_{tu}^1 \\ yq_{pq} & yq_{rs} & -p_{tu}^2 \\ zq_{pq} & zq_{rs} & -p_{tu}^3 \end{vmatrix} + \dots + \begin{vmatrix} -p_{pq}^1 & -p_{rs}^1 & -p_{tu}^1 \\ -p_{pq}^2 & -p_{rs}^2 & -p_{tu}^2 \\ -p_{pq}^3 & -p_{rs}^3 & -p_{tu}^3 \end{vmatrix}
\end{aligned}$$

Then, any of these determinants which have more than one column involving x, y or z must vanish since any two such columns are linearly dependent. Hence, each (pq, rs, tu) is linear in x, y and z, which gives us the result. We recall that the number of terms for such a polynomial of total degree N is $C_{N+3}^3 = (N+1)(N+2)(N+3)/6$.

2.5 Implementation

2.5.1 Symbolic Algebraic Computation

We have implemented the method using system "Reduce". Our algorithm allows to implicit GPPS's of any bi-degrees in u and v as defined in (2).

Let us consider the following example.

$$\begin{cases} x = & 1 - u + uv - 3v^2 + u^2v \\ y = & 2 - u - uv^2 + u^2v^2 \\ z = & -1 + 6u - uv - u^2 - 2v^2 \end{cases} \tag{20}$$

	1	v	u	u v	u²	u²v	u³	u³v
1	0	-2x+20y +3z-35	-x-5y -z+10	-6x-3y -z+11	-5y-z+9	7x+z-6	y-2	-x+1
a	0	-3y+6	y-2	x-4	y-1	-x+2	1	-1
b	-2x+20y +3z-35	-5y+10	-6x-3y -z+11	x-2y +z+4	7x+z-6	-x+1	-x+1	-z-1
ab	-3y+6	-2y+4	x-y-2	z-1	-x+1	-z-8	-1	7
b²	-5y+10	-2x+3z +5	-2y-1	2x-3z -25	-2	23	0	-3
ab²	-2y+4	2x-3z-5	x+2z-1	20	-11	-2	2	-1
b³	-2x+3z +5	0	2x-3z -25	5	23	-3	-3	-2
ab³	2x-3z-5	0	20	-5	-3	-2	0	0

Fig. 2.1 Matrix $T(x, y, z)$ for example (20).

Some examples given in [3] are discussed in section 4.

2.5.2 Numerical Computation

For numerical applications, the evaluation of the implicit equation by an algebraic system leads to numerical problems. It is more suitable to consider the implicit equation of the surface in the matricial form $T(x, y, z)$ directly. Then, processings concerning the surface are converted into processings on matrix T by means of matrix techniques.

Thus, we avoid phases of evaluation in intersection problems and moreover, this matrix approach allows easy solving of the inversion problem.

So, we need to compute the matrix T from the GPPS coefficients. Each coefficient T_{ij}^{kl} of T is a sum of some determinants (pq, rs, tu) (with notation (19)) defined by the relation (19). So, we build a *symbolic table* which provides the concerned determinants (pq, rs, tu) for each bi-degree (n, m).

• **Symbolic table**

Data structures used (for language C) and an algorithm of construction of the symbolic table for each (n, m) is given in [3].

	1	v	u	uv	u^2	u^2v	u^3	u^3v
1	00 01 10	00 02 10	00 01 20 00 11 10	00 02 20 00 12 10	00 11 20 00 21 10	00 12 20 00 22 10	00 21 20	00 22 20
a	00 01 20	00 02 20	00 11 20 10 01 20	00 12 20 10 02 20	00 21 20 10 11 20	00 22 20 10 12 20	10 21 20	10 22 20
b	00 02 10 00 01 11	00 02 11 01 02 10	00 02 20 00 01 21 00 12 10 01 11 10	00 02 21 01 02 20 00 12 11 01 12 10	00 12 20 01 11 20 00 22 10 01 21 10	00 12 21 01 12 20 00 22 11 01 22 10	00 22 20 01 21 20	00 22 21 01 22 20
ab	00 02 20 00 01 21	00 02 21 01 02 20	00 12 20 00 11 21 10 02 20 10 01 21	00 12 21 01 12 20 10 02 21 11 02 20	00 22 20 01 21 20 10 12 20 10 11 21	00 22 21 01 22 20 10 12 21 11 12 20	10 22 20 11 21 20	10 22 21 11 22 20
b^2	00 02 11 00 01 12	00 02 12 01 02 11	00 02 21 00 01 22 01 12 10 02 11 10	00 02 22 01 02 21 01 12 11 02 12 10	01 12 20 02 11 20 01 22 10 02 21 10	01 12 21 02 12 20 01 22 11 02 22 10	01 22 20 02 21 20	01 22 21 02 22 20
ab^2	00 02 21 00 01 22	00 02 22 01 02 21	00 12 21 00 11 22 10 02 21 10 01 22	00 12 22 01 12 21 10 02 22 11 02 21	01 22 20 02 21 20 10 12 21 10 11 22	01 22 21 02 22 20 10 12 22 11 12 21	11 22 20 12 21 20	11 22 21 12 22 20
b^3	00 02 12	01 02 12	00 02 22 02 12 10	01 02 22 02 12 11	02 12 20 02 22 10	02 12 21 02 22 11	02 22 20	02 22 21
ab^3	00 02 22	01 02 22	00 12 22 10 02 22	01 12 22 11 02 22	02 22 20 10 12 22	02 22 21 11 12 22	12 22 20	12 22 21

Fig. 2.2 Symbolic table for $n = m = 2$.

We present in figure 2.2 the symbolic table obtained for $n = m = 2$ (i.e., for a biquadratic parametric surface).

Observation of these tables shows that :

REMARK 2.2 *A symbolic table of bi-degree (n', m') may be viewed as a sub-table of a symbolic table of bi-degree (n, m) where $n' \leq n$ and $m' \leq m$.*

REMARK 2.3 *Many elements of these symbolic tables do not contain determinants (pq, rs, tu) such as $pq = 00$, so that in the polynomial case all the corresponding coefficients T_{ij}^{kl} do not depend on x, y and z and are real scalars determined by the surface coefficients (see for example the figure 2.1).*

For example, when $n = m = 2$, we have hatched all these concerned elements in figure 2.3.

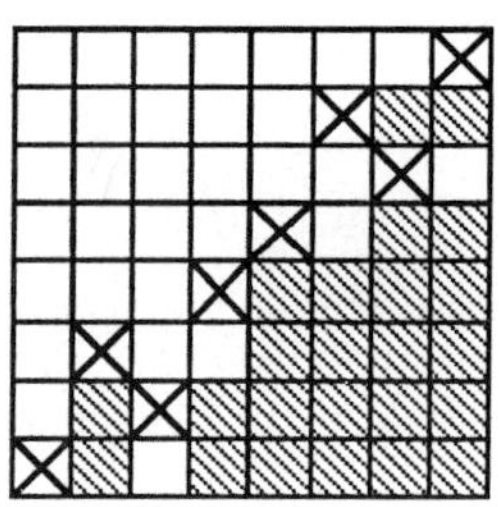

Fig. 2.3

Nevertheless, we remark on this last example that despite the large number of constant terms, the degree 8 is reached (consider the marked terms).

3 Intersection with a Ray

We consider the *general problem* and we apply the method proposed in chapter 1. According to chapter 2, each GPPS is associated with a "polynomial" matrix $T(x, y, z)$ (i.e., a matrix whose elements are polynomials in the cartesian coordinates x, y and z). The ray is defined by a parametric representation as in (10).

For a *polynomial parametric surface* (S_P) (4), or a *classic rational parametric surface* (S_{R0}) (8) of bi-degree (n, m), we get a matrix $T(x, y, z)$ of order $2nm$, whose coefficients are of total degree one in x, y and z. In these two cases, the method would be similar and we only treat here of the *polynomial problem.*

For a *general rational parametric surface* (S_R) (6) two strategies are discussed in chapter 4.

We therefore consider a (n, m) bi-degree polynomial parametric surface (S).

3.1 The Method

Remembering that every coefficient of T is a linear expression in x, y, and z, we substitute the ray equations $x(t)$, $y(t)$ and $z(t)$ in the matrix $T(x,y,z)$ so that every coefficient of T becomes a linear expression in the ray parameter t.

Thus we can write : $T = A - t.B$, where A and B are numerical matrices which depend on ray and surface coefficients.

So, intersection equation is given by :

$$g(t) = det(A - t.B) = 0$$

We treat of the intersection problem in this matricial form and we separate surface and ray computations.

We can now state the general algorithm given in chapter 1 more precisely (see figure 3.1).

Pre-Conditioning for each surface.
Compute all terms in matrices A and B which only depend on the surface.
Treatment for each ray.
Evaluation of matrices A and B.
Treatment of the intersection equation $g(t) = det(A - tB) = 0$ with :
- algebraic phases to decide of non-intersection cases,
- numerical phases (Gauss, Subdivision) to compute the roots.

Inversion for each intersection found.

Let us specify each step.

3.2 Conditioning for Every Surface

In this section, we consider the more precise following notations :

$$(PQ, RS, TU) = \begin{vmatrix} A_{PQ} & A_{RS} & A_{TU} \\ B_{PQ} & B_{RS} & B_{TU} \\ C_{PQ} & C_{RS} & C_{TU} \end{vmatrix} \text{ and } (pq, rs, tu) = \begin{vmatrix} a_{pq} & a_{rs} & a_{tu} \\ b_{pq} & b_{rs} & b_{tu} \\ c_{pq} & c_{rs} & c_{tu} \end{vmatrix}$$

where the a_{pq}'s, b_{rs}'s and c_{tu}'s are the polynomial surface coefficients (4), and where the A_{PQ}'s, B_{RS}'s and C_{TU}'s are the coefficients of the corresponding GPPS version defined in (5).

Let us recall that each coefficient T_{ij}^{kl} of matrix T is a sum of determinants (PQ, RS, TU) where only PQ may be equal to 00. Thus, from (5) and by replacing $M(x,y,z)$ by $\vec{R}_0 + t.\vec{R}_1$, we have with obvious notations :

$$\begin{aligned}
\text{if } PQ \neq 00 \text{ then } (PQ, RS, TU) &= (pq, rs, tu) = \vec{pq}.(\vec{rs} \wedge \vec{tu}) \\
&= \alpha, \text{ which only depends on the surface,} \\
\text{if } PQ = 00 \text{ then } (PQ, RS, TU) &= (\vec{pq} - \vec{R}_0 - t.\vec{R}_1, \vec{rs}, \vec{tu}) \\
&= (\vec{pq} - \vec{R}_0 - t.\vec{R}_1).(\vec{rs} \wedge \vec{tu}) \\
&= (\vec{pq} - \vec{R}_0 - t.\vec{R}_1).\vec{\beta} \\
&= \vec{pq}.\vec{\beta} - \vec{R}_0.\vec{\beta} - t\vec{R}_1.\vec{\beta} \\
&= \alpha - \vec{R}_0.\vec{\beta} - t\vec{R}_1.\vec{\beta} \\
&= a - tb,
\end{aligned}$$

where :

$$a = \alpha - \vec{R}_0.\vec{\beta} \text{ and } b = \vec{R}_1.\vec{\beta}. \tag{21}$$

In both cases, scalar α and vector $\vec{\beta}$ only depend on the surface, whereas scalars a and b also depend on the ray. Then, the evaluation of each T_{ij}^{kl} is given by formula (19) and by :

$$\begin{aligned}
T_{ij}^{kl} &= \sum (PQ, RS, TU) \\
&= \sum_{PQ \neq 00} (PQ, RS, TU) + \sum_{PQ = 00} (PQ, RS, TU) \\
&= \sum_g \alpha_g + \sum_h \left(\alpha_h - \vec{R}_0.\vec{\beta}_h - t\vec{R}_1.\vec{\beta}_h\right) \\
&= \sum_g \alpha_g + \sum_h \alpha_h - \vec{R}_0.\sum_h \vec{\beta}_h - t\vec{R}_1.\sum_h \vec{\beta}_h \\
&= \alpha_{ij}^{kl} - \vec{R}_0.\vec{\beta}_{ij}^{kl} - t\vec{R}_1.\vec{\beta}_{ij}^{kl}.
\end{aligned}$$

So, we have :

$$T_{ij}^{kl} = a_{ij}^{kl} - tb_{ij}^{kl},$$

with :

$$\begin{cases} a_{ij}^{kl} = \alpha_{ij}^{kl} - \vec{R}_0.\vec{\beta}_{ij}^{kl} \\ b_{ij}^{kl} = \vec{R}_1.\vec{\beta}_{ij}^{kl} \end{cases} \tag{22}$$

where scalars α_{ij}^{kl} and vectors $\vec{\beta}_{ij}^{kl}$ are only determined by the surface.

Thus, we associate each polynomial parametric surface of bi-degree (n, m) with the square matrix $\tilde{T}$ of order $2nm$ whose elements consist of scalars α_{ij}^{kl} and vectors $\vec{\beta}_{ij}^{kl}$ previously defined.

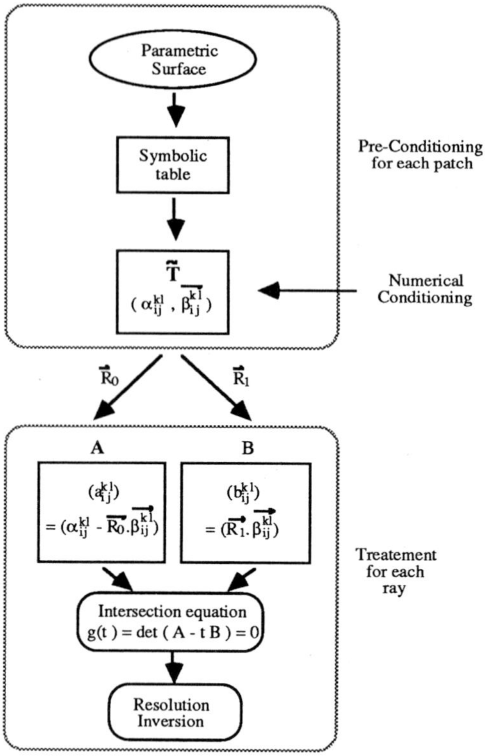

Fig. 3.1 General algorithm.

3.3 Treatment for Every Ray

3.3.1 Evaluation of Matrices A and B

For each ray, the numerical matrices A and B are obtained from relation (22) and their computation requires :

$2.N.N$ inner products,

$N.N$ additions (where $N = 2nm$).

The following two remarks are important when considering complexity optimization.

REMARK 3.1 *We note that matrix A (resp. matrix B) only depends on the origin (resp. the direction) of the ray and on the surface. So, for any ray originated at a common point (in particular for the primar rays) the matrix A is the same.*

REMARK 3.2 *We have shown at the end of chapter 2 (in remark 2.3) that many coefficients of the matrix $T(x, y, z)$ associated with a polynomial parametric surface were independent of x, y and z, so that the corresponding vectors $\vec{\beta}_{ij}^{kl}$ were null. Thus, we have directly for the corresponding terms of the matrix A and B :*

$$a_{ij}^{kl} = \alpha_{ij}^{kl} \text{ and } b_{ij}^{kl} = 0.$$

3.3.2 Treatment of the Intersection Equation

The determinant form of the intersection equation allows performing algebraic treatments [9,11] which have not yet been studied. So we proceed in the following way.

• Since $g(t) = det(A - tB)$ is a polynomial of degree $N = 2nm$, we evaluate it in $N+1$ values uniformly distributed in the given interval $[t_{min}, t_{max}]$ and express g as a Bézier curve.

• The second step consists of solving the intersection equation $g(t) = 0$. For this purpose, we apply the following method which has been developed by D. Marchepoil in [15]. The algorithm is based on the technique of Bézier subdivisions for which the proportions of subdivision are made according knots surrounding the intersection of the control polygon with the t-axis. Other methods are discussed in [15] (see also [13,16]). By a convexity argument, this method enables us to easily detect non-intersection situations and it has furthermore a high level of safety.

If $g(t)$ is expressed as $\sum_{i=0}^{N} p_i B_i^N(t)$ the following recursive procedure $Roots()$ computes all the roots of $g(t)$ in $[a,b]$ in the increasing order, which allows us to select the desired one.

```
Procedure Roots({p_0, p_1, ..., p_N}, a, b, edge)
Begin
  k = Min_{i∈{0,1,...,N-1}} {i/p_i p_{i+1} ≤ 0};
  If k does not exist Then Eliminate interval [a, b];
  Else
    Begin
      If (b - a) < ε Then
        Begin
          r = (k p_{k+1} - (k+1) p_k) / (N (p_{k+1} - p_k)) (b - a) + a;
          Give the root r ;
        End
      Else
        Begin
          If right edge Then k = k + 1;
          If k = 0 Then k = 1;
          If k = N Then k = N - 1;
          Split {p_0, p_1, ..., p_N} according to k/N;
          t = a + k(b - a)/N;
          Roots({p_0^0, p_0^1, ..., p_0^i, ..., p_0^N}, a, t, left);
          Roots({p_0^N, p_1^{N-1}, ..., p_i^{N-i}, ..., p_N^0}, t, b, right);
        End
    End
End
```

3.3.3 Inversion

Given $\bar{t}$ a root of the intersection equation $g(t) = det(A - tB) = 0$, we search for the corresponding parameters $\bar{u}$ and $\bar{v}$ of the intersection point. In fact, this step allows to check if the associated point of (S') belongs to (S). (cf. chapter 4)

We note $\overline{T}$ the numerical matrix defined by $A - \bar{t}B$.

Then $rank(\overline{T}) \leq 2nm - 1$. So, the homogeneous system $\overline{T}.\begin{bmatrix} u \\ v \end{bmatrix}_{(n,m)} = 0$ has a non-trivial solution which we hope to be in the form $\begin{bmatrix} \bar{u} \\ \bar{v} \end{bmatrix}_{(n,m)}$. In our practice, this consideration has been already verified for a suitable parametrization.

So, we apply Gauss elimination to triangularize the matrix $\overline{T}$ with permutation of the rows but without permutation of the columns, so that the unknown vector $\begin{bmatrix} \overline{u} \\ \overline{v} \end{bmatrix}_{(n,m)}$ remains unchanged.

PROPOSITION 3.1 *If* $rank(\overline{T}) = 2nm - 1$, *then the system* $\overline{T}.\begin{bmatrix} u \\ v \end{bmatrix}_{(n,m)} = 0$, *where the order of the columns has been reversed, triangularize on the following form :*

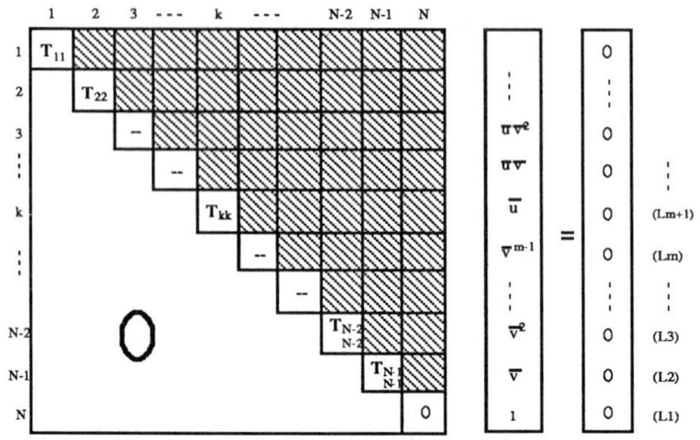

Fig. 3.2

where $T_{kk} \neq 0$ *for* $k = 1, 2, ..., N - 1$ $(N = 2nm)$.

In other word, in Gauss elimination without permutation of columns, the zero pivot is pushed back to the last position.

Hence, the last equations (L_2) to (L_{m+1}) leads us to an easy computation of the desired parameters $\overline{u}$ and $\overline{v}$.

For example, consider a biquadratic parametric surface for which we obtain :

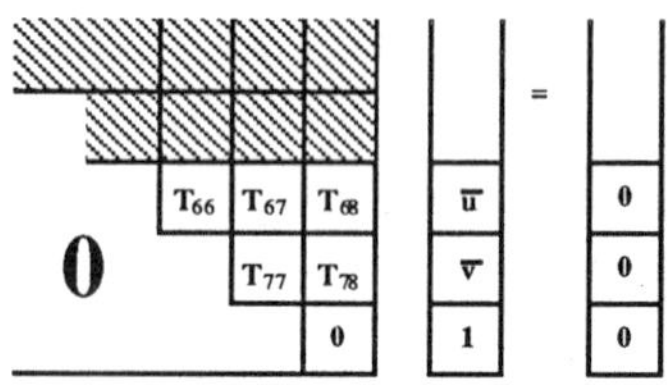

Fig. 3.3

which immediately gives $\overline{u}$ and $\overline{v}$.

4 Discussion and Results

As in the existing methods, the proposed one involves an iterative process. Here, an iterative process is used only at the end to solve a single variable equation by Bézier subdivision. In theory, this method is of a great accuracy. Nevertheless, we must control many numerical phases.

- Numerical conditioning.

  First of all it is important to notice that the array $\tilde{T}$ has been correctly computed so as to guarantee numerical stability. Secondly, most of our numerical computations use Gauss algorithm. Stability requires normalization of the concerned matrices. These normalizations are a little expensive. Nevertheless, it may be noticed that all operations performed on these matrices are carried out up a scalar factor. So, normalizations are performed directly on the numerical matrix $\tilde{T}$ during the conditioning step.

- Computation optimization.

  From remark 3.1 we keep in memory the numerical *origin* matrix A for all rays starting from a common origin. Moreover, from remark 3.2 the evaluation of *origin* and *direction* matrices A and B are simplified.

- Treatment of the intersection equation.

  The classical approach in this situation consists first in isolating the roots in the given interval with algebraic tools [1,8]. The main purpose of this step is to detect non-intersection situations.

  The subdivision algorithm used in our method allows us to quickly detect non-intersection cases from the convex hull property and it is numerically stable since we subdivise according the knots. Furthermore, this algorithm allows us to calculate any desired level of precision. A precision of d binary digits requires $dN(N+1)/2$ combinations, where N is the degree of the Bézier curve.

  Experimentations of this algorithm can be found in [15]. Let us consider in particular results obtained with the following polynom :

  $$g_\lambda(t) = t(t-0.1)(t^2+1)(t^2+2)((t-0.5)^2+\lambda)$$

  which has a double root in 0.5 for $\lambda = 0$. The subdivision algorithm can separate the roots for any negative λ until $-1E-12$. Furthermore, this algorithm detects when there is no root for any positive λ until $1E-12$. For all these tests, the number of subdivisions cannot exceed 15, and precision required is $1E-5$.

- Comparison with other implicitization methods.

  • *Sylvester's method.* The two following dual Sylvester methods have been implemented with system Reduce on Sun work station : *Sylvest1* (resp. *Sylvest2*) consists in first eliminating the parameter u (resp. v) and then the parameter v (resp. u).

  Results are presented in the following table where the implicit equations obtained have been factorized. The desired implicit equation of the surface is denoted by $S^p = S^p(x,y,z)$ where p is the total degree. The added factors are noted by $P^q = P^q(x,y,z)$ in the same way. In general, Dixon's method of computation is three times faster than Sylvester's. But, as soon as the degrees of expressions increase (see examples) Sylvester's methods do not work (Head Space Low : *HSL*).

Parametric Polynomial Surface	Bi-degree	*Dixon*	*Sylvest1*	*Sylvest2*
$1-u+uv-3v^2+u^2v$ $2-u-uv^2+u^2v^2$ $-1+6u-uv-u^2-2v^2$	$(2,2)$	S^8	*HSL*	*HSL*
$1+u+v+uv$ $2+uv+u^2$ $-1+uv^2$	$(2,2)$	S^5	P^6S^5	$(y-2)^2S^5$
$1+u+v+uv^2+u^2v^2$ $uv-v^2-2u^2v$ $3+uv^2-u^2v$	$(2,2)$	S^7	*HSL*	*HSL*
$1-u+v-2uv+u^2-v^2$ $-1+2u-v+uv+2u^2+v^2$ $3-u-v+2uv-u^2+2v^2$	$(2,2)$	S^4	S^4P^4	S^4P^4
$1+u+2uv-v^3$ $-2+uv^3$ $5-u-uv+uv^2+v^3$	$(1,3)$	S^6	$(y+2)^3S^6$	*HSL*
$1+u^3$ $1+v^3$ $(1+u^3)(1+v^3)$	$(3,3)$	$(xy-z)^9$	*HSL*	$(xy-z)^{27}$
$1+u+v^3$ $1+u^3+v$ $-1+u^2v^2$	$(3,3)$	S^{12}	*HSL*	*HSL*

- *Gröbner basis algorithm.* Let us consider the following example proposed by Buchberger in [7].

$$\begin{cases} x = & uv \\ y = & uv^2 \\ z = & u^2 \end{cases}$$

Evaluation of Gröbner basis provides the implicit equation : $x^4 - y^2z$. With system Reduce we obtain :

Dixon	*Sylvest1*	*Sylvest2*
x^4-y^2z	$-y^4(x^4-y^2z)$	$-z^2(x^4-y^2z)^2$

- *Rational example.* Let us consider the following parametrisation of a sphere :

$$\begin{cases} x = \frac{1-u^2}{1+u^2}\frac{1-v^2}{1+v^2} \\ y = \frac{1-u^2}{1+u^2}\frac{2v}{1+v^2} \\ z = \frac{2u}{1+u^2} \end{cases}$$

for which we obtain :

Gröbner	*Dixon*	*Sylvest1*	*Sylvest2*
$(z-1)(z+1)$ $(x^2+y^2+z^2-1)$	$y^4(z-1)^2(z+1)^2$ $(x^2+y^2+z^2-1)^2$	$y^8(z-1)^4(z+1)^4$ $(x^2+y^2+z^2-1)^4$	$(z-1)^4(z+1)^4$ $(x^2+y^2+z^2-1)^4$

– Extension of implicitization.

We will now discuss how the method can be applied for implicitization of GPPS of any bi-degrees in u and v. In [10], methods are proposed to treat most particular cases, however we hope for a general algorithm.

First, let us consider what happens if some of monoms u^iv^j do not appear in the parametric representation.

Suppose for example a biquadratic polynomial parametric surface (i.e., $n=2, m=2$). The associated matrix T must be of order 8. But, observation of the symbolic table given in figure 2.2 shows that missing only one of the monoms u^2, v^2 or u^2v^2 in the parametric representation, leads to a matrix $T(x,y,z)$ in which one row and one column are identically zero. After elimination of this row and this column, we obtain a seventh order matrix which provides an implicit equation of degree seven. Then, if two of these monoms (resp. all these monoms) miss, we obtain a sixth order (resp. a fifth order) matrix which provides an implicit equation of degree six (resp. five).

Second, let us consider a Steiner surface which is a parametric surface of total degree two (as in remark 1.2 where $N_1 = N_2 = N_3 = 2$). We may consider it as a biquadratic parametric surface where the monoms u^2v, uv^2 and u^2v^2 are not present in the parametric representation. As above, observation of the symbolic table shows that three rows and three columns are identically zero. So we get a fifth order matrix which provides an implicit equation of degree four (as expected! [18]).

More generally, *any GPPS of bi-degrees* (n_1,m_1), (n_2,m_2), (n_2,m_2) *as defined in (2) may be viewed as a GPPS of bi-degree* (n,m), *where* $n = sup(n_1,n_2,n_3)$ *and* $m = sup(m_1,m_2,m_3)$ *and where the missing coefficients are put to* 0.

In the same way, *any GPPS of total degrees* N_1, N_2, N_3 *may be viewed as a GPPS of bi-degree* (n,n) *where* $n = sup(N_1,N_2,N_3)$.

Experimentation of many examples (see [3]) in this way provides matrices $T(x,y,z)$ where several rows and columns are identically zero. Nevertheless, all the studied examples show that we can extract a square matrix which provides the desired implicit equation (which is checked by other methods).

For example, let us consider the following surface of bi-degrees $(1,1)$, $(1,1)$, $(2,1)$:

$$\begin{cases} x = & 1+u+v-uv \\ y = & 2-u+v-3uv \\ z = & -2+u-v-2uv-u^2+u^2v \end{cases}$$

which viewed as a surface of bi-degree $(2,1)$ provides the matrix $T(x,y,z)$:

-2y-2z	-6x+4z +14	4x-4	0
-5x+3y -2z-5	x-y+11	-4	0
-x+y-1	3x-y +1	-4	0
x-y+1	-3x+y -1	4	0

Fig. 4.1 Matrix T.

for which one column is identically zero and the last two rows are dependent. We thus obtain :

Dixon	*Sylvest1*	*Sylvest2*
$S^3(x,y,z)$	$(3y-5)^2 S^3(x,y,z)$	$(3y-5)S^3(x,y,z)$

In numerical applications, inspection of coefficients of the matrix $\tilde{T}$ provides the effective rank and the desired sub-matrix.

– Comparison between the implicit and the parametric representations of the surface.

Let (S) be a parametric surface and (S') the implicit one obtained $((S) \subset (S'))$. Generally $(S) \neq (S')$, this is emphasized in real non-projective geometry and is independent of the chosen implicitization method. Nevertheless, here, we can check if a given point of (S') (for example, an intersection point) belongs to (S). For this purpose, notice that $\overline{M}(\overline{x},\overline{y},\overline{z}) \in (S')$ if and only if $det\,(T(\overline{x},\overline{y},\overline{z})) = 0$, so that the homogeneous system $T(\overline{x},\overline{y},\overline{z}).X = 0$ has a non-trivial solution $\overline{X}$ in $\mathbb{R}^N$ $(N = 2nm)$. Then, if this solution $\overline{X}$ cannot be expressed in the form $\begin{bmatrix} \overline{u} \\ \overline{v} \end{bmatrix}_{(n,m)}$ for some $\overline{u}$ and $\overline{v}$, we are sure that this point is not on (S).

On the other hand, if the parametrization of (S) is not minimal, we can find points of (S') which do not belong to (S) but for which there exist parameters $\overline{u}$ and $\overline{v}$ as verified in the previous check [3].

In all cases, it is possible to check if $\overline{M} = \varphi(\overline{u},\overline{v})$ where φ stands for the parametric representation $(\varphi_1, \varphi_2, \varphi_3)$ of the surface.

– Rational parametric surfaces.

Given a general rational parametric surface as in (6) of bi-degree (n,m), we have not completely studied the following two numerical approaches :

- the first approach consists of applying the implicitization on the associate GPPS defined in (7) which leads to a matrix $T(x,y,z)$ of order $2nm$ but whose coefficients are polynomials of total degree 3 in x, y and z.

- the second approach consists of transforming the parametrization to the classical form which provides a matrix $T(x,y,z)$ of higher order, but whose coefficients are linear.

5 Conclusion

The purpose of our paper is to check numerical and qualitative aspects of such algebraic methods which do not seem to have been done previously. Our objective was not so much the comparison of our algorithm with the others in terms of complexity, but rather, to investigate the possibility of providing extremely precise results for ray tracing of complex surfaces. However, experimental results using concrete examples, shows that high quality images can be obtained without an exagerated increase in cost. These results suggest that further improvements in our implementation would be profitable and make the method more attractive.

Acknowledgment. The author is working under the able guidance of Patrick Chenin and wishes to thank Kadi Bouatouch for his helpful comments.

References

[1] A.G. AKRITAS and S.D. DANIELOPOULOS. An unknown Theorem for the Isolation of the Roots of Polynomials, *Indian Society for History of Mathematics*, Vol 2, Nos 3-4, (1980), 41-49.

[2] A.H. BARR. Ray Tracing Deformed Surfaces, *Computer Graphics*, Volume 20, no 4, pp. 287 - 297, August 1986.

[3] L. BIARD and P. CHENIN. Implicitization of Parametric surfaces, Research Report, L.M.C. IMAG Grenoble, to appear, July 1990

[4] K. BOUATOUCH. Theoritical Development on Polygonal Approximation of Parametric Surfaces for Ray Tracing, *Computer Graphics Forum*, December 88, Eurographics

[5] C. BOUVILLE, R. BRUSQ, J.L. DUBOIS and I. MARCHAL (CCETT). Synthèse d'Images par Lancer de Rayons : Algorithmes et architecture, *ACTA ELECTRONICA* - Volume 26, no 3-4, pp.249 - 259, 1984

[6] M. BRONSTEIN. The elimination property of Gröbner bases and applications to Computer Aided Design, Computer Science Division, Department of Electrical Engineering and Computer Science. University of California, Berkeley 94720,1986

[7] B. BUCHBERGER. Applications of Gröbner Bases in Non-Linear Computational Geometry, *Mathematical Aspects Scientific Software*, Springer Verlag, Editor: J.R. Rice,1988

[8] G.E. COLLINS and R LOOS. Real Zeros of Polynomials, *Computing, Suppl.*,4, 83-94, by Springer Verlag, (1982)

[9] Eugene D. DENMAN and Alex BEAVERS,Jr. The Matrix Sign Function and Computation in Systems, *Appl. Math. Comput.*, 2:63-94 (1976)

[10] A.L. DIXON. The Eliminant of Three Quantics in Two Independent Variables, *Proc. London Math Soc.*, (2), 76, 1908, 49 - 69

[11] J.L. HOWLAND. The Sign Matrix and the Separation of Matrix Eigenvalues, Linear Algebra and its applications 49: 221-232 (1983) *Elsevier Science Publishing Co., Inc.*

[12] J.T. KAJIYA. Ray Tracing Parametric Patches, *Computer Graphics*, Volume 16, no 3, pp. 245 - 254, July 1982

[13] J.M. LANE and R.F. RIESENFELD. Bounds on a Polynomial, BIT September 1980, pp. 112-119

[14] A. LE MEHAUTE and P. SABLONNIERE. Courbes et Surfaces Bézier / B-Splines, Colloque de l'A.T.P. du C.N.R.S. sur le thème "Outils Mathématiques et Informatiques des Modèles Géométriques", I.N.S.A. de Rennes 11, 12, 13 Mai 1987

[15] D. MARCHEPOIL and P. CHENIN. Algorithmes de Recherche de Zéros d'une Fonction de Bézier, Reseach Report, L.M.C. IMAG Grenoble, (to appear)

[16] Alyn ROCKWOOD. Constant Component Intersections of Parametrically Defined Curves, *Silicon Graphics Computer Systems*, 1989

[17] T.W. SEDERBERG and D.C. ANDERSON Ray Tracing of Steiner Patches, *Computer Graphics*, Volume 18, no 3, pp. 159 - 165, July 1984

[18] T.W. SEDERBERG and D.C. ANDERSON. Steiner Surface Patches, *I.E.E.E. Computer Graphics and Applications*, pp. 23 - 36, May 1985

[19] T.W. SEDERBERG, D.C. ANDERSON and R.N. GOLDMAN. Implicit Representation of Parametric Curves and Surfaces, *Computer Vision, Graphics, and Image Processing*, Volume 28, pp. 72 - 84, 1984

[20] M.A.J. SWEENEY and R.H. BARTELS. Ray Tracing Free Form B-Spline Surfaces, *I.E.E.E. Computer Graphics and Applications*, Volume 6, no 2, pp. 41 - 49, February 1986

[21] D.L. TOTH. On Ray Tracing Parametric Surfaces, *Computer Graphics*, Volume 19, no 3, pp. 171 - 179, July 1985

[22] C.G. YANG. On Speeding Up Ray Tracing of B-Spline Surfaces, *Computer Aided Design*, Volume 19, no 3, pp. 122 - 130, April 1987

Chapter 2

Theory of Global Illumination Models

A Theoretical Analysis of Global Illumination Models

Christian Bouville*, Kadi Bouatouch, Pierre Tellier†, Xavier Pueyo‡

Abstract

This paper provides a general theoretical framework in which any previous global illumination model can be described. It gives a theoretical background which is based on radiometric quantities and on a physical approach to insure generality and consistency. A system of energy balance equations is obtained. Two approaches are possible depending on the way the radiometric properties of surfaces are characterized. Furthermore, the problem of solving this system of equations with the two-component method is addressed, and we show how we can take advantage of the characteristics of each component to select an appropriate method.

1 Introduction

In the recent literature, significant progresses have been made in the field of rendering techniques through the use of improved global illumination model. A global illumination model describes the light transport mechanism between surfaces, that is, how each surface element interacts with the others. Therefore, the global illumination model is a key problem when accuracy is needed in the rendering process (photorealism or photosimulation). So far, two approaches have been proposed to solve this problem : the former is based on ray tracing and the latter is based on the so-called radiosity solution. As these two approaches are complementary, several authors have tried to deal efficiently with all the light transport mechanisms by mixing both approaches in their model. Generally, these papers present their solution as an improvement to traditional ray tracing or radiosity approach and therefore they emphasize the algorithmical aspect to the detriment of the theoretical background. It is thus difficult to appreciate what assumption or what approximation the authors are making, which makes it difficult to compare one model with the other.

The primary goal of this paper is to provide a very general theoretical framework in which any global illumination model can be described. The rendering equation of Kajiya [10] is an attempt in this direction, however, the author did not use the usual radiometric quantities and some points remain unclear in his theory. In the following, all the theoretical background will be based on radiometric quantities to insure generality and consistency. Then, we will show how to make use of this theory to derive appropriate photometric algorithms.

This paper addresses the following subjects. First, the general system of equations describing the global energy balance is derived. Actually, two equivalent systems of equations can be stated depending on the used photometric quantity, namely light power and

*CCETT, Rue du Clos Courtel, 35510 Cesson Sévigné

†IRISA, Campus de Beaulieu, 35042 Rennes Cedex

‡IRISA, Campus de Beaulieu, 35042 Rennes Cedex / Sec. Inf. Gràfica, Dept. LiSI, Univ. Politèc. Catalunya

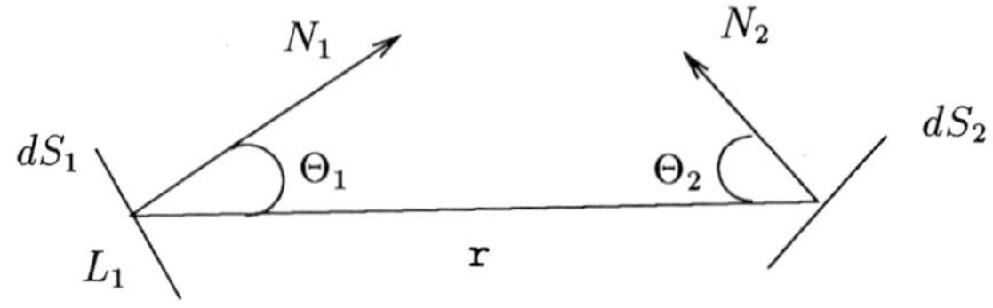

Fig. 1: Geometry for radiometric quantities

radiance. Starting from the systems of equations, the different classes of solutions are presented and discussed.

2 Global Energy Balance Equation

2.1 Generalities

Our goal is to derive a system of equations that decribes how surfaces interact with each others. To be general, these equations must be based on the theory of radiometry and account for all type of light transport mechanisms [16]. The solution of this system provides the radiometric characteristics of all surfaces in the scene. However, these equations precisely depend on the radiometric quantity used to characterize the radiometric properties of surfaces.

Most well-known illumination models assume that the radiometric properties of surfaces are described by their radiances because the human eye is only sensitive to this quantity. The radiance (sometimes called intensity) is the light power leaving a surface per unit surface and per unit projected solid angle. The radiance value is a function of the coordinates of the point on the surface and of the direction of observation.

In the radiosity approach, the radiometric properties of surface are characterized in terms of power rather than radiance because radiosity takes its origin into the thermal radiation theory. Power is simply the light energy per unit time. However, it is still necessary to compute radiance at a final step to conform to the human eye perception. Radiance and power are related by the following relation (see figure 1) :

$$\begin{aligned} d^2\Phi &= L_1 \cos\Theta_1 dS_1 d\Omega_1 \\ &= L_1 \cos\Theta_1 \cos\Theta_2 \frac{dS_1 dS_2}{r^2} \end{aligned}$$

The application of this equation will be analysed in more details in the following, however it is already obvious that the evaluation of the radiance function from power implies the subdivision of all surfaces into small enough patches because of the differential nature of the above equation.

2.2 The Radiance Approach

2.2.1 The Light Transport Equation

Our goal is now to derive an expression of the light power leaving a surface S_i at a point P_i and reaching surface S_j at a point P_j (figure 2). This light power is due to the self emittance of S_i but also to its reflective properties. At this point, we leave out of account the occlusion problem and consider that any surface S_k contributes entirely to the illumination of surface S_i.

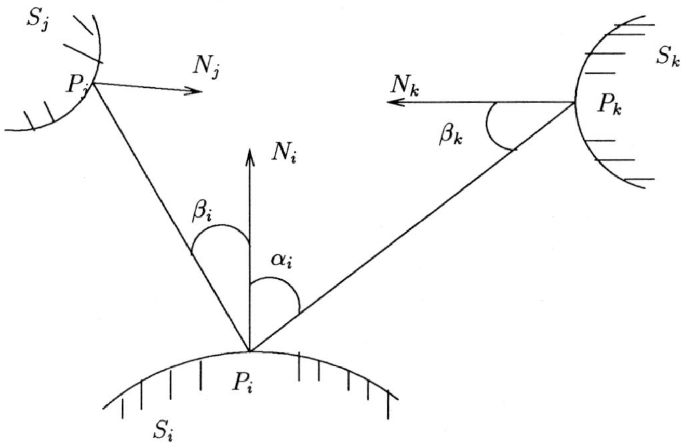

Fig. 2: Geometry of light transport mechanism

From now on, the following conventions will be adopted in all our notations :

- α_i and β_i refer, respectively, to angle of incidence and angle of reflection at point P_i of a surface S_i.
- in all our subscript or function argument notations, the order of the subscripts or the arguments follows the propagation of light with the source being the leftmost.

Let us call $L(P_i, P_j)$ the radiance of surface S_i at point P_i as seen from point P_j at surface S_j. Summing the contributions of all surfaces S_k, we have , using the definition of bidirectional reflectance [8, 3] (figure 2),

$$L(P_i, P_j) = L^E(P_i) + \sum_k \int_{\Omega_{ik}} R(P_k, P_i, P_j) L(P_k, P_i) \cos \alpha_i d\Omega_{ik} \tag{1}$$

where $R(P_k, P_i, P_j)$ is the bidirectional reflectance value for direction of incidence $\vec{P_k P_i}$ and direction of reflection $\vec{P_i P_j}$. Ω_{ik} is the solid angle under which surface S_k is seen at point P_i. $L^E(P_i)$ is the radiance due to self-emittance. In this equation, self-emittance is assumed to be lambertian, that is, independent of direction.

As

$$d\Omega_{ik} = \frac{dS_k \cos \beta_k}{||P_k P_i||^2},$$

we have

$$L(P_i, P_j) = L^E(P_i) + \sum_k \int_{S_k} R(P_k, P_i, P_j) L(P_k, P_i) G(P_k, P_i) dS_k \tag{2}$$

where $G(P_k, P_i)$ is a purely geometric term as

$$G(P_k, P_i) = \frac{\cos \alpha_i \cos \beta_k}{||P_k P_i||^2}.$$

The light occlusion effect can be accounted for by introducing a function $h(P_i, P_j)$ taking the value 1 if point P_i is visible from point P_j and 0 otherwise. Equation 2 then becomes

$$L(P_i, P_j) = h(P_i, P_j)[L^E(P_i) + \sum_k \int_{S_k} R(P_k, P_i, P_j) L(P_k, P_i) G(P_k, P_i) dS_k] \tag{3}$$

A similar equation can easily be derived from the solid angle formulation of equation 1. The above equation completely describes the light transport mechanisms between surfaces. The knowledge of $L(P_i, P_j)$ is sufficient to describe the spatial distribution of the light radiating from surface S_i. Note that the radiance functions $L(P_i, P_j)$ are in fact dependent on four variables that are the parametric coordinates of point P_j on surface S_j and of point P_i on surface S_i.

2.2.2 The Light Energy Balance System of Equations

If equation 3 is applied for all couples (S_i, S_j), a system of integral equations is obtained with the $L(P_i, P_j)$ as unknown functions. This system of equations expresses no more than the energy balance between self-emittance, absorption and reflection. Using a more condensed notation, this system can be written as follows

$$L_{ij} = h_{ij}[L_i^E + \sum_k T_{kij}(L_{ki})], \quad i, j \in [1, N] \tag{4}$$

where $L_{ij} = L(P_i, P_j)$, $L_i^E = L^E(P_i)$ and $h_{ij} = h(P_i, P_j)$. As for the term $T_{kij}(L_{ki})$, it is an integral operator which can be expressed as

$$T_{kij}(L_{ki}) = \int_{S_k} R(P_k, P_i, P_j)L(P_k, P_i)G(P_k, P_i)dS_k.$$

The solution of this system provides the radiance function of a surface as seen from any other surface.

2.2.3 The Case of Diffuse Reflection Only

The above equation greatly simplifies in case of diffuse reflection because the bidirectional reflectance $R()$ depends only on P_i, and L is independent of view direction (Lambert's law). Thus :

$$R(P_k, P_i, P_j) = R^d(P_i)$$

$$L(P_i, P_j) = L^d(P_i)h(P_i, P_j)$$

where the exponent d denotes the diffuse component.

Thus, we have :

$$\begin{aligned} T_{kij}(L_{ki}) &= R^d(P_i)\int_{S_k} L^d(P_k)G(P_k, P_i)h(P_k, P_i)dS_k \\ &= D_{ki}(L_k^d) \end{aligned}$$

For small surfaces, we may assume that $L^d(P_k)$ is constant over surface S_k. Then we get:

$$D_{ki}(L_k^d) = R^d(P_i)L^d(P_k)\tilde{F}_{ki}^d,$$

where :

$$\tilde{F}_{ki}^d = \int_{S_k} G(P_k, P_i)h(P_k, P_i)dS_k$$

is the point to surface form-factor from point P_i to surface S_k.

In this case, the system of equations (4) becomes linear :

$$L_i^d = L_i^E + R^d \sum_k L_k^d \tilde{F}_{ki}^d$$

2.3 The Light Power Approach

2.3.1 The System of Equations

The above system of equations expresses all light energy transport between surfaces in terms of radiance because the human eye is only sensitive to radiance. However, the radiosity approach expresses the exchanges of light energy in terms of power transfer because this approach takes its origin into the theory of thermal radiation [14]. For the visible parts of surfaces, the radiance values can then be derived from light power using the radiance definition equation given previously although it can only be applied for small enough surfaces. With this restriction, it will be shown that a system of equations similar to system 3 can be solved for the power transfer between surfaces. Using the equations given in subsection 2.1, the light power transferred from surface i to surface j can be be expressed as follows (see figure 2)

$$\Phi_{ij} = \int_{S_i} \int_{\Omega_{ij}} L_i h(P_i, P_j) \cos \beta_i d\Omega_i dS_i$$

where L_i is the radiance function of the surface and $d\Omega_i$ is the differential solid angle of apex P_i and subtented by dS_j. The radiance function is composed of two terms :

$$L_i = L_i^E + L_i^R.$$

L_i^E is produced by self-emittance. This term is assumed to be constant across the surface and is independent of direction (Lambertian emission). Therefore, we have

$$L_i^E = \frac{E_i}{\pi S_i},$$

where E_i is the total light power produced by self-emittance. The term L_i^R is due to reflection and can only be expressed in a differential form. Using the definition of the bidirectional reflectance, we have :

$$dL_i^R = \sum_k R(P_k, P_i, P_j) dA_{ki},$$

where dA_{ki} is the differential irradiance due to surface k and $R(P_k, P_i, P_j)$ is the bidirectional reflectance function.

From the above equations and using (see figure 2)

$$dA_{ki} = \frac{d^2\Phi_{ki}}{dS_i}$$

we have

$$\begin{aligned} \Phi_{ij} &= \sum_k \int_{S_i} \int_{\Omega_{ij}} h(P_i, P_j) \cos \beta_i d\Omega_i dS_i \int_{S_k} R(P_k, P_i, P_j) \frac{d^2\Phi_{ki}}{dS_i} \\ &+ \frac{E_i}{\pi S_i} \int_{S_i} \int_{\Omega_{ij}} h(P_i, P_j) \cos \beta_i d\Omega_i dS_i. \end{aligned} \quad (5)$$

In the above equation, we have separated the integrand of the first term into two parts so as to emphasize the role of each part of the integrand. The right part, namely the integral over S_k corresponds to the incoming light power while the left part characterizes the outgoing light power. The term $\frac{1}{\pi} \int_{S_i} \int_{\Omega_{ij}} h(P_i, P_j) \cos \beta_i d\Omega_i dS_i$ is constant and is called form factor [14, 17, 1, 9, 5]. From this equation, we can thus derive a system of equations that we can solve for the Φ_{ij}'s. Compared to equation 3, note the additional complexity introduced by the differential terms $d^2\Phi_{ki}/dS_i$. The total light power Φ_i radiated by surface i can be obtained by summing the Φ_{ij}'s over j or by using the following expression derived from equation 5 :

$$\Phi_i = \sum_k \int_{S_i} \int_{2\pi} \cos\beta_i d\Omega_i dS_i \int_{S_k} R(P_k, P_i, P_j) \frac{d^2\Phi_{ki}}{dS_i} + E_i. \tag{6}$$

As opposed to radiance which is a function, the Φ_{ij}'s and the Φ_i's are constants. Therefore, the total radiated power Φ_i does not provide sufficient information on the distribution of this power over the surfaces except if we subdivide the surfaces into very small patches (see section 2.1). To avoid this problem, it is sometimes useful to use radiant emittance or radiosity B which is related to power Φ by the following equation :

$$B(P) = \frac{d\Phi}{dS}.$$

The radiosity is the total power leaving a surface per unit surface at a given point P. From (5) and (6), we get :

$$\begin{aligned}\frac{d\Phi_{ij}}{dS_i} &= \sum_k \int_{\Omega_{ij}} h(P_i, P_j) \cos\beta_i d\Omega_i \int_{S_k} R(P_k, P_i, P_j) \frac{d^2\Phi_{ki}}{dS_i} \\ &\quad + \frac{E_i}{\pi S_i} \int_{\Omega_{ij}} h(P_i, P_j) \cos\beta_i d\Omega_i,\end{aligned}$$

and

$$\begin{aligned}B_i &= \frac{d\Phi_i}{dS_i} \\ &= \sum_k \int_{2\pi} \cos\beta_i d\Omega_i \int_{S_k} R(P_k, P_i, P_j) \frac{d^2\Phi_{ki}}{dS_i} + \frac{E_i}{S_i}.\end{aligned}$$

2.3.2 *The Case of Pure Diffuse Reflection*

This case correponds to the basic application of the radiosity approach as defined by Goral et al. [9]. In this case, the bidirectional reflectance is independent of the directions of incidence and reflection and from [8, 3], we have :

$$R^d(P_i) = \frac{\rho_i^d}{\pi}$$

where :

- $R^d(P_i)$ is the diffuse component of the bidirectional reflectance $R(P_k, P_i, P_j)$ of patch i,
- ρ_i^d is the reflectance of patch i.

Let us write :

$$\begin{aligned}\int_{S_k} R^d(P_k, P_i, P_j) \frac{d^2\Phi_{ki}}{dS_i} &= \frac{\rho_i^d}{\pi} \int_{S_k} \frac{d^2\Phi_{ki}}{dS_i} \\ &= \frac{\rho_i^d}{\pi} \frac{d\Phi_{ki}}{dS_i}\end{aligned}$$

Note that $\frac{d\Phi_{ki}}{dS_i} \approx \frac{\Phi_{ki}}{S_i}$ for small surfaces if we assume that the lighting does not vary too much over a surface.

We have then :

$$\int_{S_k} R^d(P_k, P_i, P_j) \frac{d^2\Phi_{ki}}{dS_i} \approx \frac{\rho_i^d}{\pi} \frac{\Phi_{ki}}{S_i},$$

and as

$$\int_{2\pi} \cos\beta_i d\Omega_i = \pi,$$

we have from equation 6

$$\Phi_i^d = \rho_i^d \sum_k \Phi_{ki} + E_i \tag{7}$$

Moreover, we have from equation 5

$$\Phi_{ij}^d = \rho_i^d F_{ij}^d \sum_k \Phi_{ki} + F_{ij}^d E_i \tag{8}$$

where

$$F_{ij}^d = \frac{1}{\pi S_i} \int_{S_i} \int_{\Omega_{ij}} h(P_i, P_j) \cos\beta_i d\Omega_i dS_i$$

are the geometric form factors [14]. Using equations 7 and 8, we get

$$F_{ij}^d = \frac{\Phi_{ij}^d}{\Phi_i^d} \tag{9}$$

which represents ratios of powers. If all the patches are perfectly diffuse, the use of equations 8 and 9 gives

$$\Phi_i = \rho_i^d \sum_k F_{ki}^d \Phi_k + E_i$$

which is the well-known radiosity equation introduced by Goral et al [9] for diffuse objects only.

A similar set of equations can easily be derived in the same way as above with radiosities instead of powers :

$$\tilde{F}_{ij}^d = \frac{B_{ij}^d}{B_i^d}$$

with

$$\tilde{F}_{ij}^d = \frac{1}{\pi} \int_{\Omega_{ij}} h(P_i, P_j) \cos\beta_i d\Omega_i.$$

The $\tilde{F}_{ij}^d$'s are the point to surface form-factors previously seen in section 2.2.3. For small surfaces, we have $B \approx \frac{\Phi}{S}$ and then :

$$B_i^d = \frac{\rho_i^d}{S_i} \sum_k \tilde{F}_{ki}^d S_k B_k + \frac{E_i}{S_i}.$$

2.3.3 The Link with Radiance

As we have seen above, the radiance values must be computed from the B_{ij}'s or Φ_{ij}'s. For diffuse reflection, the radiance is independent of direction and is given by :

$$L_i = \frac{B_i}{\pi} \approx \frac{1}{\pi} \frac{\Phi_i}{S_i}.$$

In all other cases, we must assume small enough surfaces to apply (see figure 2) :

$$L_{ij} \approx \Phi_{ij} \frac{r^2 h_{ij}}{S_i S_{ij} \cos\beta_i \cos\alpha_j}.$$

where S_{ij} is the visible surface of S_j as seen from P_i. As $\frac{\pi}{S_j}F_{ij}^d$ can be interpreted as the average of

$$\frac{\cos\beta_i \cos\alpha_j h_{ij}}{r^2}$$

over S_i and S_j, we have :

$$L_{ij} \approx \frac{\Phi_{ij} h_{ij}}{\pi S_i F_{ij}^d} = \frac{B_{ij}}{\pi \tilde{F}_{ij}^d}.$$

3 The Resolution of the Energy Balance System of Equations

3.1 View-Dependent Versus View-Independent Approaches

A straightforward method of solving this set of equations consists in subdividing all surfaces into small enough patches so that the radiance function does not change within the patch surface. The system of integral equations then becomes a system of linear equations. As detailed below, the radiosity approach uses this approximation for solving the special case of diffuse illumination and reflection.

However, this is not sufficient to determine the image of the scene as seen by the observer unless the viewing system is included into the system of equations. This can be performed by placing a small non reflecting surface at the observer location or by adding a non reflecting surface that covers the whole virtual screen as suggested by Neumann et al. [11]. In this last method, the additional computations can be limited to the L_{ij} between the screen surface and the visible surfaces of the screen. To some extent, this solution can be considered as view independent because only the L_{ij} between the observer and the visible surfaces need to be computed if the viewing system is changed.

In the ray tracing approach, this system is solved in a recursive manner by iterating the equations 4 :

$$L^n = h[L^E + T(L^{n-1})]$$

In the usual backward ray tracing approach, the first iteration starts from the observer location. Therefore, the ray tracing approach concentrates on the L_{ij} values of visible surfaces in direction of the observer, which makes the ray tracing solution totally view-dependent. However, many other radiance values need to be computed to evaluate the $T(L)$ integral operators. The traditional simple ray tracing approach greatly simplifies the problem by assuming perfect specular reflection with no scattering effects. A more general solution consists in making use of the Monte-Carlo approach for computing the integrals as shown in [2, 4, 12, 7]. This method is efficient for specular reflection but slow in the case of diffuse reflection because many samples are necessary to obtain a sufficiently accurate evaluation of the integrals. To solve this problem, Ward et al [18] suggests taking advantage of the smooth variations of the diffuse component across the same surface. Therefore, the diffuse component can be interpolated from neighboring points whenever an adequate proximity criterion is satisfied. This method greatly reduces the computing time of the diffuse component with ray tracing.

By and large, view-dependent methods do not require the breaking down of all surfaces into patches because the sampling is governed at the image level rather than on object surfaces. Consequently, a radiance-based illumination model is more appropriate in this case because no small surface assumption is necessary (see sections 2.1, 2.3.2 and 2.3.3).

3.2 Two-Component Approach

3.2.1 A Radiance-Based Solution

We shall see why the global diffuse and global specular components may be separated. In other words, why the specular component of the radiance of a patch can be computed after having completely evaluated the global diffuse component. For this purpose, we shall use an approach nearly similar to the one proposed in [15]. In the following, we only use radiance quantities. The same demonstration can be made for power quantities.

From [8] we have :

$$R(P_k, P_i, P_j) = d_i R^d(P_i) + s_i R^s(P_k, P_i, P_j). \tag{10}$$

Let us rewrite system 4 as :

$$L = h[T(L) + L^E]$$

where $L = \{L_{ij}\}, T = \{\sum_k T_{kij}\}, h = \{h_{ij}\}$ and $\{\}$ represents tensor. Separating the diffuse and specular components, the above system becomes

$$L = h[L^E + D(L)] + T_s(L), \tag{11}$$

where the integral operators used in this system are given by :

- $T_s = \{h_{ij} \sum_k T^s_{kij}\}$,
- $T^s_{kij} = h_{ij} s_i \int_{S_k} L(P_k, P_i) R^s(P_k, P_i, P_j) G(P_k, P_i) dS_k$,
- $D = \{\sum_k D_{kij}\}$,
- $D_{kij} = d_i \int_{S_k} L(P_k, P_i) R^d(P_i) G(P_k, P_i) dS_k = d_i D_{ki}(L)$ (see section 2.2.3).

Let us call L^D the global diffuse component :

$$L^D = L^E + D(L).$$

Thus we have :

$$L = hL^D + T_s(L).$$

Assuming that L^D is known, system 11 can be solved in a recursive manner by iterating the equation :

$$L^n = hL^D + T_s(L^{n-1}.) \tag{12}$$

We see that the solution of equation 12 is :

$$L = (\sum_{m=0}^{\infty} T_s^m) \cdot (hL^D) = S \cdot (hL^D), \tag{13}$$

where $S = \sum_{m=0}^{\infty} T_s^m$ is the global specular operator. Note that D is the global diffuse operator.

Since

$$L^D = L^E + D(L),$$

we obtain :

$$L^D = L^E + D \cdot S(hL^D). \tag{14}$$

From equation 14, we see that we can separate the computation of the global diffuse component from the global specular component.

The notion of form factor can then be extended so as to take into account the specular effects contributing to the global diffuse component. These extended form factors are obtained by a Rieman's sum approximation of the integral operator $D \cdot S$.

In conclusion, the global illumination model can be computed in two passes :

- compute the extended form factors ($D \cdot S$) for each patch, and solve the radiosity equation 14 to evaluate the global diffuse component of each patch [16, 15].
- evaluate the total radiance values (using equation 13) by means of either a combination of both Z-buffer and ray tracing techniques [16] or simple ray tracing [15] or distributed ray tracing [7].

However, the operator $D \cdot S$ involves complex computations [15].

3.2.2 A Radiosity-Based Solution

The light power can be broken down into two components as follows :

$$\Phi_{ij} = \Phi_{ij}^d + \Phi_{ij}^s. \tag{15}$$

Although the power transfer equations are not well suited to the handling of the specular component, the radiosity equations can be extended to account for the specular component. Using equation 15 and 9, the general expression of Φ_{ij} is :

$$\Phi_{ij} = F_{ij}^d \Phi_i^d + \Phi_{ij}^s. \tag{16}$$

Shao et al [13] propose the following definition of a specular form factor :

$$\Phi_{ij}^s = F_{ij}^s \Phi_i^s.$$

Hence the definition of an extended form factor :

$$\Phi_{ij} = F_{ij} \Phi_i,$$

where

$$F_{ij} = f_i^d F_{ij}^d + f_i^s F_{ij}^s$$

and

$$f_i^d = \frac{\Phi_i^d}{\Phi_i}, f_i^s = \frac{\Phi_i^s}{\Phi_i}.$$

From equations 5 ,6 and 10 it is obvious that f_i^d and f_i^s are not constant in general, and in particular $f_i^d \neq d_i$ and $f_i^s \neq s_i$ contrary to the assumption made by Shao et al [13]. This assumption implies that the ratio of the specular component of the reflected light power to the diffuse one remains constant, which cannot be true since the specular component depends strongly on incidence. Therefore, we suggest a more accurate solution.

Using equation 16 we have :

$$\begin{aligned} \Phi_{ij} &= \Phi_i^d [F_{ij}^d + \frac{\Phi_{ij}^s}{\Phi_i^d}] \\ &= F_{ij} \Phi_i^d \end{aligned} \tag{17}$$

where our general form factor is defined by :

$$F_{ij} = F_{ij}^d + \frac{\Phi_{ij}^s}{\Phi_i^d} \tag{18}$$

Replacing Φ_{ki} by $F_{ki}\Phi_k^d$ in equation 7, we get :

$$\Phi_i^d = d_i \rho_i^d \sum_k F_{ki} \Phi_k^d + E_i. \tag{19}$$

Note that the extended form factors depend on the total power distribution in the environment, therefore the above equations cannot be solved as they are. However, a method, similar to the one described in [13] and proceeding by successive refinements of the F_{ij}'s, can be used. Such an approach leads to the following algorithm :

1. Given $F_{ij}^{(n-1)}$, solve the following system for the Φ_i^d's

$$\Phi_i^{d(n)} = d_i \rho_i^d \sum_k F_{ki}^{(n-1)} \Phi_k^{d(n)} + E_i,$$

2. Compute the specular components $\Phi_{ij}^{s(n)}$ from the new values of the Φ_i^d's (see below),
3. If $max||\Phi_{ij}^{(n)} - \Phi_{ij}^{(n-1)}||$ is below a given threshold then stop the iterative process,
4. Update the values of the extended form factors :

$$F_{ij}^{(n)} = F_{ij}^d + \frac{\Phi_{ij}^{s(n)}}{\Phi_i^{d(n)}}$$

5. Go to step 1.

The computation of the Φ_{ij}^s's in step 2 can be performed using distributed ray tracing [2, 16]. A less accurate solution consists in using the hemi-cube approach as suggested by Shao et al [13].

3.3 Comments on Resolution Methods

A close examination of both two-component approaches reveals that they actually proceed the same way. They first compute the global diffuse component taking into account the diffuse to diffuse (geometrical form factors) and specular to diffuse (extended form factors) light transport mechanisms, and specular to specular light paths. Then, the specular component is computed from the global diffuse component by taking into account all specular to specular light paths. The radiosity-based approach iterates each step, the one after another, for each surface thus adding the effects of new bounce for all specular light paths. In the method described in section 3.2.1, the kernel representing the effect of specular to specular light paths is precomputed, which allows the computation of both components separately.

Note that in both methods, the specular to specular light transport mechanism comes into play in both steps. However, the effects of these light paths need not be computed with the same accuracy. In the first step, only a sparse sampling is necessary because all light paths end up with a diffuse reflection which scatters the light in all directions, which amounts to filtering with a narrow pass-band filter. Therfore, the images of reflected objects are not perceptible.

As opposed to the the first step, all light paths necessarly end up with a specular reflection in the second step which tends to create reflected images with distinct outlines. Consequently, a sufficient dense sampling is necessary in this case to avoid aliasing impairments (jagged edges) or excessively blurred outlines. The latter case occurs when interpolating on a too sparse set of samples.

From this observation, it clearly appears that a view-dependent approach is more effective for computing the specular components in the second step because the sampling rate can be easily adapted to the required screen definition. From this point of view, the radiance-based method is more interesting because it allows the use of different methods for computing the two components.

4 Some Implementation Reflections

In this section we present our position about some aspects of illumination models implementation, related to the attempt of separating subsets of the environmemt in order to reduce the problem's complexity (form factor computation, systems of equations resolution) and to explore parallel solutions. In fact, implementation details are not discussed because of the generality of the proposed illumination model. So we are only introducing the directions in which we are currently working, for a specific implementation, that could be applied to other cases.

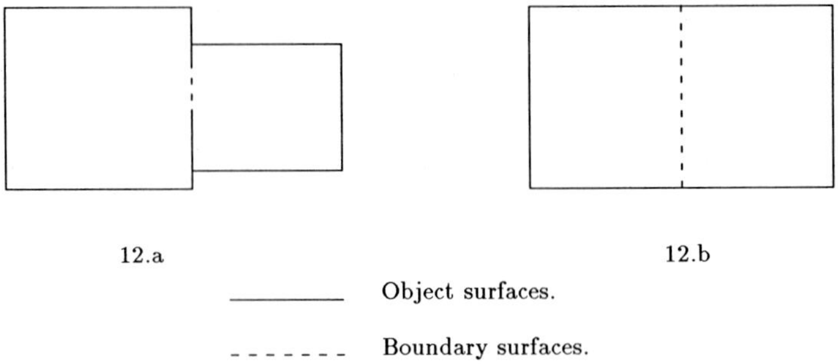

Fig. 3: Two different exemples of *local environment*

Because both, form-factor computation and system of equations solution are $O(N^2)$, it seems obvious that one of the goals of research in this field is to reduce N. Two contributions [11, 19] have been made recently in this direction. In both papers authors propose to subdivide the environment in *subsystems* or *local environments.* Boundaries must then be defined to separate local environments, in order to be able to formulate the radiosity equations for each subsystem. In this way, patches of a subsystem are of two types: *object patches* and *boundary patches* (figure 3).

To solve the different local systems of equations, the characteristics of boundary patches must be defined. It is easy to see intuitively that these characteristics depend on the properties of neighbouring local environments. So local radiosity equations can not be solved independently in the general case; even though they may become almost independent under special circumstances.

This kind of techniques must mainly deal with to aspects:

- Boundary patches modelisation.
- Systems of equations resolution.

In [11] authors propose a method (for special cases) where boundary patches are modelled by black surfaces, whereas [19] consider boundaries as being transparent. To solve the equations, the former propose to compute an approximated solution for each subsystem considering the others as light emitters. When all the subsystems have been treated, the process starts again with the first subsystem using the previous approximation. Nevertheless, [19] use the subdivision technique to express form factors between a patch i of a local environment and patch j of another as a combination of form factors of i and j to boundary patch k ($F_{ij} = f(F_{ik}, F_{kj})$). Finally they solve a set of global equations.

Next we analyse the problem using a simple example and propose alternative solutions under study. Let's suppose an environment S subdivided into two local environments S_1 and S_2 (figure 4). The boundary between these local environments is going to be considered as two different surfaces (I and II) belonging each one to one of the local environments. Assuming for simplicity that surfaces I and II are composed by only one patch, we obtain the following equations representing each local environment (we use in this example the radiosity).

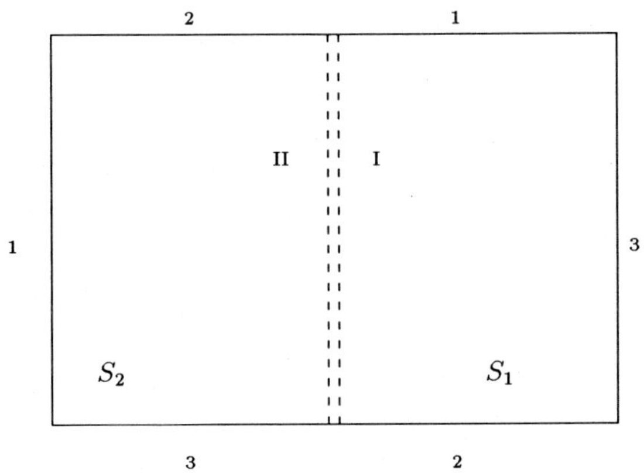

Fig. 4: Local environment notation

$$\begin{bmatrix} 1-\rho_1^1F_{1,1}^1 & -\rho_1^1F_{1,2}^1 & \cdots & -\rho_1^1F_{1,I}^1 \\ -\rho_2^1F_{2,1}^1 & 1-\rho_1^1F_{2,2}^1 & \cdots & -\rho_2^1F_{2,I}^1 \\ \vdots & & & \vdots \\ \vdots & & & \vdots \\ -\rho_I^1F_{I,1}^1 & -\rho_I^1F_{I,2}^1 & \cdots & 1-\rho_I^1F_{I,I}^1 \end{bmatrix} \begin{bmatrix} B_1^1 \\ B_2^1 \\ \vdots \\ \vdots \\ B_I^1 \end{bmatrix} = \begin{bmatrix} E_1^1 \\ E_2^1 \\ \vdots \\ \vdots \\ E_I^1 \end{bmatrix} \tag{20}$$

$$\begin{bmatrix} 1-\rho_1^2F_{1,1}^2 & -\rho_1^2F_{1,2}^2 & \cdots & -\rho_1^2F_{1,II}^2 \\ -\rho_2^2F_{2,1}^2 & 1-\rho_1^2F_{2,2}^2 & \cdots & -\rho_2^2F_{2,II}^2 \\ \vdots & & & \vdots \\ \vdots & & & \vdots \\ -\rho_{II}^2F_{II,1}^2 & -\rho_{II}^2F_{II,2}^2 & \cdots & 1-\rho_{II}^2F_{II,II}^2 \end{bmatrix} \begin{bmatrix} B_1^2 \\ B_2^2 \\ \vdots \\ \vdots \\ B_{II}^2 \end{bmatrix} = \begin{bmatrix} E_1^2 \\ E_2^2 \\ \vdots \\ \vdots \\ E_{II}^2 \end{bmatrix} \tag{21}$$

In these systems appear the parameters ρ_I, F_{iI} and EI (respec II) modeling patch I (respec. II) in local environment 1 (respec. 2). In fact, F_{iI} depends on the location (L_I), the normal (N_I) and the area (A_I) of patch I.

Depending on the values given to these parameters the solution obtained for equations 20 and 21 will be more or less accurate. In our current work we study the effect of different definitions of these parameters which can:

- be expressed as functions of the complementary (neighbour) local environment (*virtual boundaries*). For exemple, we are experimenting with some estimations of *local environment reflectivity, patch to neighbour local environment form factor* based in the idea of the ambient term proposed in [6].

or

- be derived from the geometry of the boundary and some physical assumptions like boundary reflectivity, transmision,... (*geometric boundaries*), as done in [11, 19].

With regard to the equation's resolution, we must account for the interaction between both local environments. Instead of solving each system separately a number of times using the result of each system to define new initial guess for the other or solving a set of global equations; we will make cooperate intermediate results of each system. In this way, both systems would converge simultaneously and a global criterium of convergence could be used.

In addition to equation's resolution and local environment boundary modelling, other ongoing work focuses on:

- Criteria of subdivision into local environments.
- Cooperation of subdivision with a suitable scene organisation (data structure).

as pointed in [11, 19].

The former should be guided by scene's elements of major contribution to the environment's illumination and the latter should account for other eventual local environment's boundaries not related to illumination criteria.

5 Conclusion

From the purely mathematical point of view, a power-based or radiosity-based system of equations does not differ from a radiance-based solution. However, as radiance must be computed in the end, the use of power-based or radiosity system of equations entails additional computations. Note also that this conversion step implies a discretization at the object surface level. From this point of view, the radiance-based system of equations offers a more general statement of the global illumination problem. This remains true with the two-component approach : we have seen that the power-based solution is equivalent to the radiance solution but with more restrictions with regard to sampling techniques. This aspect is particularly critical when dealing with the specular component which requires a very dense sampling of the radiance function. The computational cost of this may be very high when a view-independent aproach is used. Therefore, we suggest the specular component be computed by a view-dependent method in the second step.

References

[1] D. R. Baum, H. E. Rushmeier, and J. M. Winget. Improving radiosity solution through the use of analytically determined form-factors. *Computer Graphics*, 23(3):335–344, July 1989.

[2] C. Bouville and K. Bouatouch. Introduction to new ray tracing techniques. EUROGRAPHICS'88 Tutorial.

[3] C. Bouville and K. Bouatouch. A unified approach to global illumination models. In *PIXIM'89 Conference*, page , September 1989.

[4] C. Bouville, J. L. Dubois, I. Marchal, and M. L. Viaud. Monte-carlo method applied to an illumination model. In *EUROGRAPHICS'88 Conference Proceeding*, pages 483–497, September 1988.

[5] M. Cohen and D. Greenberg. The hemi-cube, a radiosity solution for complex environments. *ACM Computer graphics*, 19(3), 1985.

[6] Michael F. Cohen, Shenchang E. Chen, John R. Wallace, and Donald P. Greenberg. A progessive refinement approach to fast radiosity image generation. In *SIGGRAPH'88 Conference Proceeding*, pages 75–84, august 1988. Computer Graphics vol.22 num.4.

[7] R. L. Cook, T. Porter, and L. Carpenter. Distributed ray tracing. *ACM Computer graphics*, 18(3), 1984.

[8] R.L. Cook and K.E. Torrance. A reflectance model for computer graphics. *ACM transactions on graphics*, 1(1):7–24, January 1982.

[9] C. M. Goral, D. P. Greenberg K. E. Torrance, and B. Battaile. Modeling the interaction of light between diffuse surfaces. In *SIGGRAPH'84 Conference Proceeding*, pages 213–222, ACM, August 1984.

[10] J.T. Kajiya. The rendering equation. In *Proceedings of SIGGRAPH'86 in computer graphics*, pages 143–150, SIGGRAPH, August 1987.

[11] László Neumann and Attila Neumann. Photosimulation: interreflection with arbitrary reflectance models and illumination. *Computer Graphics Forum*, 8(1):21–34, 1989.

[12] R. Y. Rubinstein. *Simulation and the Monte-Carlo Method.* Jhon Wiley and Sons, New York, 1981.

[13] M. Shao, Q. Peng, and Y. Liang. A new radiosity approach by procedural refinements for realistic image synthesis. In *SIGGRAPH'88 Conference Proceeding*, pages 93–101, ACM, August 1988.

[14] R. Siegel and J. R. Howell. *Thermal Radiation Heat Transfer.* Hemisphere Publishing Corporation, New York, 1981.

[15] F. Sillion and C. Puech. A general two-pass method integrating specular and diffuse reflection. *Computer Graphics*, 23(3):335–344, July 1989.

[16] J. R. Wallace, M. F. Cohen, and D. P. Greenberg. A two-pass solution to the rendering equation : a synthesis of ray tracing and radiosity methods. In *SIGGRAPH'87 Conference Proceeding*, pages 311–320, ACM, August 1987.

[17] J. R. Wallace, K. A. Elmquist, and E. A. Haines. A ray tracing algorithm for progressive radiosity. *Computer Graphics*, 23(3):335–344, July 1989.

[18] G. J. Ward, F. M. Rubinstein, and R. D. Clear. A ray tracing solution for diffuse interreflection. In *Proceedings of SIGGRAPH'88 in computer graphics*, pages 85–92, SIGGRAPH, August 1988.

[19] Hau Xu, Qun-Sheng Peng, and You-Dong Liang. Accelerated radiosity method for complex environments. In *EUROGRAPHICS'89 Conference*, pages 51–61, september 1989.

Physically Based Lighting Calculations for Computer Graphics: A Modern Perspective

Peter Shirley*

Abstract

The light transport problem is discussed and formulated in a form convenient for Computer Graphics. Basic physical units are presented, and the rendering equation is formulated in these units. A survey of view dependent and zonal methods is presented, and the extension of these methods to non-diffuse surfaces and non-isotropically scattering media is outlined.

1 Introduction

In the 1980s lighting calculations methods in computer graphics have undergone tremendous changes. Ray tracing methods have been introduced that work well for predominantly specular environments[9, 38]. Radiosity methods have yielded good results for diffuse environments[6, 12]. More recently researchers have attempted to find algorithms that calculate lighting for environments that are both diffuse and specular[2, 17, 22, 32, 34, 36], or contain surfaces that are neither diffuse nor specular[15, 17, 27, 31]. The radiosity approach has also been applied to environments with isotropically scattering participating gasses[28].

Many researchers are now examining how to best do lighting calculations for environments with arbitrarly scattering surfaces and gasses. In this paper the problem is put in a suitable theoritical frame, and recent lighting calculation methods are examined in that context. The extension of these methods to general surfaces and gasses is then discussed. Some practical issues of generated realistic images are treated in the appendices.

2 Terms and Units

In this section some terms and definitions that form a basis for physically based lighting calculations useful for illumination calculations are presented. Assuming that we use the rule of geometric optics, then the standard quantities of the field of Illumination Engineering can be used[10, 16, 19, 39]. A good description of these quantities in a computer graphics context was recently given by Neumann and Neumann[25]. Some of the notation used in this paper has been modified to be more convenient for computer graphics. All the quantities apply to multiple wavelengths and should technically be preceded by the word 'spectral'.

The fundamental unit useful for graphics is *radiant energy*, denoted by $Q(\lambda)$. Radiant energy is simply a measure of light energy per unit wavelength at wavelength λ. Since we are interested in the amount of light hitting a surface or film plane during a set time period, *radiant power* (also called *radiant flux*), the radiant energy per unit time, $\Phi(\lambda)$,

*Center for Supercomputing Research and Development, 305 Talbot Lab, University of Illinois, Urbana, Illinois 61801 USA, shirley@iuvax.cs.indiana.edu

is often used. The amount of light traveling from a source in a certain direction can be measured as *radiant intensity*:

$$I(x,\psi,\lambda) = \frac{d\Phi(\lambda)}{d\omega}$$

where x is the position of the source, and ω is the differential solid angle originating x. The quantity most often used in graphics is the *radiance*, L. For a small surface, the radiance in direction ψ can be expressed:

$$L(x,\psi,\lambda) = \frac{dI(x,\psi,\lambda)}{dA(x)\cos\theta(\psi)} \tag{1}$$

where x is the location of the surface, ψ is an outgoing direction, $dI(x,\psi)$ is the radiant intensity in direction ψ, $dA(x)$ is the area of the patch, and $\theta(\psi)$ is the angle between ψ and the surface normal at x.

Radiance shares many characteristics of the perceptual measure *luminance*; it gives an indication of surface brightness, dependent upon neither the size of the object being viewed, nor the distance to the viewer (the radiance will only stay constant along a line of sight if there is no atmosphere between the viewpoint and the surface being viewed. Otherwise there will be filtering effects that will diminish the measured radiance of the object, and scattering effects that will add radiance causing a bleaching effect. This is why mountains in the distance often appear faded). Radiance is often called intensity in the graphics literature; in the heat transfer literature the term *intensity* is used, while the lighting design community uses *radiance.* Because the lighting design community has addressed their terminology problems by adopting an ANSI standard[16], their use of radiance (and other terms) may be preferable for graphics practitioners. Because the pioneering work in radiosity work at Cornell University had its roots in the heat transfer literature, adopting the lighting design terminology may be problematical.

A simple way to describe the reflectance of a surface is by the absolute reflectance $R(\psi_{in},\lambda)$, the fraction of light at wavelength λ incident from direction ψ_{in} that is not absorbed. The reflectance is often too simple a measurement because the distribution of the reflected light is not described. To overcome this shortcoming, the bidirectional reflectance-distribution function (*BRDF*), ρ, can be used. Written in terms of radiance the expression for the bidirectional reflectance is:

$$\rho(x,\psi_{in},\psi_{out},\lambda) = \frac{dL(x,\psi_{out},\lambda)}{L(x,\psi_{in},\lambda)d\omega(\psi_{in})\cos\theta(\psi_{in})} \tag{2}$$

Here x is the point of reflection, ψ_{in} is the incident direction, ψ_{out} is the direction of reflectance, $d\omega_{in}$ is the differential solid angle the incoming light arrives through, and $\theta(\psi_{in})$ is the angle between ψ_{in} and the surface normal at x. The denominator in this expression is simply the radiant flux density incident on the reflecting surface.

Sometimes it is more convenient to work with the radiant power Φ than with the radiance L. On these occasions the *BRDF* is cumbersome. It is more natural to view the surface reflection properties in terms of the probability distribution of the reflected light. This can be called the *scattering probability function* (*SPF*), s:

$$s(x,\psi_{in},\psi_{out},\lambda) = \frac{dI(x,\psi_{out},\lambda)}{R(x,\psi_{in},\lambda)d\Phi(x,\psi_{in},\lambda)}$$

The *SPF* directly describes the amount of energy scattered in each direction ψ_{out}. The term $R(x,\psi_{in},\lambda)$ appears in the denominator to scale the function to a valid probability density function over the solid angles ω. Thus the probability of an energy packet of wavelength λ incident on point x from direction ψ_{in} being scattered in direction ψ_{out} is $R(x,\psi_{in},\lambda)s(x,\psi_{in},\psi_{out},\lambda)d\omega(\psi_{out})$, and the probability of it being absorbed is $(1 - R(x,\psi_{in},\lambda))$. The *BDRF* and the *SPF* have the simple relationship $\rho = Cs\cos(\theta(\psi_{out}))$, where C is the constant that enforces the unit area constraint for a probability density.

Although the reflectance characteristics of real surfaces are quite varied and complex, there are two simple surface types that are usually used to approximate real reflection distributions. The first is an idealized matte surface, the diffuse reflector. The diffuse reflector is sometimes called a Lambertian surface because it obeys Lambert's Law, which states that the *BRDF* is constant. The *BRDF* can only be constant if the numerator in Equation 2 is constant. This implies that a diffuse reflector has a constant spectral radiance at all viewing angles under steady lighting conditions. We can see that this is a decent approximation for many materials such as matte paint, which do not noticeably change *color* (the perceptual approximation to spectral radiance) as we change our viewpoint. Quantitatively, the rule for the radiance of a diffuse reflector located at point x is:

$$L(x, \lambda) = \frac{R(x, \lambda)\Phi(x, \lambda)}{\pi A} \tag{3}$$

Here $\Phi(x, \lambda)$ is the power hitting the surface and A is the area of the surface.

The other surface used is the specular surface. Specular surfaces include polished metals, glasses, and any smooth reflective surface. The specular surface is most easily described by its *SPF* which is a delta function times an attenuation term. The attenuation will typically vary with incident angle as discussed in Appendix A.1. This is evident in the extreme reflectivity of glass viewed at an acute angle, and its transparency when viewed straight on.

3 Rendering Equation

Constructing a realistic image for a raster display is usually thought of as finding a continuous image function defined over a rectangular window or film plane and then filtering this image for display on a finite raster. The image function for a pinhole camera or a point viewer is determined exactly from the radiance values seen from the eye or camera aperture (pin-hole) in directions that are being 'looked at'. More precisely, the image function is known once we have $L^\star = L(x_0, \psi, \lambda)$, where x_0 is the eye or pin-hole, ψ are all directions within the viewing pyramid, and λ ranges over the visible spectrum. If a finite aperture model is used, then x_0 will vary over the area of the aperture.

The most common way to view radiance calculations to attempt to solve for $L^\star$ is using the *rendering equation.* The rendering equation describes the light transport between all the surfaces in an environment. It can be written down in any radiometric units, but radiance is convenient because radiance is the quantity we will finally assign to each point on the screen. The equation is fairly easy to derive for a differential surface at point x being viewed from direction ψ_{out}. We can begin be dividing the radiance into reflected and emitted components:

$$L(x, \psi_{out}, \lambda) = L_e(x, \psi_{out}, \lambda) + L_r(x, \psi_{out}, \lambda)$$

Here L_e is the emitted component of spectral radiance, and L_r is the reflected component. Since all the reflected light must come from the set of all directions $\psi_{in} \in \Omega_\psi$, the expression for L_r comes straight from the definition of ρ (Equation 2). If direction ψ_{in} is the only source of non-zero radiance, then,

$$L_r(x, \psi_{out}, \lambda) = \rho(x, \psi_{in}, \psi_{out}, \lambda) L(x, \psi_{in}, \lambda) \cos\theta(\psi_{in}) d\omega(\psi_{in})$$

If there are many incoming directions with non-zero radiance, then we must integrate over all incoming directions:

$$L_r(x, \psi_{out}, \lambda) = \int_{\psi_{in} \in \Omega_\psi} \rho(x, \psi_{in}, \psi_{out}, \lambda) L(x, \psi_{in}, \lambda) \cos\theta(\psi_{in}) d\omega(\psi_{in}) \tag{4}$$

The rendering equation is often called the *transport equation* in the heat transfer literature. The recursive nature of this equation makes it non-trivial to solve. The form of Equation 4 is most similar to Immel et al.'s formulation of the rendering equation[15].

Kajiya's differs in that it integrates over all surfaces rather than angles, and it doesn't use radiance[17]. Modifying Kajiya's representation to use radiance yields:

$$L_r(x, \psi_{out}, \lambda) = \int_{x' \in \Omega_x} g(x', x)\rho(x, \psi', \psi_{out}, \lambda)L(x, \psi', \lambda) \cos\theta \frac{dA(x')cos\theta'}{\|x' - x\|^2} \tag{5}$$

Here x' varies over all points of all surfaces, $g(x', x)$ is a geometry term that is one if x' can 'see' x and zero otherwise, and ψ' is the direction from x' to x.

Equation 5 is usually more convenient for zonal methods that find relationships between all surface pairs as is done by Wallace et al.[37].

4 Non-Zonal Methods

Classic projection methods are a direct way to estimate L^*. In these methods a scanline or Z-buffer is used to determine what location x is seen in each incoming direction ψ from the eye at x_0. Because the radiance does not vary along an uninterrupted line of sight, the radiance seen in direction ψ is simply the radiance of the surface seen in that direction:

$$L(x_0, \psi, \lambda) = L(x, \psi, \lambda)$$

In these projection methods, the radiance at the point x is set to be a direct lighting component plus an ambient term. The direct lighting can be calculated by using Equation 5 and evaluating the integral only for light sources.

In Whitted style ray tracing, a ray is sent from x_0 in direction ψ, and an ray intersection calculation determines the point x seen from point x_0 in direction ψ. If x is diffuse, then the same direct lighting calculation used by projection methods is employed. If the surface is specular, then a new ray is sent in the reflection direction ψ_r, and the the radiance is:

$$L(x_0, \psi, \lambda) = L_e(x, \psi, \lambda)R(x), \psi, \lambda)L(x, \psi_r, \lambda) \tag{6}$$

This process is applied recursively until a non-specular surface is encountered.

Thus, projection methods give pictures of directly lit objects, and ray tracing yields pictures of directly lit objects and reflections of directly lit objects. Neither method gives true global illumination terms.

Distributed ray tracing extended Whitted-style ray tracing by letting rays reflect probabilistically off almost-specular surfaces[9]. Many important aspects of implementing distributed ray tracing can be found in the paper by Cook[8] and the paper by Bouville et al.[4]. Kajiya extended the distributed ray tracing idea to include any surfaces with arbitrary *BRDF*[17]. To do this Kajiya uses a Monte Carlo method to get a statistical estimate of $L(x_0, \psi, \lambda)$:

$$\begin{aligned} L(x_0, \psi_0, \lambda) \approx\ & L_e(x_1, \psi_0, \lambda) + \\ & R(x_1, \psi_0, \lambda)L_e(x_2, \psi_1, \lambda) + \\ & R(x_1, \psi_0, \lambda)R(x_2, \psi_1, \lambda)L_e(x_3, \psi_2, \lambda) + \\ & R(x_1, \psi_0, \lambda)R(x_2, \psi_1, \lambda)R(x_3, \psi_2, \lambda)L_e(x_4, \psi_3, \lambda) + \cdots \end{aligned} \tag{7}$$

Here ψ_i is a random direction with probability density $s(x_i, \psi_i, \psi_{i+1}, \lambda)$, and x_i is the point seen from x_{i-1} in direction ψ_i. Since each R is at most one, and the L_e values have a known maximum for a given environment, the series can eventually be terminated. Since the identity of x_i is found by firing a ray from x_{i-1}, the term 'Monte Carlo method' is often used interchangeably with 'ray tracing method'. In effect, instead of choosing random points, we choose random paths. It is usually assumed that the *SDF* s is the same for all λ, so one scattered ray can be used for all wavelengths.

In order to reduce variance, Kajiya calculated a direct lighting term analytically at each x_i. This means that the *SDF* must be modified to exclude directions that will hit light sources so that direct lighting is not counted twice.

5 Zonal Methods for Diffuse Environments

In zonal methods, a preprocessing stage estimates the radiance at a finite number of points in the environment and then interpolates for a complete solution[12]. These precomputed radiance values are then queried in the viewing stage, simplifying the viewing process.

If all of the surfaces in a scene are diffuse, then we need only find $L(x_i, \lambda)$ for all points x_i. Commonly the points are viewed as the centers of finite area zones, and the radiance of each zone is assumed to be constant. Once the radiances are found, they are interpolated to radiance values at the vertices shared by zones. In the viewing stage Gouraud shading can be used to give an image a smoother appearance[6, 27]. Wallace et al. presented a method to find the radiances directly, which avoids the first interpolation step[37].

Since the radiance of each point depends on all other visible points, the radiances of the $x_i s$ can be formulated as a set of N linear equations, where N is the number of points. Unfortunately, the explicit solution of this system requires $O(N^2)$ storage, which is not acceptable for complex scenes. This problem can be avoided by calculating the coefficients of the matrix on the fly, which yields $O(N)$ storage, but recomputes each coefficient several times[5]. This process can be viewed as an explicit energy transport simulation, where each zone in turn shoots its accumulated energy to other zones until most of the energy has been absorbed (an exact physical simulation would involve immediate reflection of the light. If we assume the light is absorbed and then immediately re-emitted, giving the same apparent behavior, then the accumulation step can be viewed as simulation. This shooting would start with the light sources, which can shoot their initial energy in non-diffuse distributions[6]. Because we only want to send power received by the current source zone since the previous shooting phase for that zone, we must keep track both of the total power $\Phi(x_i, \lambda)$, and the unsent power $\Phi_{new}(x_i, \lambda)$. After the Φ_{new} has been shot, it is set to zero. When a shooting scheme is employed, the mathematics is simplified if we work in units of radiant power Φ, and then convert the power values to radiance using equation 3 before the viewing phase[32].

Several strategies have been used to determine how much energy each target zone receives during the shooting phase for a source zone. The earliest method used a Hemicube to determine which zones were seen by the source zone through each directional bin of the Hemicube[5, 6]. Wallace et al. sent energy explicitly to every target vertex visible to the source zone[37]. Visibility is determined by sending rays from the source to the target vertex and testing for obstructing objects between the source and the target vertex. Several researchers have sent energy using a Monte Carlo approach by emitting energy bundles as rays sent in a diffuse distribution, and giving the energy to whatever target zones are hit by the rays[1, 2, 22, 32, 34]. The mechanics of generating the random rays according to a diffuse distribution are discussed in Appendix A.2.

One optimization used for sending the energy is to choose the zone with the most energy to send as the next source. This might not be wise if the Monte Carlo approach is used. Airey and Shirley have empirically observed that the Monte Carlo approach has $O(N \log N)$ time complexity for room environments, but finding the maximum energy source will increase the time complexity to $O(N^2)$. This problem can be avoided by letting the zones send in random order, or by sorting the set of patches for each reflection phase. Another optimization used for zonal methods is to let the zones send energy in groups, so that the there are a few large source zones and many small target zones. In the radiosity literature, the large zones are called *patches* and the small target zones are called *elements*[7]. Because the amount of energy shot varies with each zone, the proportional error for some 'hot' zones is more important than others. If the Hemicube strategy is employed, a higher resolution raster can be used for high power zones such as the light sources[3]. In the method of Wallace et al., shadow testing can be avoided if the amount of power being sent is below some tolerance[37]. If the Monte Carlo Method is used, then the number of energy packets (rays) sent can be proportional to the energy being sent from the source zone[1, 2, 32].

6 Zonal Methods for General Environments

If the energy shooting scheme of the last section is employed, the extension of zonal methods to non-diffuse environments is straightforward. In addition to solving for the total power coming from each zone, we must also find the distribution of power coming from each surface. This can be done in a manner similar to the method of Immel et al.[15], but some modifications can make the method faster.

In diffuse environments each incoming energy packet adds to the total power of target zone. If the zone is not diffuse, then the energy packet adds to the radiant intensity $I(x_i, \psi, \lambda)$ for the zone. When it comes time for the zone to send, it can send the power it has received since the previous shooting step for that step according to $I_{new}(x_i, \psi, \lambda)$.

Thus, general radiosity sends energy according to a directional function $I_{new}(x_i, \psi, \lambda)$, rather than as a cosine distribution as is done in the diffuse case. If a Hemicube is used, then $I_{new}(x_i, \psi, \lambda)$ is stored in the 'pixels' of the hemicube, where each pixel corresponds to some ψ_j, and all of the power sent in direction ψ_j is sent to the zone seen through the center of that directional bin. This is very similar to the method Immel originally employed, but the shooting concept was not used.

Wallace et al.'s method of sending rays to all target vertices could also be extended to non-diffuse environments. Instead of weighting rays with a cosine distribution, the power received by a visible target vertex would be:

$$\Phi_{received}(x_j, \lambda) = I_{new}(x_i, \psi, \lambda)\omega_j$$

where x_j is the location of the target vertex and ω_j is the solid angle subtended by x_j as seen from x_i. The power received by x_j will be attenuated by $R(x_j, \psi, \lambda)$ and loaded into the table for $I_{new}(x_j, \psi_{out}, \lambda)$ according to the *SPF* $s(x_j, \psi, \psi_{out}, \lambda)$.

The Monte Carlo method can also be extended easily by shooting power packets as rays distributed randomly with a density proportional to $I_{new}(x_i, \psi, \lambda)$. An advantage of this is that the rays can be concentrated where I is large. A complication arises because the shape of $I_{new}(x_i, \psi, \lambda)$ will probably be different for each λ. One way to deal with this is to calculate the luminant intensity (a quantity integrated over all visible wavelengths) and use this for the distribution of emitted rays.

During the viewing phase, the functions $I_{new}(x_i, \psi, \lambda)$ can be queried for ψ_0 that point toward the viewpoint and the radiance can be calculated from Equation 1.

A problem with all three of these methods is that when the *SPF* of a zone is close to specular, then it will have to be stored at very high resolution or with great imprecision[15]. One way to get around this is to ignore the table entries for specular surfaces during the viewing stage as done in [31]. Unfortunately, the zonal shooting phase will still have problems for specular surfaces. The Monte Carlo method will not have this problem if there are no tables for specular surfaces and power is simply reflected off the specular surfaces during the zonal calculations, and Equation 7 is used for viewing specular surfaces, with the ray tree terminating with a query of the I function at the first specular surface. This strategy has been successfully used for diffuse-specular scenes[22, 34], and for almost-specular surfaces[32].

For optimization, the $I(x_i, \psi, \lambda)$ tables should vary in resolution according to the regularity of the *SPF* at x_i. A diffuse surface can have one table entry (total spectral power), and almost-diffuse zones can have a small I tables. The resolutions of the tables can increase for zones that are more specular in nature.

7 Zonal Methods for Participating Media

A zonal method has been applied to the case of an isotropically scattering media by Rushmeier[28]. Her approach was not based on the energy shooting strategy, so arbitrary scattering functions were not allowed.

The ray tracing techniques of the last section can be extended to media with general scattering functions. As with surfaces, the media can be divided into zones, where each zone located at x_i is considered to contain small particles with number density N (number of particles per unit volume), scattering cross sectional area A, and a *SPF* $s(x_i, \psi_{in}, \psi_{out}, \lambda)$. Values for A and s for many real world gasses as well as an excellent treatment of scattering in general can be found in the paper by Klassen[20].

When a ray carrying power Φ passes a distance t through a zone, it will have some amount of power Φ_s scattered by the zone:

$$\Phi_s = \Phi(1 - e^{-NAt})$$

This energy can be entered into the $I(x_i, \psi, \lambda)$ table for the zone. During the shooting phase of the algorithm, volume zones can fire their accumulated power according to $I(x_i, \psi, \lambda)$.

After the zonal phase is finished, the radiant intensity functions can be interpolated to zone vertices. When a viewing ray passes through the media, it will pick up some of the radiance of the zones, and some of the background radiance will be attenuated.

If the radiant intensity functions $I(x_i, \psi, \lambda)$ of the zones are converted to $L(x_i, \psi, \lambda)$ radiance functions for the particles, then calculating the color seen along a viewing ray is:

$$L(x, \psi, \lambda) = L_b(\psi, \lambda)e^{-NAt} + (1 - e^{-NAt})L(x_i, \psi, \lambda)$$

Where the ray passes through a distance t of the zone, and L_b is the radiance seen through the zone. If N, A, or $L(x_i, \psi, \lambda)$ vary along the ray (which will happen if we interpolate between zone vertices), then ray integration can be done in small steps as done by Kajiya and Von Herzen[18]. This machinery is also used for scalar volume visualization, though the lighting models used are not necessarily physically motivated[21, 35].

Because the volume zones are treated similarly to surface zones, it is straightforward to allow volume zones to be light sources such as fire.

One possible problem that arises when volumes are used is that a volume and surface object may overlap. This means care must be taken when emitting energy from a volume element to avoid sending energy from the inside of an opaque object. A possible solution is to allow volume geometries that are not rectilinear, so the volumes can be wrapped around a surface. This unfortunately makes ray tracking more difficult[33].

8 Conclusion

Because of the physical simulation nature of the progressive refinement Radiosity algorithm[5], it is particularly suitable for extension to non-diffuse environments with participating media. Because of its nice treatment of perfectly specular surfaces, the Monte Carlo zonal method[22] is best suited for general environments that include specular objects. In the absence of near-specular surfaces, any zonal method will work. Kajiya's path tracing can be used to view zonal solutions that have some surfaces not accounted for in the zonal solution.

For ray tracing based zonal methods, the extension to participating gasses is straightforward. If units of radiant power are used, then the scattering probability function (*SPF*) is a convenient way to express the scattering character of surfaces or gasses.

9 Acknowledgements

Thanks to William Kubitz, Dennis Gannon, Allan Tuchman, Greg Rogers, Bill Brown, and Kelvin Sung for their help and encouragement. This work was partially supported by the Air Force Office of Scientific Research Grant AFOSR-90-0044.

A Appendices

A.1 Fresnel Equations

To scientifically generate reflection coefficients for smooth conductors (metals) and dielectrics, the fresnel equations can be used. The Fresnel equations for light incident to a dielectric-conductor interface as presented by [29] are

$$R_s = \frac{a^2 + b^2 - 2a\cos\theta + \cos^2\theta}{a^2 + b^2 + 2a\cos\theta + \cos^2\theta} \tag{8}$$

$$R_p = R_s \frac{a^2 + b^2 - 2a\sin\theta\tan\theta + \sin^2\theta\tan^2\theta}{a^2 + b^2 + 2a\sin\theta\tan\theta + \sin^2\theta\tan^2\theta} \tag{9}$$

Where R_s and R_p are the reflectivities for the two planes of polarization, θ is the angle of incidence, and a and b are given by

$$a^2 = \frac{1}{2n_i^2}\left\{\sqrt{(n^2 - k^2 - n_i^2\sin^2\theta)^2 + 4n^2k^2} + n^2 - k^2 - n_i^2\sin^2\theta\right\} \tag{10}$$

$$b^2 = \frac{1}{2n_i^2}\left\{\sqrt{(n^2 - k^2 - n_i^2\sin^2\theta)^2 + 4n^2k^2} - n^2 + k^2 + n_i^2\sin^2\theta\right\} \tag{11}$$

Here n_i is the index of refraction of the dielectric, n and k are the optical constants of the metal. The reflectance for unpolarized light is simply the average of R_s and R_p. The equations for a dielectric-dielectric interface can be found by setting k to zero and using n as the index of refraction for the second dielectric.

Values of n and k can vary with wavelength, so the color properties of materials are treated automatically. Values of n and k for many materials at optical and other wavelengths can be found in [26].

A.2 Generating Random Ray Sets

For Monte Carlo methods we must often generate random points according to some probability density function, or random rays according to a directional probability density. In this section a method for one and two dimensional random variables is described. The discussion closely follows that of Shreider[30].

If the density is one dimensional $f(x)$ defined over the interval $x \in [a, b]$, then we can generate random numbers α_i that have density f from a set of uniform random numbers ξ_i, where $\xi_i \in [0, 1]$. To do this we need the probability distribution function $F(x)$:

$$F(x) = \int_a^x f(x')dx' \tag{12}$$

To get α_i we simply transform ξ_i:

$$\alpha_i = F^{-1}(\xi_i) \tag{13}$$

where F^{-1} is the inverse of F. If F is not analytically invertable then numerical methods will suffice because an inverse exists for all valid probability distribution functions.

If we have a two dimensional density (x, y) defined on $[a, b : c, d]$ then we need the two dimensional distribution function:

$$F(x, y) = \int_c^y \int_a^x f(x', y')dx'dy' \tag{14}$$

We first choose an x_i using the marginal distribution $F(x, d)$, and then choose y_i according to $F(x_i, y)/F(x_i, d)$. If $f(x, y)$ is not seperable (expressable as $g(x)h(y)$), then this will normally be handled numerically.

To choose reflected ray directions for zonal calculations or distributed ray tracing, we can think of the problem as choosing points on the unit sphere or hemisphere (since each ray direction ψ can be expressed as a point on the sphere). For example, suppose that we want to choose rays according to the density:

$$p(\theta, \phi) = \frac{n+1}{2\pi} \cos^n \theta \tag{15}$$

Where n is a Phong-like exponent, θ is the angle from the surface normal and $\theta \in [0, \pi/2]$ (is on the upper hemisphere) and ϕ is the azimuthal angle ($\phi \in [0, 2\pi]$). The distribution function is:

$$P(\theta, \phi) = \int_0^{\phi} \int_0^{\theta} p(\theta', \phi') \cos \theta' d\theta' d\phi' \tag{16}$$

The $\cos \theta'$ term arises because on the sphere $d\omega = \cos \theta d\theta d\phi$. When the marginal densities are found, p (as expected) is seperable and we find that a (r_1, r_2) pair of uniform random numbers can be transformed to a direction by:

$$(\theta, \phi) = (\arccos((1 - r_1)^{\frac{1}{n+1}}, 2\pi r_2) \tag{17}$$

One nice thing about this method is that a set of jittered points on the unit square can be easily transformed to a set of jittered points on the hemisphere with a distribution of Equation 15. If n is set to 1 then we have a diffuse distribution needed for a Monte Carlo zonal method.

A.3 Image Display

There are several color issues that must be addressed for the sake of realism. It has been observed that the three color values usually used in graphics is sometimes inadequate[14]. Instead Hall and Greenberg[14] use several evenly placed spectral values in the visible spectrum. Meyer[24] has proposed an unevenly spaced set of sample locations that are in some perceptual sense optimal. Both of these authors then convert their spectral values to CIE XYZ values[39] and the XYZ values can then be transformed to the color representation for a particular device. For a generic RGB monitor Meyer[23] suggests starting with

$$\begin{bmatrix} R \\ B \\ G \end{bmatrix} = \begin{bmatrix} 1.910 & -0.532 & -0.288 \\ -0.985 & 1.999 & -0.028 \\ 0.058 & -0.118 & 0.898 \end{bmatrix} \begin{bmatrix} X \\ Y \\ Z \end{bmatrix} \tag{18}$$

When the image is finally displayed, the accuracy of the color calculations must not be ruined by improperly handling screen gamma correction. If banding occurs in parts of the image, jittering is called for, even if the display has 24-bit color resolution. Both of these issues are discussed clearly in Hall's book[13].

One problem encountered when using a spectral color model is that it does not allow direct use of RGB reflection data or texture maps. This issue is addressed by Glassner by choosing one of the infinite mappings from RGB to spectral descriptions[11].

References

[1] J. M. Airey and M. Ouh-young. Two adaptive techniques let progressive radiosity outperform the traditional radiosity algorithm. *Tech Report, University of North Carolina at Chapel Hill*, 1989.

[2] J. M. Airey, J. H. Rohlf, , and F. P. Brooks. Towards image realism with interactive update rates in complex virtual building environments. *ACM Workshop on Interactive Graphics*, pages 41–50, 1990.

[3] D. R. Baum, H. E. Rushmeier, and J. M. Winget. Improving radiosity solutions through the use of analytically determined form-factors. *Computer Graphics*, 23(3):325–334, July 1989. ACM Siggraph '89 Conference Proceedings.

[4] C. Bouville, J. L. Dubois, I. Marchal, and M. L. Viaud. Monte-carlo integration applied to an illumination model. *Eurographics '88*, pages 483–497, 1988.

[5] M. F. Cohen, S. E. Chen, J. R. Wallace, and D. P. Greenberg. A progressive refinement approach to fast radiosity image generation. *Computer Graphics*, 22(4):75–84, August 1988. ACM Siggraph '88 Conference Proceedings.

[6] M. F. Cohen and D. P. Greenberg. The hemi-cube: a radiosity solution for complex environments. *Computer Graphics*, 19(3):31–40, July 1985. ACM Siggraph '85 Conference Proceedings.

[7] M. F. Cohen, D. P. Greenberg, D. S. Immel, and P. J. Brock. An efficient radioisty approach for realistic image synthesis. *IEEE Computer Graphics and Applications*, 6(2):26–35, 1986.

[8] R. L. Cook. Stochastic sampling in computer graphics. *ACM Transactions on Graphics*, 5(1):51–72, January 1986.

[9] R. L. Cook, T. Porter, and L. Carpenter. Distributed ray tracing. *Computer Graphics*, 18(4):165–174, July 1984. ACM Siggraph '84 Conference Proceedings.

[10] W. G. Driscoll. *Handbook of Optics*. McGraw-Hill, New York, N.Y., 1978.

[11] A. S. Glassner. How to derive a spectrum from an rgb triplet. *IEEE Computer Graphics and Applications*, 9(7):95–99, 1989.

[12] C. M. Goral, K. E. Torrance, and D. P. Greenberg. Modeling the interaction of light between diffuse surfaces. *Computer Graphics*, 18(4):213–222, July 1984. ACM Siggraph '84 Conference Proceedings.

[13] R. Hall. *Illumination and Color in Computer Generated Imagery*. Springer-Verlag, New York, N.Y., 1988.

[14] R. Hall and D. P. Greenberg. A testbed for realistic image synthesis. *IEEE Computer Graphics and Applications*, 3(8):10–20, 1983.

[15] D. S. Immel, M. F. Cohen, and D. P. Greenberg. A radiosity method for non-diffuse environments. *Computer Graphics*, 20(4):133–142, August 1986. ACM Siggraph '86 Conference Proceedings.

[16] A. N. S. Institute. Nomenclature and definitions for illumination engineering. ANSI Report, 1986. ANSI/IES RP-16-1986.

[17] J. T. Kajiya. The rendering equation. *Computer Graphics*, 20(4):143–150, August 1986. ACM Siggraph '86 Conference Proceedings.

[18] J. T. Kajiya and B. P. V. Herzen. Ray tracing volume densities. *Computer Graphics*, 18(4):165–174, July 1984. ACM Siggraph '84 Conference Proceedings.

[19] J. E. Kaufman, editor. *The Illumination Engineering Society Lighting Handbook, Reference Volume*. Waverly Press, Baltimore, MD, 1984.

[20] R. V. Klassen. Modeling the effect of the atmosphere on light. *ACM Transactions on Graphics*, 6(3):215–237, July 1987.

[21] M. Levoy. Display of surfaces from volume data. *IEEE Computer Graphics and Applications*, 8(3):29–37, 1988.

[22] T. J. V. Malley. A shading method for computer generated images. Master's thesis, University of Utah, June 1988.

[23] G. W. Meyer. Color issues in synthetic image generation. *A Consumer's and Developer's Guide to Image Synthesis*, pages 49–80, 1988. ACM Siggraph '88 Course Notes.

[24] G. W. Meyer. Wavelength selection for synthetic image generation. *Computer Vision, Graphics, and Image Processing*, 41:57–79, 1988.

[25] L. Neuman and A. Neumann. Photosimulation: Interreflection with arbitrary reflectance models and illumination. *Computer Graphics Forum*, 8:21–34, 1989.

[26] E. D. Palik. *Handbook of Optical Constants of Solids*. Academic Press, New York, N.Y., 1985.

[27] H. E. Rushmeier. *Realistic Image Synthesis for Scenes with Radiatively Participating Media*. PhD thesis, Cornell University, May 1988.

[28] H. E. Rushmeier and K. E. Torrance. The zonal method for calculating light intensities in the presence of a participating medium. *Computer Graphics*, 21(4):293–302, July 1987. ACM Siggraph '87 Conference Proceedings.

[29] L. G. Schultz and F. R. Tangherlini. Optical constants of silver, gold, copper, and aluminum ii. the index of refraction n. *Journal of the Optical Society of America*, 44(5):362–368, May 1954.

[30] Y. A. Screider. *The Monte Carlo Method*. Pergamon Press, 1966.

[31] M.-Z. Shao, Q.-S. Peng, and Y.-D. Liang. A new radiosity approach by procedural refinements for realistic image synthesis. *Computer Graphics*, 22(4):93–102, August 1988. ACM Siggraph '88 Conference Proceedings.

[32] P. Shirley. A ray tracing algorithm for global illumination. *Graphics Interface '90*, May 1990.

[33] P. Shirley and H. Neeman. Volume visualization at the center for supercomputing r & d. *Proceedings of the Chapel Hill Workshop on Volume Visualization*, pages 17–20, May 1989.

[34] F. Sillion and C. Puech. A general two-pass method integrating specular and diffuse reflection. *Computer Graphics*, 23(3):335–344, July 1989. ACM Siggraph '89 Conference Proceedings.

[35] C. Upson and M. Keeler. V-buffer: Visible volume rendering. *Computer Graphics*, 22(4):59–64, July 1988. ACM Siggraph '88 Conference Proceedings.

[36] J. R. Wallace, M. F. Cohen, and D. P. Greenberg. A two-pass solution to the rendering equation: a synthesis of ray tracing and radiosity methods. *Computer Graphics*, 21(4):311–320, July 1987. ACM Siggraph '87 Conference Proceedings.

[37] J. R. Wallace, K. A. Elmquist, and E. A. Haines. A ray tracing algorithm for progressive radiosity. *Computer Graphics*, 23(3):335–344, July 1989. ACM Siggraph '89 Conference Proceedings.

[38] T. Whitted. An improved illumination model for shaded display. *Communications of the ACM*, 23(6):343–349, June 1980.

[39] G. Wyszecki and W. S. Stiles. *Color Science: Concepts and Methods, Quantitative Data and Formulae.* Wiley, New York, N.Y., 1982.

Efficient Radiosity Methods for Non-Separable Reflectance Models

Lazlo Neumann*, Attila Neumann†

Abstract

Determination of interreflection of non-diffuse environments looks back to a few years. In case of N patches, separable (or, in particular, diffuse) reflectance leads to an equation system of N unknowns ; in case of general bidirectional reflectance there are $O(N^2)$ unknowns. This paper will describe two new, efficient methods for this latter extended, sparse matrix problem. Applying decomposition to diffuse + specular, sorted gathering + shooting methods is rather effective in case of small specular cones. The other method, relying on albedo-equivalent separable reflectance, offers a fast approximating radiosity solution, primarity suiting specular reflectances, with flat, undistinctive characteristics, for that any method is too slow. The two methods may be combined, the error term for the iterative solution of the first method defines a problem, offered a rapid approximate solution by the second method.

1 Introduction

The radiosity method is a finite approximation of the rendering equation describing interreflections kajiya [4], Neumann et al. [5]. Scene objects are decomposed into patches to be considered as about homogeneous. A finite approximate solution leads to a linear equation system. In case of general bidirectional reflectance, an extended, sparse matrix problem arises, with as many $O(N^2)$ unknowns as there are pairs of unoccluded patches (seeing each other). Physical purport of variables may be either *radiance* (intensity) or radiant *power*. The former was comprised in the equation system by Immel at al. [3], and the latter in that by Neumann et al. [6]. The radiance variable equation system can be solved by the Gauss-Seidel method, but the power variable equation system may not. Convergence of classic or Jacobi iteration [6] [5], for both types of equation systems is doubtless. Then, however, also the previous and the actual vectors have to be stored, through the solution has an illustrative purport : iteration k yields the *image of order* k, if the zeroth approximation is a constant vector forming the right-hand side of the equation system. Also the version of the conjugated gradient method introduced by Neumann et al. [5] suits to solve both types of equation systems. For clear environments this is the fastest among the available methods.

A novel radiosity solution has been introduced for non-diffuse environment by Min-Zhi Shao et al. [7] approximating the solution by a set of problems of the size of the diffuse equation system, involving variable matrices. This method is effective if in addition to the diffuse component, surfaces also comprises a mirror-like specular component or one with a small specular cone. Otherwise, computation of small-size matrices comprises $0(N^3)$ operations. In general case, there is no exact method able to dispense with $0(N^3)$ operations per iteration. Accordingly, the method presented in Section 3 below (equation

*OKTATREND Ltd, VAROSMAJOR U.52 H-1122 BUDAPEST
†RAILWAY RESEARCH INSTITUTE, MUZEUM U.11 H-1088 BUDAPEST

system with one power variable), also applying the diffuse + specular decomposition, is effective in the same cases as the method above. The method to be introduced applying Jacobi iteration (of proven convergence) offers a somewhat faster convergence than the method above. Furthermore, it may be solved by the conjugated gradient method, with advantages manifest, for clear inner environments.

The real advantage of radiosity equations in power variable form is obvious for shooting-type solution methods. The sorted shooting method has been introduced by cohen at al. [2] for diffuse environments. This paper will present, generalisation of this method for non-diffuse environments, and prove its convergence. Thereafter, the method of sorted gathering + shooting will be introduced, where power transport from all the other unoccluded patches to a patch and reradiated to them will be computed in a single step. In selecting the actual patch, a skill radically reducing computation costs will be applied, making use of albedo functions pre-tabulated for bidirectional reflectances in the system. The usual diffuse + specular decomposition will further reduce the need in operations by an order for a small-space-angle cone included by essential directions (outside of that the specular component may be taken as zero, at a slight error).

A class of non-diffuse models, hardly accessible numerically, comprises general reflectance models where, after separating diffuse or separable reflectance components, an undistinctive component of flat characteristic is left. For them, an efficient approximate method will be introduced, exact at the level of zero-order, and first-order image components, while for higher-order image components it is approximative. This method also suits specular-type materials, at an increased approximation error. The gist of the method is to introduce a separable model with the same albedo function as that of the former. While separable systems, similarly to diffuse systems, lead to equation systems with N unknowns. In this paper, they will be applied in the form where variable do not comprise the zero-order component. Thereby the effect of point-like light sources is simple and exact to handle, the image contains the classic ray-tracing image (of pixel resolution) as an additive component. The first-order image can be computed simultaneously to reflections of higher-order components by adaptive refinement at pixel level.

Starting from generally non-diffuse (non-separable) radiosity solutions, the image can be computed either by the coupling method or by complete two-pass method (Neumann et al. [5]). these procedures applying adaptive refinement permit a display of pixel resolution. This paper will be exclusively concerned with radiosity methods.

2 Basics

Radiometric magnitude fundamental for the description is spectral radiance [1]
definable at a point of surface A, in a give direction, at a fixed wavelengh λ :

$$S = \frac{d^2 P}{d\omega dA \cos\theta} \left[W sr^{-1} m^{-2}\right] \tag{1}$$

where P is the absolute value of the radiant power leaving from, or arriving at the surface A at a solid angle ω, and θ is the incidence angle. Two monochromatic sights are equivalent. If the observer perceives spectal radiance equal in any direction. So, in computing synthetic images, the final goal is to determine radiances in directions tending to the pupil.

Given surfaces of the scene are optically described by *bidirectional response* $\rho(L, V)$ (reflectance / transmittance). With usual symbols, L and V are unit vectors pointing from a definite surface point to the light source, and to the view point, respectively. The

[1]Notation of *spectral radiance* is not uniform in the special litterature. here symbol S will be applied throughout. Standard rediometric notation after Wyszecky et al. [10] : $L_{e,\lambda}$ will be avoided since also the vector of light source direction is denoted L.A. quality of radiance in radiosity solutions based on radiant heat transfer analogies is *intensity* I, e.g. after Wallace et al. [9]

bidirectional response is in $[\rho] = [sr^{-1}]$ units. Bidirectional response has two important features in case of linear, passive optical materials. One is essential symmetry following from Helmholtz's principle of *reciprocity* :

$$\rho(L, V) = \rho(V, L) \tag{2}$$

The other feature relies on *energy conservation*, that is,the total reflected and transmitted energy is less than or equal to the input energy. Their difference is energy dissipated or absorbed by the material. Non-dissipated energy proportion will be denoted $a(L)$ where L is direction of the point source. Now

$$a(L) = \int_{V \in F} \rho(L, V)|NV| d\omega_V \tag{3}$$

The $a(L)$ value is *albedo* for direction L. In its classic meaning, this term is used for diffuse materials where $a(L) \equiv a \equiv \pi \cdot \rho \equiv constant$, irrespective of direction L. For reflecting materials, albedo may also be called *reflectivity*. With these notations, the conservation of energy $a(L) \leq 1$ for each $L \in F$, where F means any direction in the half-space or space, depending on whether there is transmittance or not. N is the normal unit vector of the surface, hence $|NV| = \cos\theta_V$ i.e. cosine of the angle of incidence of V. The absolute value is needed since there is no stipulation on the direction of N.

Let us have a point source of radiant power P at a distance r in direction L from the tested point of surface A. Now, output radiance in direction V is:

$$S^{out} \cdot (V) = \frac{P}{4\pi r^2} \rho(L, V)\ |NL| \tag{4}$$

Remind that in case of visibility, radiance $S^{in}(V)$ at the pupil equals $S^{out}(V)$, irrespective of the pupil distance and direction of its normal vector. In case of illumination by a distributed light source, radiance typical of the light source $S^{in}(L)$ (eventually zero in given solid angle domains) has to be known for any direction $L \in F$. For a distributed light source:

$$S^{out}(V) = \int_{L \in F} \rho(L, V)\ |NL|\ S^{in}(L) d\omega_L \tag{5}$$

Surfaces within the scene may have emissions of their own. These are the so-called *self-illuminating* surfaces expressed by radiance function $S_E(V)$. Combined effects of the self-emission of the surface and of lights reflected/transmitted by point-like light sources will be termed *zero-order illumination component*:

$$S_0^{out}(V) = S_E(V) + \sum_{i=1}^{M} \frac{P_1}{4\pi r_i^2} \rho(L_1, V)\ |NL_1|\ h(L_i) \tag{6}$$

where factor $h(L_1)$ $(0 \leq h(L_i) \leq 1)$ depends on occluding conditions of the scene composed of several surfaces. If light source i is occluded, then it is zero ; if it is perfectly visible then it is 1. If the considered point is just on the borderline between light and shadow, then its value is between zero and 1. The effect of light-absorbing medium d may be incorporated in $h(L_i)$ as a multiplying factor. Equation (6) is illustrative by missing surface-to-surface interreflections. Conventionally it is displayed by the ray-tracing method at a pixel resolution.

Some notations will be introduced to write the *rendering equation* for determining radiance incident on any point of the scene from any other (unoccluded) point. Let T' be a surface point of the scene, and let T and T" be visible from T' (figure 1). Let us determine output radiance from T' toward T. It has two components : zero-order illumination conform to (6) and light reflected from all the possible points T" across T' to Tdescribed by (5). Let unit vectors be $L = (T" - T')^0$ and $V = (T - T')^0$, and let bidirectional response at T' be $\rho_{T'}$ then :

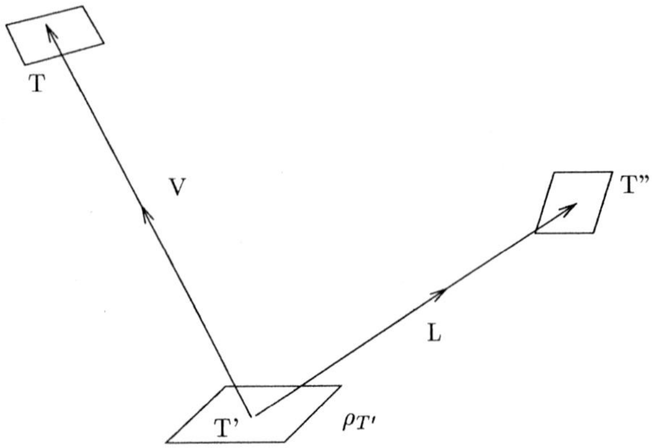

Fig. 1:

$$S^{out}(V) = S_0^{out}(V) + \int_{L \in F(T')} \rho_{T'}(L,V)\, |NL|\, S^{in}(L) d\omega_L \tag{7}$$

Equation (7) is the *rendering equation* from which the radiosity equation can be deduced.

3 The Radiosity Method

Let us introduce some notations. Let A_i $(i = 1, 2, ...N)$ be the area of a patch considered as homogeneous, as for the radiosity solutions. Let T_i be a preferential point on patch i, for instance, the centre for rectangles. The solid angle of view of the part of patch j *visible* from T_i is ω_{ij}. If A_j is completely visible, then

$$\omega_{ij} \approx \frac{A_j \cdot |N_j V_{ji}|}{r_{ij}^2} \quad [sr] \tag{8}$$

where r_i, j is the spacing between T_i and T_j, and $V_{i,j}$ is unit vector from T_i to T_j. If patch j is but partly visible from T_i then let A_j be th area of the visible part in (8). Let us write [2]

$$F_{ij} = \omega_{ij}\, |N_i V_{ij}| \quad [sr] \tag{9}$$

The absolute value in (9) is needed because of transparent models where normal vector N_i has no preferential direction. The z-buffer-type hemi-cube method has been generalized in practice to compute form factors (Cohen et al. [1]. An other approach of form factor computation has been introduced by Sillion et al. [8]. Obviously, in equality

$$A_i F_{ij} = A_j F_{ji} \tag{10}$$

Reciprocity of form factors is true, but only approximately, because of finite approximation. For partly occluded patches, (10) may involve an important error.

[2]Form factor current in publications for diffuse environments is exactly the π−th part of that according to (9), a non-dimensional value. The modification introduced here is convenient - in addition to the formal identity maintained for the diffuse case - by beeing coherent with notations for the non-diffuse case. Here ρ is a constant value of bidirectional reflectance in the diffuse case, in sr^{-1} units

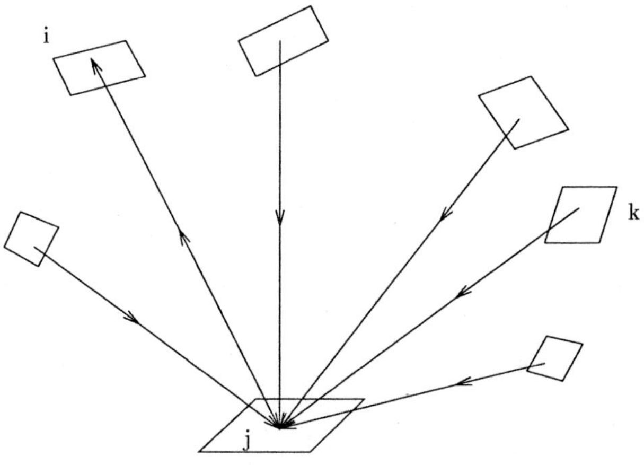

Fig. 2:

Radiant power P_{ij} is that emitted from i to patch j. Obviously, $P_{ij} \neq P_{ji}$. Radiance derived from P_{ij} :

$$S_{ij} \approx \frac{P_{ij}}{A_i F_{ij}} \left[W m^{-2} sr^{-1}\right] \tag{11}$$

The equation system for the general, non-separable case may be written according to (7). Introducing notation $\rho(k \rightarrow j \rightarrow i) = \rho_j(V_{jk}, V_{ji})$, this magnitude is required for computing the component arising from patch $k(k = 1, 2, ...N \quad k \neq j)$ of radiance S_{ji} (V_{jk} and V_{ji} are unit vectors in directions $j \rightarrow k$ and $j \rightarrow i$, respectively).

Immel et al. [3] were the first to write the equation system with *radiance* variables, with somewhat different notations :

$$S_{ji} = S_{ji}^0 + \sum_{k=1}^{N} \rho(k \rightarrow j \rightarrow i) F_{jk} S_{kj} \tag{12}$$

This equation will be written for any par (i, j) where $F_{ji} > 0$. These equations may be written not only for radiances, but also directly for *power* transport, using (10) and (11). This form of equation system has been introduced by Neumann et al. [6].

$$P_{ji} = F_{ji} \cdot \left[A_j S_{ji}^0 + \sum_{k=1}^{N} (\rho k \rightarrow j \rightarrow i) P_{kj}\right] \tag{13}$$

A row of (13) contains a single form factor $F_(ji)$ on the output side, input side factors F_{jk} are explicitely missing. Variables P_{kj} exist, however, only for patch pairs (k, j) where $F_{jk} > 0$.

Back to equation (6), let us consider the constant term, zero-order component

$$S_{ji}^0 = S_{ji}^E + S_{ji}^P \tag{14}$$

Patches have self-emissions S^E, point-like source effects are :

$$S_{ji}^P = \frac{1}{4\pi} \sum_{k=1}^{M} (\rho k \rightarrow j \rightarrow i) \left|N_j V_{jk}^*\right| \cdot \frac{P_k}{r_{jk}^2} \; h_{kj}^* \tag{15}$$

Superscript * reminds that the given magnitude refers to an outer light source affected by the subscript variable of $\sum$. Factor h^*_{kj} may assume any value from 0 to 1, depending on the proportion of the area of patch i illuminated by the given light source. Occluding conditions may be examined similarly as for the hemi-cube technique. The point-like light source will be surrounded by a full cube. Fundamentally, the point source may be a *non-isotopic* radiant. This possibility used to be ignored in classic ray-tracing, although it permits rather spectacular effects. Such a non-isotropic light source may be e.g. a light cone from a slide projector, or a stained glass window transmitting sunshine. Slides, photos of stained glass windows,or silhouettes of any real object can be digitalized. So anisotropy in any direction has a transmittance value $\theta \in [0,1]$, that can be assimilated as a multiplicative factor in factor h, together with coefficient d of the light absorbing medium. Also for θ values, patch-wise means are assumed.

In occurence of surface texture or pattern, in Equation (12) and (13) a mean ρ value surface weighted is taken for each of the patches. The effect of light absorbing medium may be involved in form factor (9) as a multiplying factor. After solution of radiosity equations, radiance values per pixel may be determined by the adaptively refining coupling method, or in some cases by the complete two-pass method (Neumann et la. [5]. These methods contain zero-order image after (14) or (15)(classic ray tracing image) as an additive component of pixel resolution. In this method, even higher-order reflections don't appear in patch decomposition (blurred by interpolation), but the radiosity solution is always joined after a least on distributive ray-tracing step.

In the general case, equations (12) and (13) are rather time consuming to solve. Immel et al. [3] expedited the Gauss-Seidel solution of (12) by a heuristic selection of the sequence of equation. Even so, run times were exorbitant. The Gauss-Seidel method can be proven to involve a sufficient condition for (12) to convergence. (12) and (13) can always be solved by Jacobi iteration and by the conjugated gradient method [5]. In case of clear environments, this latter is faster than the conventional methods. Min-Zhi Shao et al. [7] have introduced a rather ingenious solution method for cases where ρ can be decomposed to diffuse + specular, and the specular cone has a small spatial angle. It is a rapid method but its convergence has not yet been cleared. In the following, another method applying decomposition will be presented, somewhat faster than the former, and of proven convergence, the same as for(13) [6] [5].

4 A New Method of Diffuse + Specular Decomposition

In particular, let us consider diffuse + specular decomposition : $\rho = \rho^D + \rho^S$. Of course, a decomposition to separable + non-separable is also possible. With the notations above equation (13) becomes :

$$P_{ji} = F_{ji} \cdot \left[A_j \; S^0_{ji} + \rho^D_j \sum_{k=1}^{N} P_{kj} + \sum_{k \in I(j,i)}^{N} \rho^S(k \to j \to i) \; P_{kj} \right] \qquad (16)$$

where $I(j,i)$ is the set of subscripts of patches in"important directions" including subscripts k, where in case of input rays $k \to j$, direction $j \to i$ points to the "reflection cone" (to be defined as $\rho >$ given ϵ. Reciprocity of ρ involves "reciprocity of cones", that is, $k \in I(j,i)$ if $i \in I(j,k)$. Sums in (16) may be written for pairs (k,j) where $F_{j,k} > 0$. Theses are known form the hemi-cube of patch j. Variables P_{ji} a priori exist only for $F_{ji} > 0$. A single row of (16) requires N additions and as many multiplications as there are subscripts in the set $I(j,i)$ of the specular cone, may be significantly less than N. The advantage of equation (16) is manifest if variables belonging to patch j (that is P_{ji} with a given j and for $i = 1,2,...N$, provided $F_{ji} > 0$) are conveniently computed *simultaneously.* Namely, sums making up the diffuse part are identical in these rows. This skill, together with the separation of the specular part as above, *significantly* reduces the cost of computations compared to the original equation (13) (16) can be solved both by *Jacobi iteration* and by the *conjugated gradient method.* The image, or the radiance values may be computed by means of equation (11).

5 Sorted Shooting Method

5.1 Algorithm

The sorted shooting method introduced for diffuse environments (Cohen et al. [2] can be directly generalized for non-diffuse (non-separable) environments. In the classic "gathering" approach, all the ($k = 1, 2, ...N$) patches reflected /transmitted by patch j contribute to power transport $j \to i$ with weighting factors $F_{ji} \cdot \rho(k \to j \to i)$ in conformity with a row of (13) . The inverse is realized by the shooting approach. On patch j, power transport $i \to j$ ramifies to patches $k = 1, 2, ...n$ weighted by factor $F_{ji} \cdot \rho(k \to j \to i)$ for every pair (i, j) where $F_{ij} > 0$, two variables are introduced. One is power P_{ij}, with the same content as (13) the other is a parameter : *unshot power* P^u_{ij}. Initially :

$$P_{ij} = P^u_{ij} = A_i \; F_{ij} \; S^0_{ij} \tag{17}$$

That is, the zero-order component from which the constant is started. At start, every form factor has to be computed. 207zhe s The procedure consists in filing unshot power for every pair $i \to j$ with $F_{ij} > 0$. Among $O(N^2)$ unshot powers the maximum value (e.g. P^u_{ij}) is selected. This is reflected by patch j to be irradiated into all directions $j \to k \quad (k = 1, ...N)$. After shooting, the selected power is set to zero.

Contribution of unshot power P^u_{ij} to power P_{jk} and to unshot power P^u_{jk} is:

$$\Delta P_{jk} = \rho(i \to j \to k) F_{jk} P^u_{ij} \tag{18}$$

To select the maximum unshot power, it is advisable to apply a sorted data structure e.g. a Fibonacci heap. After pointing out the maximum P^u_{ij}, for every pair (j, k) with $F_{jk} > 0$, variables P_{jk} and P^u_{ij} are increased by ΔP_{jk}. At last, by the end of shooting, variable P^u_{ij} is zeroed.

5.2 Display

the non-diffuse ambient term [5] image may be added, by and by refreshed, to the image. Thereby, by analogy to the skill introduced with the diffuse method, an approximate representation is already available in computation. During initial form factor computation, the classic ray tracing image (zero-order component) and sum of the non-diffuse ambient term may be considered in pixel resolution. Interrupting the algorithm after a given number of steps, an image may be computed as follows. Radiance toward the observer can be computed from power variables P_{ij} according to (11). This image can be corrected in several ways. Either, by simply adding radiance arising from unshot power P^u_{ij}. Or, the quoted ambient term image may be added. The former perfectly omits further interreflections of unshot powers, the latter reckons with them applying a rough estimation. It is a much closer estimation to write a separable problem in terms of unshot powers. The separable model will be introduced in Section 6, here it will be simply referred to S^E_{ij} in (28)or (29) and has to be replaced by radiance values computed from unshot powers P^u_{ij} by (11).

5.3 Convergence

Next, the convergence of the method will be demonstrated. By analogy to this proof, on one hand, also convergence of the sorted shooting method known for diffuse environments, on the other hand, also that in Section 5, are conceivable. Obviously, sum of unshot powers tends to zero. Let :

$$P^U = \sum_{i,j=1}^{N} P_{ij}^U \tag{19}$$

There are at most $\leq (N-1) \cdot N$ variables. Let $A < 1$ be the highest albedo value in the system. After a single shooting, the P^u value drops by c times. A rough estimation of c is given by:

$$c < 1 - \frac{1-A}{N^2} < 1 \tag{20}$$

Namely, the highest unshot power is $\geq \frac{P^U}{N^2}$–. A-fold is re-radiated to the system (4) is simply a proof of the existence of convergence estimable by a geometric series. Of course, the estimation somewhat better approximates the real speed of convergence if A means the mean rather than the max albedo value of the system, without going into details of what is understood by mean. Accuracy of the estimation is improved by replacing the mean efficiency [5] value for A. Namely thereby (in addition to light absorption by the surface) energy irradiated outside the system, and light absorption in space, are taken into consideration. After a "big cycle" i.e. about N^2 steps, product of factors c may be assessed as :

$$\left[1 - \frac{1-A}{N^2}\right]^{N^2} \approx \exp(A-1) \tag{21}$$

For instance, for a real environment of mean efficiency $A = 0.2$, after a big cycle, P^U may be (again, roughly) estimated to decrease by $\exp(-0.8) = 0.45 \ times$. In reality, P_{ij}^U values are not uniform by distribution, and (in particular, initially) perfectly independent of albedo distribution. Therefore in reality, iteration converges much faster.

Finally, let us notice that shooting methods (by analogy to overrelaxation methods) may be theoretically modified to under and overshooting methods. That is s-times the absolute maximum unshot power is shot (where $s \neq 1$, advisably examining $0 < s < 2$). That is, either a power residue is left, or P_{ij}^U is overshot, to become negative. These feasible methods are worth to be examined from the aspect of the existence or speed of convergence.

6 Sorted Gathering + Shooting for Non-Diffuse Environments

In the gathering + shooting approach, methods in Section 2 and 4 are combined. Even, they have been applied in Section 3 concerned with simultaneous computation of rows for patch j of the radiosity equation system. In this approach, powers incident on, and irradiated by, the given patch will be simultaneously handled. This approach is more realistic, namely both approaches of gathering and shooting are higher abstractions, farther from the real parallel process.

Compared to Section 3, here selection of the actual patch is novel, made by means of sorting parameter (U_j) "single-index unshot" powers assigned to every patch. Variables are powers P_{ij} and P_{ij}^U just as before. Let $U_j (j = 1, 2, ..., N)$ be the overall unshot power gathered by patch j from every direction of the space and irradiable controlled by the type of reflectance/transmittance. In case of general ρ_j the computation of U_j would need $O(N^2)$ operations by convertional approximation. The method to be presented permits to reduce the number of operations to $0(N)$. Out of power P_{ij}, patch j emits a power $P_{ij} \cdot a_j(V_{ji})$ to the full (or half-) space where a_j is albedo function (equation 3) of patch j. Its values are easy to tabulate by preprocessing for isotropic materials, with respect ot variable $\alpha = \arccos(NL)$. "Patch-wise approximation" of power U_j may have a minimum of deviation from that can be computed by (22). Exceptionnaly this fact may result in a minimum sorting error, essentially inaffecting the method. Namely variables U_j are exclusively applied for sorting, their values are omitted in real power computation. At start, P_{ij} and P_{ij}^U are valued after (17), and

$$U_j = \sum_{i=1}^{N} a_j(V_{ji}) P_{ij}^U \tag{22}$$

where $(j = 1, 2, ..., N)$ are "single-subscript" unshot powers. Let us select maximum U_j and patch j. Then variations of all the P_{jk} and P_{jk}^u are determined by means of ΔP_{jk} in (18), with successive effects of powers P_{ij}^u for every i, where $F_{ji} > 0$. Also separation to diffuse + specular proven in (16)may be applied. Now ΔP_{jk} is computed with ρ^S restricted to the cone of reflection, and separately, the diffuse term. Denoting $J(j)$ the set of subscripts of patches seen from patch j, the algorithm becomes after this initialization :

1. select max u_j, given ϵ
then displaying and END

2. $P_j^D \quad = \quad \rho_j^D \cdot \sum_{i=1}^{N} P_{ij}^u$ (parameter of the diffuse component)

3. $\Delta P_{jk} \quad = \quad F_{jk} \cdot \left[P_j^D + \sum_{i \in I(j,k)}^{N} \rho^S(i \to j \to k) P_{ij}^u \right]$

4. $P_{jk} \quad := \quad P_{jk} + \Delta P_{jk}$

5. $P_{jk}^u \quad := \quad P_{jk}^u + \Delta P_{jk}$

6. $U_k \quad := \quad U_k + A_k(V_{kj}) \cdot \Delta P_{jk}$ (steps 3,4,5,6 are performed for every $k \in J(j)$)

7. $U_i \quad := \quad U_i - a_j(V_{ji}) \cdot P_{ij}^u$ (substraction of shot power)

8. $P_{ij}^u \quad := \quad 0$ (steps 7 and 8 are performed for every $i \in J(j)$)

9. $U_j \quad := \quad 0$; GOTO 1

For $\rho^S \equiv 0$, the algorithm above offers a solution for purely diffuse systems. Now, $a_j(V_{ji}) \equiv a_j \equiv \pi \cdot \rho_j$. This method is not the same as sorted shooting [2] known for diffuse environments. Requireing $O(N^2)$ variables, this algorithm is of a rather theoretical importance for diffuse cases.

7 Approximation with Albedo-Equivalent Separable Reflectance

7.1 Equation System for Separable Reflectance

Separable bidirectional reflectance/transmittance and the relevant equation system have been introduced by Neumann et al. citeNEUMANN89. Separable models may be written in the form

$$\rho(L, V) = a(L) \cdot r(V) \tag{23}$$

If reciprocity condition (2) holds, then function "a" is constant times the function "r". Separable models are the *widest class* of bidirectional responses where *output* light distribution is *independent* of the spatial distribution of *input* light power. Total input light power weighted by function "a" is dispersed in semi-space (or in full space) according to density function"r". $a(L)$ always denotes (dimensionless) albedo as in (3), while $r(V)$ is density function of output light distribution in $[sr^{-1}]$ units, provided :

$$\int_{V \in F} r(V)|NV|d\omega_V = 1 \tag{24}$$

The most special separable model is a diffuse model. Here $a(L) = a = constant$, and $r(V) = \pi^{-1}[sr^{-1}]$. Isotropic, separable ρ meeting reciprocity may be formally constructed by assuming an arbitrary albedo function $a(L) = \tilde{a}(\alpha) \leq 1$ $(0 \leq \alpha \leq \frac{\pi}{2})$ where $\alpha = \arccos(NL)$. Now using notation $\beta = \arccos(NV)$:

$$r(V) = \tilde{r}(\beta) = \frac{\tilde{a}(\beta)}{\pi \cdot \int_0^{\frac{\pi}{2}} \tilde{a}(\alpha) \cdot sin2\alpha d\alpha} \tag{25}$$

Integral in the denominator can be numerically determined (in case of transmittance, the range of integration is $[-\pi/2, \pi/2]$). *In the case of N patches of separable models, an equation system with N unknowns may be written, just as for diffuse environments.* Let us introduce notations $a_{ij} = a_i(V_{ij}), r_{ji} = r_j(V_{ji})$, where a_i is albedo function of patch i ; r_j is density function of output for patch j. First, let patches have special self-emissions, where *radiosity* $B_i^E[Vm^{-2}]$ is irradiated at a distribution $r_i(V)$. the complete zero-order component may be written as in equation (15).

$$E_i = B_i^E + \frac{1}{4\pi} \cdot \sum_{k=1}^{M} a_i(L_{ik}^*) \cdot |N_i L_{ik}^*| \cdot \frac{P_k^*}{r_{ik}^2} h_{ki}^* \tag{26}$$

It is not hard to see that in this case the linear equation system becomes :

$$B_i = E_i + \sum_{j=1}^{N} F_{ij} \ a_{ij} \ r_{ji} \ B_j \tag{27}$$

where radiosity B_i is dispersed at a distribution r_i, thereby in direction$V$, radiance is $B_i r_i(V)$. In the *diffuse case* $r_{ji} = \frac{1}{\pi}$ and $a_{ij} \equiv a_i = \rho_i \pi$. In this case the direction-independent, *constant radiance* is $\frac{1}{\pi}$ times the radiosity B_i.

Radiance $S_i^E(V)$ describing patch self-illumination may have an arbitrary *direction-dependence.* Now, the equation system will be written (at a difference from the conventional approach) for zero-order components *without* illumination P_i and B_i of powers and radiosities, resp., emitted by patches :

$$P_i = \sum_{j=1}^{N} F_{ji} \ a_{ij} \ (r_{ji} P_j + S_{ji}^E A_j) \tag{28}$$

or, in radiosity form :

$$B_i = \sum_{j=1}^{N} F_{ij} \ a_{ij} \ (r_{ji} B_j + S_{ji}^E) \tag{29}$$

To compute the image, radiance in an arbitrary direction V has to be known B_i dispersed according to r_i is added the zero-order component :

$$S_i(V) = S_i^E(V) + B_i r_i(V) \tag{30}$$

Of course, (28) and (29) may also be written for diffuse environments. What is new in it is that inherent emission may be direction-dependent. In addition to inherent emission, the constant term may include point sources, now, in formula above, S^E has to be replaced by zero-order component S^0 involving these effects.

7.2 An Efficient Approximate Solution for Non-Separable Environments

For non-separable (non-diffuse) models, where direction-dependence of the reflected light is rather irrelevant, no procedure requiring less than $O(N^3)$ operations is known. Next, an approximate, view-dependent procedure requiring $O(N^2)$ operations without computing form factors, suiting for them (e.g. for a phong-like model of the form $\rho(L, V) = NH$) will be presented.

Let us introduce the concept of albedo equivalence. Bidirectional responses ρ_1 and ρ_2 are albedo equivalent if for any $L \in F$, $a_1(L) \equiv a_2(L)$ where a_1 and a_2 are albedo functions after (3) of ρ_1 and ρ_2 rep. In different terms, albedo function of formally derived (at times, negative) $\rho = \rho_1 - \rho_2$ is zero throughout. Albedo equivalence has a rather unique illustrative meaning. In case of point source distributed illumination, the ratio of overall powers incident on, and leaving, the surface is the same for ρ_1 and for ρ_2. Of course, outputs have different spatial distributions.

For any bidirectional response ρ there is an unambiguously defined albedo equivalent separable model. Let $a(L)$ be the albedo function of ρ.Then the separable model is of the form $\rho^* = a(L) \cdot r(V)$ where function r is constant-times function "a" and meets (24). For an isotropic bidirectional reflectance ρ, r may be computed from (25), preceded by tabulating the albedo according to :

$$a(L) = \tilde{a}(\alpha) = \int_{\phi=0}^{\pi} \int_{\beta=0}^{\frac{\pi}{2}} \tilde{\rho}(\alpha, \beta, \phi) \cdot sin2\beta \ d\beta \ d\phi \tag{31}$$

where : $\alpha = \arccos(NL)$ and $\beta = \arccos(NV)$ are incident angles, and ϕ is the difference of horizontal polar coordinates ϕ_1 and ϕ_2 of L and V, respectively. Furthermore, $\tilde{\rho}(\alpha, \beta, \phi,) = \rho(L, V)$. Thus, in case of isotropic reflectance, abledo-equivalent separable model ρ^* can be numerically determined from (31) and (25).

Let us consider a complex environment, with arbitrary non-separable reflectances ρ. Let illumination S^0 be a direction-dependent, self-illumination according to (14) and (15), sum of point source effects. Using this zero-order component, let us write the equation system of albedo-equivalent separable model ρ^* belonging to ρ for radiosities B_i in form (29) :

$$B_i = \sum_{j=1}^{N} F_{ij} \ a_{ij} \ (r_{ji} B_j + S_{ji}^0) \tag{32}$$

(32) beeing solved, looking at patch i from direction V, radiance value of computed image is, by analogy to (30) :

$$S_i(V) = S_i^0(V) + B_i r_i(V) \tag{33}$$

where the zero-order component (that is, the classic ray-tracing component) belongs to the original ρ, but interreflections result from an optimally approximative separable model. For ρ other than clear and specular, equation (33) yields an acceptable, rapid approximate solution. The second term may be computed by adaptative refinement. In knowledge of the solution of (32) a significatly better, yet inexpensive approximation is possible :

$$S_i(V) = S_i^0(V) + \sum_{j=1}^{N} \rho_i(V_{ij}, V) \ F_{ij} \ S_{ji} \tag{34}$$

where $S_{ji} = S_j^0(V_{ji}) + B_j \cdot r_j(V_{ji})$ (34) yields an image where zero-order and first-order components are exact, and the higer-order components are approximate. For instance, let sunshine across the window (far point source) have a dull reflection at the floor to the opposite wall where its reflection appears as a blurred spot. Now, not only the floor is seen with an exact reflection according to ρ but also the blurred spot. In case of a point source, the first-order image is formed by twice refracted rays according to ρ, undergoing simple surface to surface interreflection. Furthermore, also the higher-order reflections have only been approximated but they reach the pupil at a reflection exactly conform to ρ_i. The first term in (34) is easy to display at pixel resolution. Sums are known patch-wise hence an approximate pixel-level image pay be computed by interpolation, and an exact one by the coupling method [5], by adaptive refining.

It has to be remarked here, even without separable problem (32), an image exactly describing rays coming from point-like sources with simple or double refraction but perfecty omitting higher-order interreflections may be computed. Now, S_{ji} has to be replaced by $S_j^0(V_{ji})$ in (34). This method is a deterministic variant of the distributed ray tracing method, where, after the first refraction, a ray ramifies to every visible patch, i.e. in direction $0(N)$.

8 Future Problems

The presented methods finally result in a finite solution of the rendering equation. The derivation beween the radiosity solution and the exact solution depend on the patch subdivision. The problem of fineness required for patch subdivision has not yet been solved, the resulting error is but partly corrected by ulterior adaptive refinement. Nearer, coupling method applying adpative refinement may shift the appearance of error to the level of higher-order components. Similarly, also two-pass-type methods only reduce the error, without giving a solution of principle. The gist of the problem is that higher-order components of the Neumann series of the radiosity equation system finite form of the rendering equation, higher powers of matrices, increasingly differ from operator powers yielding series of exact solution. An essential feature of radiosity methods is this *degeneration*.This is more marked for e.g. highly specular materials, for very clear environments. This problem awaits to be theoretically cleared, and to be given a practical method, e.g. an on-line adaptive subdivision procedure. This problem is related to the development of decomposition methods suiting solution of large systems, expected to become an important trend of evolution for radiosity methods.

By now, several types of feasible radiosity solution methods have been developped. It would be advisable to develop a decision tree or expert system (based on numerical analysis and great many practical tests) for selecting a given algorithm for a given problem. Aspects of decision may be mean clearness of the complex environment, complexity of occluding condition, type of reflectance/transmittance models, the expected exactness level (may be separatly for levels of zero- , first- and higher-order images), storage needs, and computation speed. Actually, there is no rapid, exact radiosity solution for non-separable (e.g. specular) reflectances with flat, undistinctive characteristics. Again the problem of radiosity solution of low degeneration for clear environments with reflectances comprising very specular components, or complex occluding conditions still awaits to be developed. In general, however, the main problem is due to large-size systems, irregarding relatively dark diffuse systems suiting the sorted shooting method.

References

[1] M. F. Cohen, D. P. Greenberg, D. D. Immel, and P. J. Brock. An efficient radiosity approach for realistic image synthesis. *IEEE Computer Graphics and Applications*, 6:26–35, March 1986.

[2] Michael F. Cohen, Shenchang E. Chen, John R. Wallace, and Donald P. Greenberg. A progessive refinement approach to fast radiosity image generation. In *SIGGRAPH'88 Conference Proceeding*, pages 75–84, august 1988. Computer Graphics vol.22 num.4.

[3] D. S. Immel, M. F. Cohen, and D. P. Greenberg. A radiosity method for non-diffused environments. *Computer Graphics*, 20(4):133–142, July 1986.

[4] J.T. Kajiya. The rendering equation. In *Proceedings of SIGGRAPH'86 in computer graphics*, pages 143–150, SIGGRAPH, August 1987.

[5] László Neumann and Attila Neumann. Hybrid methods in photosimulation. *Submitted to ACM TOG*, 21–34, June 1989.

[6] László Neumann and Attila Neumann. Photosimulation: interreflection with arbitrary reflectance models and illumination. *Computer Graphics Forum*, 8(1):21–34, 1989.

[7] M. Shao, Q. Peng, and Y. Liang. A new radiosity approach by procedural refinements for realistic image synthesis. In *SIGGRAPH'88 Conference Proceeding*, pages 93–101, ACM, August 1988.

[8] F. Sillion and C. Puech. A general two-pass method integrating specular and diffuse reflection. *Computer Graphics*, 23(3):335–344, July 1989.

[9] J. R. Wallace, M. F. Cohen, and D. P. Greenberg. A two-pass solution to the rendering equation : a synthesis of ray tracing and radiosity methods. In *SIGGRAPH'87 Conference Proceeding*, pages 311–320, ACM, August 1987.

[10] G. Wyszecky and W. S. Stiles. *Color Science, Concepts and Methods, Quantitative Datas and Formulas.* J. Willey and sons, 2nd Edition, 1982.

Chapter 3

Photometric Algorithms

A Progressive Ray-Tracing-based Radiosity with General Reflectance Functions

Christophe Schlick Bertrand LeSaec [1]

Abstract — In this paper, we present a progressive and interactive rendering method to solve the global illumination problem. Our method, currently under implementation, can be considered as an extension of Wallace's recent paper, at the SIGGRAPH'89 conference, about a Progressive Ray-Tracing-based Radiosity. The method is intended to remove the limitation to purely diffuse phenomenons that exists in Wallace's paper and allow the use of general reflectance functions.

1 Introduction

Two great goals to achieve for computer graphics are *photorealism* and *interactivity*. Photorealism consists in simulating, as exactly as possible, the light propagation from the light sources to the observer's eye, taking all the reflection / transmission / absorption phenomenons into account. Interactivity, on the other hand, means computing and displaying the image, as quickly as possible, in order to allow the user to virtually walk through the scene, in real time. But improving photorealism implies an increase of computing time and thus, a drop of interactivity. On the other hand, improving interactivity means a smaller response time and so, a loss of photorealism. In fact, a trick devised in [2] and later improved in [6] enables a conciliation of photorealism and interactivity. This trick, called "Progressive Refinement Rendering" consists in a fast display of a rough but immediatly useful image that transforms itself progressively and gracefully into the final and correct image.

The mixing of photorealism and interactivity, known as "Photorealistic Rendering with Interactive Walkthrough" is an important challenge for the next few years. If it is not intended for computer animation (since moving an object forces the whole image to be recomputed), *PRIW* is made for applications such as architecture, house decorations, street lighting simulation...

In this paper, we propose a progressive and interactive rendering method that goes beyond the purely diffuse phenomenons limitation that existed until now. In Section 2, some classical rendering methods are recalled, insisting on their advantages and drawbacks, both on the photorealism and the interactivity point of view. In Section 3, principles of *Progressive Radiosity* and *Ray-Tracing-based Radiosity* are recalled. In Section 4, we detail the first part of our algorithm, and in Section 5, the second part.

2 Background

Early image synthesis methods ([9], [13]) were all one-pass methods, that accounted only for direct illumination. Later, ray-tracing-based algorithms improved photorealism by allowing indirect illumination and interreflections (specular ([20], [7] or diffuse ([11], [19]).

[1] *Pmail :* LaBRI 351, Cours de la Libération 33405 Talence (FRANCE)
Email : schlick@geocub.greco-prog.fr

Today, a limit seems to have been reached in the one-pass algorithms field. To get photorealistic images, computation becomes more and more complex and goes always further from the interactivity given by Gouraud and Phong shading. Moreover, all that cost serves for one image only, because the slightest movement of the observer implies to compute the whole image again.

That's why in ([8], [4]) a new approach is presented. That new approach divides the computation in two passes. During the first pass, global illumination is computed for the whole scene. During the second pass, the only thing that remains to do is to extract the illumination informations concerning the view point and display the scene. The first pass uses a so-called radiosity method, that consists in writing the energy exchange equation between surfaces and solving the resulting linear system. The second pass consists in finding the visible surfaces and interpolating the illumination computed during the first pass using Gouraud's method. Radiosity methods work well in diffuse environments, but extension to general environments ([10]) are both memory and time expensive.

Because it seems not to be possible to handle efficiently diffuse and specular phenomenons in a unique operation, recent methods ([17], [16], [15], [3]) suggest to split them in two. The diffuse part of illumination is computed by radiosity in a view-independent way during the first pass, and during the second pass, the specular part seen by the observer is computed by ray-tracing.

All these methods, and especially the most recent ones, are able to produce highly photorealistic images of several kinds of environments, but they need to solve linear systems with several thousands unknowns, and thus can not enable interactivity. But as we will see in Section 3, a rewriting of the radiosity algorithm, found in [6], offers a first version of what a future *PRIW* system will include : an useful image almost immediatly and a progressive refinement that occurs during the time the user interactively walks through the scene.

3 Progressive and Ray-Tracing-based Radiosity

3.1 The Light Transport Equation

Equations that characterize light transport in an environment are well-known in physics, and for several years now, well-known within the field of computer graphics. Traditionally, they are written under a form that shows energy exchange between surfaces — the *radiosity* equation being the most famous of them. But as recalled in [3], the human eye is only sensitive to *radiance*, and not to *energy*, thus, it is more judicious to show radiance exchange between surfaces. Therefore, we will rewrite, in terms of radiance, some results found in recent papers dealing with radiosity, taking the notations used in [3] (see Figure 1).

The *light transport equation* that completely describes the radiance exchange between surfaces, for a given wavelength, is the following :

$$L_{ij} = L_{ij}^E + \sum_k \int_{S_k} R_{kij}\, L_{ki}\, A_{ki}\, G_{ki}\, dS_k \qquad (1)$$

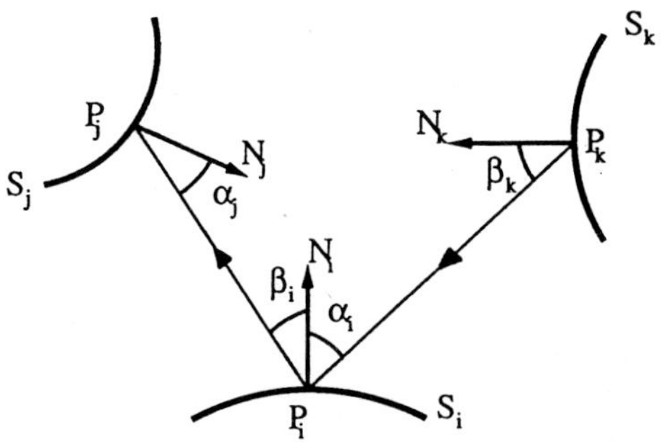

Fig. 1 : The Light Transport Geometry

- L_{ij} : Radiance leaving surface S_i at point P_i in the direction of point P_j
- L_{ij}^E : Self-emitting radiance leaving point P_i in the direction of point P_j
- R_{kij} : Bidirectional reflectance of surface S_i between directions $\vec{P_kP_i}$ and $\vec{P_iP_j}$ (bidirectional reflectance is the ratio of reflected radiance by irradiance, where irradiance is incident light power by unit surface area)
- L_{ki} : Radiance leaving surface S_k at point P_k in the direction of point P_i
- G_{ki} : Geometrical factor that represents the influence of the distance and orientation of P_i and P_k. The geometrical term is given by :

$$G_{ki} = \frac{cos\alpha_i \, cos\beta_k}{D_{ki}^2} \text{ where } D_{ki} = \| \vec{P_kP_i} \|$$

- A_{ki} : Absorption factor that represents the influence of the medium through which light travels from P_k to P_i (in vacuum, $A_{ki} = 1$). By convention, if P_i can not "see" P_k, $A_{ki} = 0$. The absorption term can be given either by the exact Bougher law or by a more empirical one, for instance :

$$A_{ki} = e^{-\tau D_{ki}} \text{ where } \tau \text{ is an arbitrary constant characterizing the medium}$$

It should be noted that L_{ij} does not represent the radiance that *reaches* P_j but the one that *leaves* P_i. To get the former, absorption has to be applied to L_{ij}, that means L_{ij} has to be scaled by A_{ij}. This is different from the [3] formulas that are only correct in vacuum, when $A_{ij} = 1$.

When you have an environment divided into a set of patches S_k, an intuitive interpretation to Equation (1) can be given. It describes the influence of all those patches on the radiance of a differential surface dS_i around the point P_i. As shown in [18], computing illumination at the vertices P_i of a patch, and interpolating the result inside the patch causes less error than computing average illuminations for patches and bring them to vertices, as with classical radiosity approaches.

3.2 Purely Diffuse Environment

When the whole environment is purely diffuse, several simplifications occur to Equation (1) :

- L_{ij} does no longer depend on j and L_{ki} on i (radiance is constant, whatever the direction). Moreover, when the environment is divided into a set of sufficiently small patches S_k, L_k can be considered constant over the whole patch.

- R_{kij} does no longer depend on k and j (bidirectional reflectance is constant, whatever the couple of directions)

Thus, Equation (1) becomes less complex :

$$L_i = L_i^E + R_i \sum_k L_k \, I_{ki} \tag{2}$$

- I_{ki} : Illuminance between surface S_k and differential surface dS_i (illuminance is the ratio of radiance leaving S_k by the irradiance of dS_i). In fact, we call I_{ki} the illuminance because it represents the way S_k illuminates dS_i (depending on all the intervening factors : shape, position, orientation, medium). The illuminance is given by :

$$I_{ki} = \int_{S_k} A_{ki} \, G_{ki} \, dS_k$$

Let us examine similitarities between Equation (2) and the more classical equation, found in radiosity papers :

$$\Pi_i = \Pi_i^E + \rho_i \sum_k \Pi_k \, F_{ki} \tag{3}$$

- Π_i : Power leaving differential surface dS_i

- Π_i^E : Self-emitting power leaving differential surface dS_i

- ρ_i : Reflection factor of differential surface dS_i (ratio of reflected power by incident power)

- Π_k : Power leaving surface S_k

- F_{ki} : Form factor from surface S_k to differential surface dS_i (ratio of power reaching dS_i by power leaving S_k)

Equation (2) describes light transport by expressing radiance transfer, whereas Equation (3) describes the same light transport by power exchange. The product $\rho_i F_{ki}$ represents the total loss from power leaving S_k to power leaving S_i after reflection. In the same manner, the product $R_i I_{ki}$ represents the total loss from radiance leaving S_k to radiance leaving S_i after reflection. For a purely diffuse environment, $\rho_i = \pi R_i$ and $F_{ki} = I_{ki}/\pi$ that means $\rho_i F_{ki} = R_i I_{ki}$. Therefore, there is no difference between thinking in term of power (or energy) and in term of radiance. But for non purely diffuse environment, it isn't true any longer...

3.3 Ray-Tracing-based Radiosity

Since the radiosity method has become popular, several algorithms have been proposed in order to compute F_{ki} using numerical integration techniques ([8], [4], [12], [1]). In [18], the authors present a way to compute F_{ki} by using ray-tracing. The method has an interesting feature, it gives a parametrizable precision (the more rays you cast, the more precision you get). That method can be easily adapted to compute I_{ki} instead of F_{ki} :

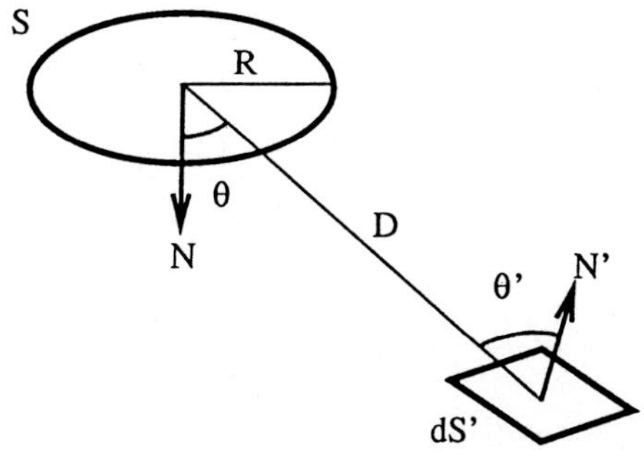

Fig. 2 : Form-factor between disk and differential surface

Let S be a disk of radius R and dS' a differential surface (Figure 2).

When S and dS' are parallel ($\theta = \theta' = 0$), and visibility does not change over the whole disk, $I_{S\,dS'}$ has got an analytical solution :

$$I_{S\,dS'} = A\frac{\pi R^2}{D^2 + R^2} = A\frac{S}{D^2 + \frac{S}{\pi}}$$

When S and dS' are not parallel, $I_{S\,dS'}$ can be approximated when R is small compared to D :

$$I_{S\,dS'} \simeq A\frac{S}{D^2 + \frac{S}{\pi}} cos\theta\, cos\theta'$$

When S is arbitrary shaped, S can be approximated by a set of n small disks, each of surface $\delta S = S/n$ spread over the whole surface. Thus $I_{S\,dS'}$ becomes :

$$I_{S\,dS'} \simeq \frac{1}{n}\sum_{p=1}^{n} A_p \frac{\delta S}{D_p^2 + \frac{\delta S}{\pi}} cos\theta_p\, cos\theta'_p = \frac{S}{n}\sum_{p=1}^{n} A_p \frac{cos\theta_p\, cos\theta'_p}{D_p^2 + \frac{S}{n\pi}}$$

In our context :

$$I_{ki} = \frac{S_k}{n}\sum_{p=1}^{n} A_{ki_p} \frac{cos\alpha_{i_p}\, cos\beta_{k_p}}{D_{ki_p}^2 + \frac{S_k}{n\pi}} \tag{4}$$

By substituing Equation (4) in Equation (2), an approximated light transfer equation is obtained :

$$L_i = L_i^E + R_i \sum_k L_k \frac{S_k}{n}\sum_{p=1}^{n} A_{ki_p} \frac{cos\alpha_{i_p}\, cos\beta_{k_p}}{D_{ki_p}^2 + \frac{S_k}{n\pi}} \tag{5}$$

Equation (4) gives us a way to compute I_{ki} by using ray-tracing. The algorithm can be expressed in the following manner :

```
I_ki := 0;
Choose n sample points on S_k;
For each sample point P_kp do
    Trace a ray from P_i to P_kp;
    If the ray intersects nothing then
        Compute D_kip, cosα_ip, cosβ_kp, A_kip;
        I_ki := I_ki + A_kip (cosα_ip cosβ_kp)/(D²_kip + S_k/(nπ));
    Endif;
Endfor;
I_ki := I_ki * S_k/n;
```

Note that the number n of sampling points does not need to be the same for all vertices P_i. It can be high or low, depending on several factors : area of S_k, distance or orientation between S_k and S_i, amount of emitted radiance, partial occlusion of the patch... Wallace got some impressive results with as few as one to five sampling points for each source.

3.4 Progressive Radiosity

Once illuminances I_{ki} have all been computed, Equation (2) can be interpreted as a linear system whose unknowns are L_i (the radiance leaving every vertex P_i of the scene). Thus any existing linear system solver can be used to find the global illumination solution (Gauss-Seidel iterative scheme seems to be particulary well-suited). That method, used in the classical radiosity papers, has a major drawback on the interactivity point of view : before the first useful image is available, all the illuminances have to be computed and the whole system has to be solved.

A second method, much more efficient, introduced in [6] consists in solving the linear system of Equation (2) by successive refinements, using the following algorithm :

```
For each vertex P_i do L_i := L_i^E;
Repeat
    Select patch S_k with greatest radiance
    For each vertex P_i in the environment do
        Compute I_ki;
        L_i := L_i + R_i L_k I_ki;
    Endfor;
Until convergence;
```

Moreover, Cohen proposed to add an ambient term during the second pass in order to lighten the images at the early stages of the resolution, when only a few light sources have been taken in account. That ambient term decreases as computation goes on, and the image transforms itself, progressively and gracefully from an almost immediate approximated solution of the global illumination system to the final accurate one.

Mixing Ray-Tracing-based and Progressive Radiosity, as done in [18], can achieve excellent results, both on the photorealism and on the interactivity point of view. But that method is currently limited to purely diffuse reflectance. Therefore we present in the next sections, the two parts of an algorithm based on the same scheme that brings an extension to general reflectance functions.

4 First Part

4.1 Extension to General Reflectance Functions

As shown in [10], the global illumination problem is much more complex when one goes beyond purely diffuse environments, because no simplification occurs anymore to Equation (1).

Let us take Equation (1) and suppose that we split both bidirectional reflectance and self-emitting radiance into a diffuse part and a specular one :

$$R_{kij} = d_i\, R_i^d + s_i\, R_{kij}^s \tag{6}$$

$$L_{ij}^E = d_i\, L_i^{Ed} + s_i\, L_{ij}^{Es} \tag{7}$$

- d_i (resp. s_i) : Weight of the diffuse (resp. specular) part of surface S_i properties
- R_i^d : Diffuse bidirectional reflectance of surface S_i at point P_i
- R_{kij}^s : Specular bidirectional reflectance of surface S_i at point P_i between direction $\vec{P_k P_i}$ and $\vec{P_i P_j}$
- L_i^{Ed} : Diffuse self-emitting radiance leaving surface S_i
- L_{ij}^{Es} : Specular self-emitting radiance leaving surface S_i in direction $\vec{P_i P_j}$

Then Equation (1) becomes :

$$L_{ij} = d_i\, L_i^d + s_i\, L_{ij}^s \tag{8}$$

where

$$L_i^d = L_i^{Ed} + R_i^d \sum_k \int_{S_k} L_{ki}\, A_{ki}\, G_{ki}\, dS_k$$

$$L_{ij}^s = L_{ij}^{Es} + \sum_k \int_{S_k} R_{kij}^s\, L_{ki}\, A_{ki}\, G_{ki}\, dS_k$$

When one deals with general reflectance functions, not only L_i^d but also each L_{ij}^s have to be stored for every point P_i. Suppose that we have got a way to store L_i^d and L_{ij}^s at each point P_i, the scheme presented in Section 3 can be used again : loop until convergence, selection of the most illuminating patch, computing of the contribution of that patch to every vertex.

So there are only three problems to solve, to extend progressive ray-tracing-based radiosity for general reflectance functions :

- How to store directional radiance leaving point P_i
- How to choose the most illuminating patch S_k
- How to compute the contribution of patch S_k to the radiance leaving P_i

4.2 Storage of Directional Radiance

In [10], the authors proposed to put a cube, whose faces were divided into square pixels, around every vertex. Each pixel serves both to store the patch visible through that pixel and the illumination leaving a point in the corresponding direction. Immel had to use a regularly sampled cube because he used it for hidden part removal with a depth-buffer algorithm. With ray-tracing-based radiosity, this is no longer the case because only a storing structure for radiance is needed. Thus we can use a true hemisphere (or a sphere, when the surface is transparent). That hemisphere can be more or less sampled (using meridians and parallels) according to the specularity of the surface — variation of reflected radiance when going away from the exact reflection direction.

In fact, one can distinguish three kinds of surfaces :

- Class-1 (non specular surfaces) : No hemisphere is needed because only L_i^d has to be stored
- Class-2 (surfaces with low or middle specularity) : A sampled hemisphere can be used to store the directional radiances L_{ij}^s
- Class-3 (surfaces with high specularity) : Sampling required to insure a good precision can become very fine and thus very expensive. Moreover, for perfectly mirror surfaces, the number of samples should be infinite. For this kind of surfaces, a particular treatement has to take place as we will see in the next section.

Another question to answer is how to sample efficiently the hemisphere. The ideal sampling, is the one for which the sum of reflected radiance leaving a point of the surface over the projected area of each pixel (in fact, the radiosity per pixel) is constant. The sampling has to be done at the beginning, before the resolution starts, when the incoming direction of light reaching a point on a surface are not known yet. Therefore, all the methods that sample directions according to the incident direction and the bidirectional reflectance ([11]) can not be used here. Our sampling should not favour one particular direction but has to suppose that the light can come from anywhere around the point.

Therefore, to establish how that sampling should look like, let suppose that, for a given point, the same incident radiance L comes from every direction and that bidirectional reflectance function R of the surface on that point is the same whatever the incoming direction.

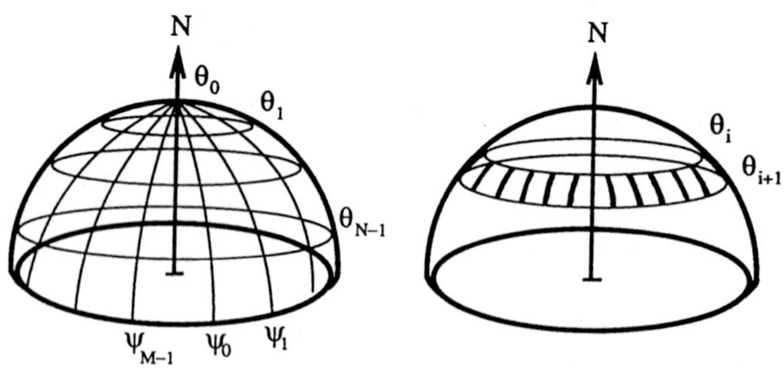

Fig.3 : (a) Sampling of the hemisphere (b) Summation between two parallels

Let M be the number of meridians, N the number of parallels and $P = M * N$, the number of pixels. Let ψ be the angle between the initial and the current meridian, and θ be the angle between the normal vector and the current parallel. Sampling the hemisphere requires to find two series of angles $0 = \theta_0, \theta_1 \cdots \theta_N = \pi/2$ and $0 = \psi_0, \psi_1 \cdots \psi_M = 2\pi$ (see Figure 3.a)

Radiosity leaving the point through the whole hemisphere is :

$$B_{Hemisphere} = \int_{2\pi} R\,L\,cos\theta\, d\Omega = R\,L \int_0^{\pi/2} cos\theta\, 2\pi\, sin\theta\, d\theta = \pi\, R\,L$$

We want radiosity leaving the point through each pixel to be constant :

$$B_{Pixel} = \int_{Pixel} R\,L\,cos\theta\, d\Omega = \frac{\pi\, R\,L}{P}$$

For symetry reasons, meridians have to be regularly sampled around the normal vector, thus we have :

$$\forall i = 0 \cdots M-1,\ \psi_i = \frac{2\pi\, i}{M}$$

Let B_i be the radiosity through the portion of the hemisphere limited by θ_i and θ_{i+1} (see Figure 3.b). We have :

$$B_i = R\,L \int_{\theta_i}^{\theta_{i+1}} cos\theta\, 2\pi\, sin\theta\, d\theta = \pi\, R\,L\,(cos^2\theta_i - cos^2\theta_{i+1})$$

We want that, for each i, $B_i = \frac{\pi\, R\,L}{N}$ thus :

$$\forall i = 0 \cdots N-1,\ cos\theta_i = \sqrt{\frac{N-i}{N}}$$

In order to speed up the other steps of the algorithm, rather than store simply L_i^d and L_{ij}^s, we store the following entities, for each point P_i :

- If $d_i \neq 0 : \mathcal{D}_i = d_i\, L_i^d$
- If $s_i \neq 0 : \mathcal{S}_{i_p} = s_i\, L_i^s(\theta_p, \psi_p)$ (for each pixel p of the hemisphere) and $\mathcal{T}_i = \sum_{p=1}^{P} \mathcal{S}_{i_p}$

For the moment, M and N are chosen by hand, according to the specularity of the surface. Further work should be done to find M and N automatically so as the less sampling error is done.

4.3 Choice of the Most Illuminating Patch

In order to choose the most illuminating patch, one has to compute the contribution of a patch S, that means the power ϕ_S leaving S. But for a given patch, due to spatial sampling, the contribution is only known at its vertices $P_1 \cdots P_K$, thus ϕ_S can only be approximated and not computed exactly.

$$\phi_S = \int_S B\, dS \simeq \frac{S}{K}(B_1 + \cdots + B_K)$$

where B_i is the radiosity leaving surface S at point P_i

For a given point, due to directional sampling, the contribution is only known for some directions, thus B_i can only be approximated too :

$$B_i = \int_{2\pi} L_i(\theta,\psi)\, cos\theta\, d\Omega = d_i\, \pi\, L_i^d + \int_{2\pi} s_i\, L_i^s(\theta,\psi)\, cos\theta\, d\Omega \simeq \pi\mathcal{D}_i + \sum_{p=1}^{P} \frac{\pi}{P}\mathcal{S}_{i_p} = \pi(\mathcal{D}_i + \mathcal{T}_i)$$

So, at each step of the iteration, the most illuminating patch can be found easily and at low cost. It should be noticed that finding this patch is only done to speed up the convergence. Therefore, the final solution of thew iterative scheme will not suffer from the approximation made here.

4.4 Contribution of a Patch to an Arbitrarly Point

Suppose that at a certain stage of our algorithm, we have found the most illuminating patch S_k. We now want to compute its contribution to every vertex P_i of the environment. In fact, according to Figure 4, for each point P_j, we have to compute L_{ij}^k, radiance due to patch S_k, leaving surface S_i at point P_i in direction $\vec{P_iP_j}$:

$$L_{ij}^k = \int_{S_k} R_{kij}\, L_{ki}\, A_{ki}\, G_{ki}\, dS_k \tag{9}$$

When S_k is approximated by n disks or area $\delta S = S_k/n$, Equation (9) becomes :

$$L_{ij}^k = \frac{S_k}{n} \sum_{p=1}^{n} R_{kij_p}\, L_{ki_p}\, A_{ki_p} \frac{cos\alpha_{i_p}\, cos\beta_{k_p}}{D_{ki_p}^2 + \frac{S_k}{n\pi}} \tag{10}$$

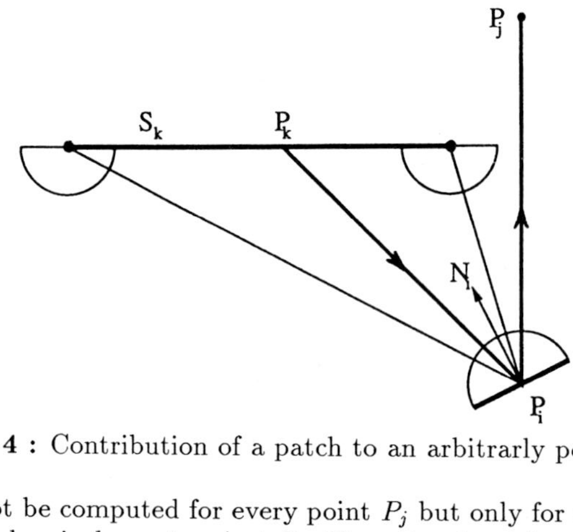

Fig. 4 : Contribution of a patch to an arbitrarly point

In fact, L_{ij}^k will not be computed for every point P_j but only for some sampled directions according to the hemisphere stored at P_i. Thus the algorithm written in Section 3 can be adapted :

```
Extract radiance leaving S_k in direction of P_i from all its vertices;
Choose n sample points on S_k;
For each sample point P_kp do
    Trace a ray from P_i to P_kp;
    If the ray intersects nothing then
        Compute L_kip by interpolation from vertices;
```

```
            Compute $D_{ki_p}$, $cos\alpha_{i_p}$, $cos\beta_{k_p}$, $A_{ki_p}$;
            $C_{ki_p}$ := $L_{ki_p} \frac{S_k}{n} A_{ki_p} \frac{cos\alpha_{i_p} cos\beta_{k_p}}{D^2_{ki_p} + \frac{S_k}{n\pi}}$;
            $L^d_i$ := $L^d_i$ + $R^d_i C_{ki_p}$;
            For each sampled direction $j$ do $L^s_{ij}$ := $L^s_{ij}$ + $R_{kij_p} C_{ki_p}$;
        Endif;
    Endfor;
```

As we have seen earlier, for class-3 surfaces (highly or perfectly specular), the hemisphere method can not be used anymore, because the number of required samples would increase dramatically. When P_i belongs to such a surface, no hemisphere is used, the incident ray is simply reflected and/or refracted and a new ray is traced (or few distributed rays, if specularity is not perfect) and if it intersects another patch S_j, radiance from S_k is transfered to S_j vertices (according to the distance between them and the impact point) after being scaled by reflection and absorption factors.

Finally, using the same iteration scheme as in Section 3, a complete (approximated) solution to the global light transport system in a environment with general reflectance functions can be found by progressive refinements.

5 Second Part

The second part of the method is quite more simple than the first one. At every stage in the first part iterative process, an approximation (more or less accurate) of a view-independent global illumination solution is available. Thus, if the computer allows it, first and second part of the algorithm can run concurrently, and informations relative to the view point can be extracted at any moment, while resolution goes on.

For all vertices that belong to class-1 or class-2 patches (diffuse or low specular), a radiance information is stored. Thus a hardware Gouraud's interpolation can achieve almost real-time walkthrough rendering. Cohen's ambient term can be added to diffuse surfaces in order to get an useful image at the early stages of the first part resolution.

For all vertices that belong to class-3 patches (highly or perfectly specular), no illumination information is stored and thus, these patches will appear black for a Gouraud shading. Here, a progressive refinement rendering can be used again. When view point changes rapidly — when the user walks through the environnemt — a simple and fast Gouraud is used, making all class-3 patches appear black. But as soon as the user stops his walk, the computation of these pixels can start, first by ray-tracing then eventually by distributed ray-tracing. Such a scheme presents two interesting advantages. First, ray-tracing is used only where it is needed and second, it creates a kind of *golden thread* as described in [2] that allows images to be quickly displayed when one walks through the scene and to be progressively and gracefully refined, when the walk stops or pauses for a moment.

6 Conclusion

In this paper, we have presented a solution to the global illumination problem that includes several features. It is a ray-tracing-based solution that means it is able to do exact shadow testing for complex objects ([18]). It is not limited to diffuse environments but can handle general reflectance functions. The first part is a progressive refinement iterative scheme that procures an approximated solution at each step of the resolution. The second part is a progressive refinement scheme too, that allows more or less accurate rendering, according to the time one is willing to spend for the image display. A general view of the implementation of our method, showing the different processes that run concurrently, can be seen in Figure 5.

Several other direction for future work can be taken. One of these direction could be to extend the method in order to include participating medium ([14]). Another direction is to find a efficient solution to the *feature missing problem* that occurs when using ray-tracing to compute form-factors. A solution may be to reuse an adaptative subdivision scheme that already exists for texture mapping or ray-patch intersecting. Thus subdivision could be made finer when the emitting patch is near the receiving vertices, and coarser when it is far. All that research directions, as well as the complete implementation of our method, is currently going on here, at LaBRI, in Bordeaux (France).

References

[1] D.R. Baum, H.E. Rushmeier, J.M. Winget, *Improving Radiosity Solution through the Use of Analytically Determined Form-Factors*, Computer Graphics, v.23, n.3, p.325-334, 1989

[2] L. Bergman, H. Fuchs, E. Grant, S. Spach, *Image Rendering by Adaptive Refinement*, Computer Graphics, v.20, n.4, p.29-38, 1986

[3] C. Bouville, K. Bouatouch, *A Unified Approach to Global Illumination Models*, Proceedings of PIXIM 89, p.250-263, 1989

[4] M.F. Cohen, D.P. Greenberg, *The Hemi-Cube: a Radiosity Solution for Complex Environments*, Computer Graphics, v.19, n.3, p.31-40, 1985

[5] M.F. Cohen, D.P. Greenberg, D.S. Immel, P.J. Brock, *An Efficient Radiosity Approach for Realistic Image Synthesis*, Computer Graphics and Applications, v.6, n.2, p.26-35, 1986

[6] M.F. Cohen, S. Chen, J. Wallace, D.P. Greenberg, *A Progressive Refinement Approach to Fast Radiosity Image Generation*, Computer Graphics, v.22, n.4, p.75-84, 1988

[7] R.L. Cook, *Shade trees*, Computer Graphics, vol 18, nb 3, pp 223-231, 1984

[8] C.M. Goral, K. Torrance, D.P. Greenberg, B. Battaile, *Modeling the Interaction of Light Between Diffuse Surfaces*, Computer Graphics, v.18, n.3, p.213-222, 1984

[9] H. Gouraud, *Continuous shading of curved surfaces*, IEEE Transactions on Computers, v.20, n.6, p.623-629, 1972

[10] D.S. Immel, M.F. Cohen, D.P. Greenberg, *A Radiosity Method for Non-Diffuse Environments*, Computer Graphics, v.20, n.4, p.133-142, 1986

[11] J.T. Kajiya, *The Rendering Equation*, Computer Graphics, v.20, n.4, p.143-150, 1986

[12] T. Nishita, E. Nakamae, *Continuous Tone Representation of Tri-Dimentional Objects taking Account of Shadows and Interreflections*, Computer Graphics, v.19, n.3, p.23-30, 1985

[13] B.T. Phong, *Illumination for Computer Graphics*, Communications of the ACM, v.18, n.6, p.449-455, 1975

[14] H.E. Rushmeyer, K.E. Torrance, *The Zonal Method for Calculing Light Intensities in the Presence of a Participating Medium*, Computer Graphics, v.21, n.4, p.293-301, 1987

[15] F. Sillion, C. Puech, *A General Two-Pass Method Integrating Specular and Diffuse Reflection*, Computer Graphics, v.23, n.3, p.335-344, 1989

[16] M. Shao, Q. Peng, Y. Liang, *A new Radiosity Approach by Procedural Refinements for Realistic Image Synthesis*, Computer Graphics, v.22, n.4, p.93-101, 1988

[17] J.R. Wallace, M.F. Cohen, D.P. Greenberg, *A Two-Pass Solution to the Rendering Equation: a Synthesis of Ray-Tracing and Radiosity Methods*, Computer Graphics, v.21, n.4, p.311-320, 1987

[18] J.R. Wallace, K.A. Elmquist, E.A. Haines, *A Ray-Tracing Algorithm for Progressive Radiosity*, Computer Graphics, v.23, n.3, p.315-324, 1989

[19] G.J. Ward, *A Ray-Tracing Solution for Diffuse Interreflections*, Computer Graphics, v.22, n.4, p.85-92, 1988

[20] T. Whitted, *An Improved Illumination Model for Shaded Display*, Communications of the ACM, v.23, n.6, p.343-349, 1980

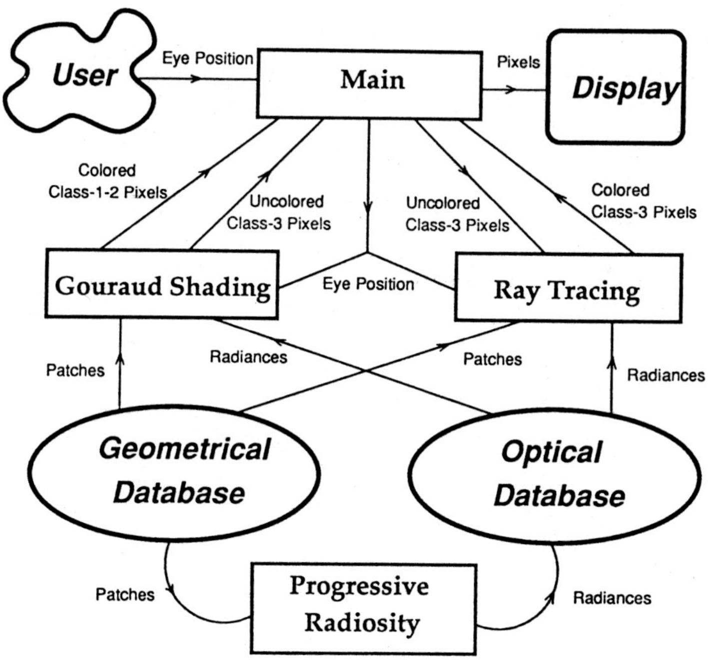

Fig. 5 General view of the implementation

A Two-Pass Radiosity Method for Bézier Patches

Arjan J.F. Kok[1], Celal Yilmaz[2], Laurens H.J. Bierens[2]

Abstract

A restriction of the radiosity method has been the difficulty of processing environments consisting of curved surfaces. In order to apply current radiosity methods, such surfaces are usually subdivided into many polygonal patches. However, as the computational complexity of the radiosity method depends on the number of patches, this approach results in a very inefficient use of the available processing time and data storage capacity. In this paper, a ray tracing based radiosity method for diffuse and specular reflective Bézier surfaces is presented. The original Bézier surface description is used throughout the entire algorithm which makes the subdivision of each Bézier patch into many polygonal patches unnecessary.

1 Introduction

A realistic image of an environment can be calculated by evaluating the distribution of light in the environment. Two commonly used approaches for high quality image synthesis are the radiosity method [3] and ray tracing [8]. They both calculate the influence of direct and indirect reflections of light. However, the radiosity method is most suited for the display of diffuse environments, while ray tracing is most suited for the display of specular environments. Hence these methods are complementing each other, and may be combined to take both diffuse and specular components into account. Therefore two-pass radiosity methods are introduced [5,6]. A two-pass radiosity method consists of a view independent preprocess (first pass) in which the diffuse intensities are calculated, and a view dependent postprocess (second pass) in which the specular intensities in the environment are calculated. Because the preprocess is view independent, the results of one preprocess can be used in several postprocesses to get pictures with different viewpoints.

To model complex environments with curved surfaces, B-spline and Bézier patches are widely used. To calculate the shading for Bézier patches with a radiosity method, the Bézier patches can, of course, be approximated with polygons. After that, the intensities of the polygons can be calculated using a polygon based radiosity method. When necessary, the polygons can be even further subdivided into elements to get more accurate intensities [2]. However, to get an accurate polygonal approximation of the Bézier patches many polygons have to be used. Also care has to be taken that no intensity discontinuities along the edges between adjacent polygons occur.

To overcome these problems one can compute the intensities of Bézier patches directly, without dividing them into polygons. In this paper a two-pass radiosity method for Bézier patches is presented. In a preprocess the diffuse intensities of the patches are calculated. The intensities are calculated for different points (sample points) of the patches by using a ray tracing based method. In order to get an accurate shading, more sample points are used where high intensity gradients occur (adaptive sampling). In the ray tracing based postprocess the actual picture, including the specular intensity components, is computed using the results of the preprocess.

---

[1] Faculty of Technical Mathematics and Informatics, Delft University of Technology, Julianalaan 132, 2628 BL Delft, The Netherlands

[2] Faculty of Electrical Engineering, Delft University of Technology, Mekelweg 4, 2628 CD Delft, The Netherlands

The organization of this paper is as follows. In section 2 a description of the preprocess is given. In section 3 a description of the postprocess is given. In section 4 an evaluation of the two-pass radiosity method for Bézier patches is given. The paper ends with the conclusions in section 5.

2 The Preprocess

The goal of the preprocess is to calculate the diffuse light intensities of all patches in the environment. For all patches so called formfactors are calculated, that are needed to determine these intensities. A formfactor represents the amount of energy leaving some patch and reaching some other patch. Because curved surfaces are used, also energy leaving a patch and reaching the same patch is possible. Formfactors can be calculated analytically, but are commonly approximated using some sort of projection method. One such method is the hemicube projection method [1]. Another method to find the formfactors is based on ray tracing [5]. We shall use the ray tracing based technique for the calculation of the formfactors. Direct energy as well as indirect energy reaching the patch via one or more specular reflections is taken into account calculating the formfactors. The intensities of the patches can be calculated with these formfactors. A summary of the preprocess is given in figure 1. A discussion of the different steps of the preprocess is given in the following sections.

```
for all patches
    create regularly distributed sample points
while new sample points exist
    for each new sample point
        calculate formfactors
    solve radiosity equations
    for all patches
        create adaptively sample points
```

Fig. 1: The preprocess.

2.1 Sample Points

In order to exhibit the intensity gradients on the Bézier patches accurately, a number of sample points for which the intensities will be calculated have to be determined. To find these points the Bézier patch can be subdivided into Bézier elements, like polygonal patches can be subdivided into elements [2]. Like the Bézier patches, the Bézier elements are defined by their control points, and also these Bézier elements give an exact representation of (a part) of the surface. Often the intensities of an element are calculated at the centre points of the element. A disadvantage of the use of centres is the discontinuity of the shading that can occur between two neighbouring Bézier patches (not elements), when the intensities of the centre points are interpolated to the corner points of the patch [7]. Furthermore, in order to get the centre of the Bézier patch extra computations have to be performed. Therefore it is more suitable to use the corner control points of the elements as sample points. If a corner point of a patch has the same coordinates and normal as the corner point of the neighbouring patch, the formfactors of the two neighbouring patches will have the same values there. So if the two neighbouring patches have first order continuity and the same physical properties, the shading is guaranteed to be continuous.

To get a regular distribution of sample points, the Bézier patch is subdivided into Bézier elements of a specified level. If, for example, the level is 2, two subdivisions are performed, and so 16 Bézier elements arise with at the most 25 different element corner points, that are regularly distributed over the original Bézier patch. These corner points will be used as sample points. Before the formfactors at a sample point can be calculated, the normal at that point must be known. The exact normal at the corner point can be determined taking the cross product of two vectors tangent to the Bézier element in the sample point. The tangent vectors can easily be calculated with the control points of the Bézier patch or element, see figure 2.

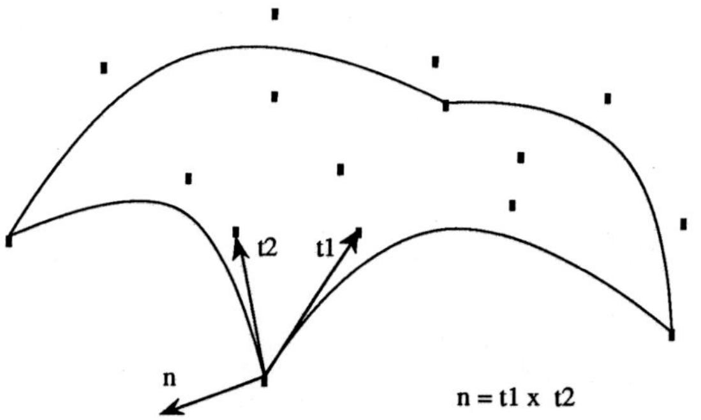

Fig. 2: Determination of normal in corner point of Bézier element.

2.2 Formfactors

As mentioned before, the formfactors of the sample points are calculated using a ray tracing based method. Instead of a plane parallel to the tangent plane in the sample point, as done in [5], we project the environment on a hemisphere [9]. Before formfactor calculation starts, a reference hemisphere is built. This reference hemisphere consists of a collection of rays and a weightfactor table. The rays of the reference hemisphere are constructed by dividing the hemisphere into a number of circles, see figure 3.

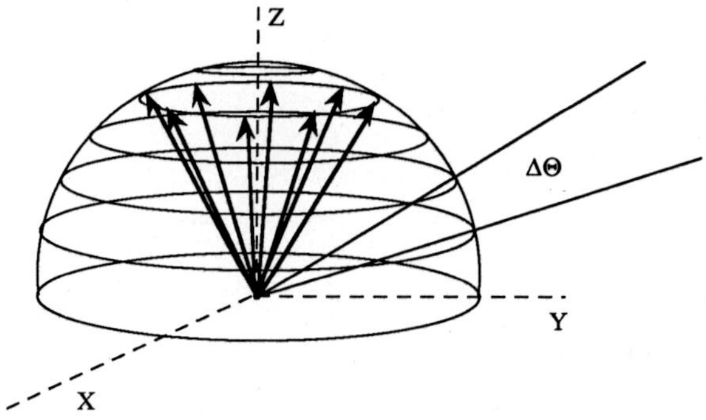

Fig. 3: Reference hemisphere with rays of one of the circles.

These circles are parallel to the xy-plane and are spaced by a constant angle $\Delta\theta$. If circle N is the circle in the xy-plane, then $\Delta\theta = 2^{-1}\pi N^{-1}$. Now the number of rays in a circle can be determined. Circle 0 has zero radius, and is represented by one ray along the z-axis, so $N_0 = 1$. The number of rays on circle j will be equal to

$$N_j = \text{trunc}(4N\sin(j\,\Delta\theta) \qquad 1 \le j \le N$$

A number of rays is defined on every circle in such a way that the distance between two rays is equal to the distance between two adjacent circles. For each circle the influence of a ray within that circle on the hemisphere is stored in the weightfactor table. Also the influence of a ray for a specified frustum size is stored in this table. A frustum consists of some of the circles of the complete hemisphere and is used for specular reflections and transmissions. The weightfactor W for a ray in circle j within a frustum with size k is:

$$W_{jk} = \frac{\cos(j\Delta\theta)}{\sum_{i=0}^{k} N_i \cos(i\Delta\theta)} \qquad 0 \le k \le N\text{-}1 \text{ and } 0 \le j \le k$$

The values for k=N-1 represent the contributions for the rays within the complete hemisphere. The circle with k=N is not relevant because of the zero contribution. The weightfactors in the table are used for determining the formfactors.

To calculate the point-to-patch formfactors for a sample point, the centre of the hemisphere is placed at the sample point. For this purpose the reference hemisphere is transformed, so that the origin of the reference hemisphere is equal to the sample point and the z-axis of the reference hemisphere has the direction of the normal of the sample point. Then all rays of the transformed hemisphere are traced.

If a ray hits a patch, the point-to-patch formfactor of the sample point with respect to the hit patch is increased with the weightfactor of the traced ray. By tracing all rays of the hemisphere for all sample points all the formfactors representing the direct energy transport can be calculated.

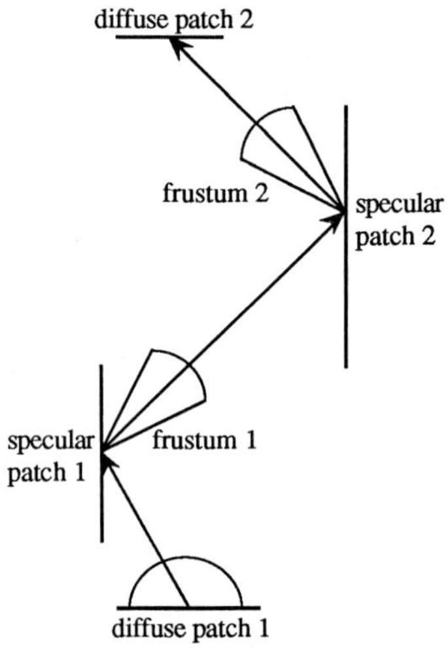

Fig. 4: Ray tracing to determine extended formfactors.

However, also the formfactors caused by indirect energy transport are important. An example of such indirect energy transport is light leaving a light source reaching a diffuse surface by a specular reflection through a mirror. Therefore extended (or extra) formfactors are calculated that take multiple reflection into account. So, if a patch is hit, the formfactor of the sample point and the hit patch is updated. However, if the patch has a specular value larger than zero, also the reflection direction is determined and a frustum (of a given frustum size) with secondary rays is traced from the intersection point in the reflection direction. If a ray of the frustum hits a patch, a contribution calculated from the weightfactors of the original ray and the frustum ray and from the specularity of the reflecting patch is added to the formfactor of the sample point and the new hit surface. If this patch is also specular, then again a frustum of rays is traced. This process is repeated until a perfectly diffuse patch is hit, see figure 4. In this way also indirect contributions to the formfactors are computed.

2.3 Intersection Point Calculation

The intersection of a ray and a Bézier patch is calculated using subdivision [4,8]. A bounding box for the Bézier patch is made and a bounding box test performed. Because a Bézier patch is always within the convex hull of its control points, a bounding box can be made by determining the minimum and maximum x-, y- and z-values of the control points of the patch. If there is a hit between the ray and the bounding box, then there is a possible hit between the ray and the Bézier patch. The Bézier patch is subdivided further, and for each new calculated patch again a bounding box is determined. These bounding boxes surround the patch more closely, because the control points of the subdivided patches are closer to the actual surface. For all these bounding boxes a bounding box test with the ray is performed, and as long as a possible hit is found, the procedure continues. If the patch, and thus also the bounding box surrounding it, is very small or a maximum subdivision level is reached, the procedure stops and the found intersection point of the bounding box and the ray is considered to be the intersection point of the ray and the Bézier patch.

2.4 Radiosity Equations

When the point-to-patch formfactors for all sample points are determined, we compute for each patch the average patch-to-patch formfactor. This is done like [2] but instead of the average of the element-to-patch formfactors of a patch, the average of the point-to-patch formfactors of a patch is computed. With the patch-to-patch formfactors a linear system of radiosity equations can be made. Because the formfactor matrix is diagonally dominant the system can be solved with a Gauss-Seidel iteration method. The solution of the matrix equation results in an average intensity value for each patch. Using the point-to-patch formfactors the actual intensity values for each sample point are obtained. In the rendering stage (the postprocess) the intensities of these sample points are used to calculate the diffuse component of the light reflection for a point on the patch.

2.5 Adaptive Sampling

When the intensities for the sample points are calculated, great intensity differences (high gradients) between the sample points of Bézier elements may occur. This, for example, can happen if an element is partially covered by a shadow or locally receives a large amount of light from a neighbouring patch. Also, if an element has a high curvature, then each of the corner points (and so sample points) will have a very different normal direction, so the hemisphere rays are traced in very different directions, see figure 5. The different directions will result in different formfactors, because different patches are hit, and consequently in different intensities.

Fig. 5: High curvature causes different tracing directions.

As with polygons [2] the Bézier elements can be subdivided into elements adaptively. For all elements on the highest level of subdivision sample points are inspected. If the sample points of an element have a gradient higher than a maximum allowed gradient, this element is subdivided into new elements. If the corner points of the elements that arise from the subdivision are not earlier used as sample points, then they are added to the collection of sample points. After the gradient test is done for all elements, the formfactors for the newly created sample points are calculated. For the already existing sample points the earlier calculated formfactors can be used. If for all sample points the formfactors are known, again the patch-to-patch formfactors can be calculated, and with these the sample point intensities as described earlier. However, to get the average patch-to-patch formfactors one now has to take into account the fact that not all sample points are equal important for determining the average. Sample points surrounded by small Bézier elements have less influence on the average than sample points surrounded by greater elements. If all points would have the same influence on the average, too much emphasis would be placed on the parts of the patch with many sample points (where the sampling is adaptively refined). Therefore each sample point has a weightfactor indicating the area of the patch on which it has influence. For each element, that is not further subdivided, of which the sample point is a corner point, a contribution is added to this weightfactor. Because the area of an element created at level i is equal to 4^{-i}, and the area of the element is distributed over the four sample points, the contribution of an element created at level i to all of it's corner points is equal to $4^{-(i+1)}$. An example of the weightfactors for the sample points of an adaptively subdivided patch is given in figure 6.

After calculation of the sample point intensities again the elements can be tested for high gradients. If some elements have high gradients, again subdivision can be done for these elements.

Adaptive sampling will result in less samples (so less computation time and memory use) than regular sampling to give a picture of the same quality, because only samples are taken where it is really needed.

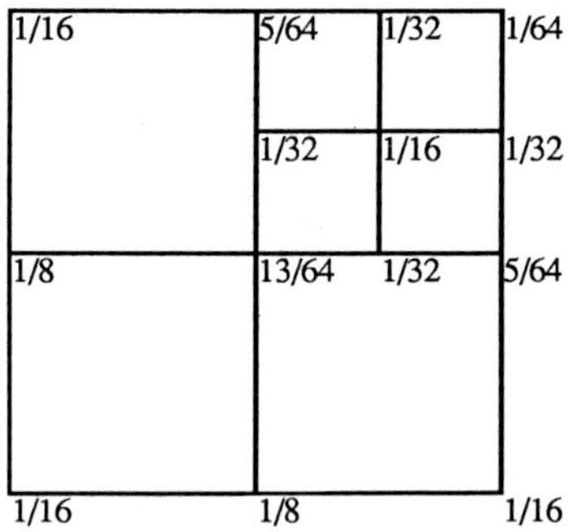

Fig. 6: Example of sample point weightfactors at a maximum subdivision level 2.

3 The Postprocess

The result of the preprocess is a collection of intensities corresponding to sample points on the Bézier patches. These sample point intensities are used to compute the pixel intensities in the postprocess. In the postprocess the intensity values to be displayed are calculated using ray tracing. For each pixel a ray is traced from the viewpoint through the pixelplane into the environment to find the first intersection of the ray with a patch. For the intersection calculation the same procedure is used as in the preprocess. If the ray hits a patch, the Bézier element in which the intersection point is situated is determined, and the u,v coordinates of the intersection point within this element are calculated, see figure 7. No shadow rays are traced, because the influences of the light emitters were already calculated in the preprocess, resulting in the sample point intensities. Using the u- en v-coordinate, an interpolation from the intensities of the sample points of the element will give the intensities of the intersection points.

If the intersected patch is (partially) specular, a frustum of secondary rays is traced from the intersection point, see figure 7. If a secondary ray hits a patch, the intensities of the new intersection point are calculated and added to the pixel values. If this patch is also specular, again a frustum of rays is traced, and so on.

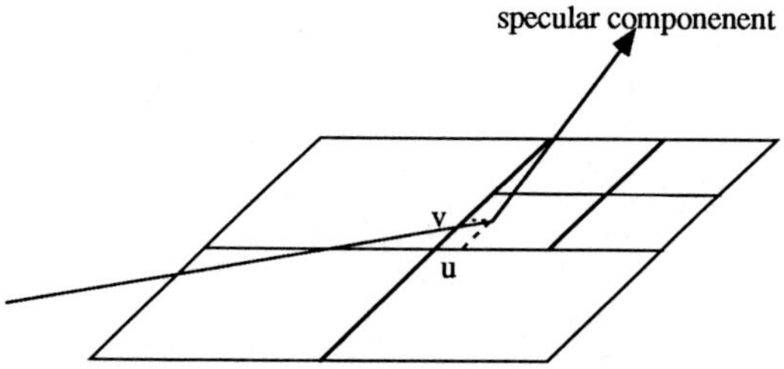

Fig. 7: Ray-patch intersection point.

4 Results and Evaluation

An environment consisting of 14 Bézier patches (no polygons are used) is displayed in both picture 1 and picture 2. It exists of a room with the complete ceiling as light source, a vase (of 7 patches) and a strangely curved perfect specular mirror. To calculate the formfactors for this environment, 10 circles (so 232 rays) are chosen on the hemisphere. Experiments [9] showed that 10 is more or less the minimal acceptable number of circles. To calculate the intersection points of rays with patches the maximum subdivision level is set to 10.

For picture 1 the sampling level is set to 2, so 25 sample points are taken on each patch. Picture 2 is the result of adaptive sampling to level 3. The statistics for the preprocess of the pictures are given table 1.

Table 1: Statistics preprocess

	picture 1	picture 2
max. sampling level	2	3
sample points	300	960
primary rays	69600	222720
secondary rays	4288	13554
bounding box tests	4557516	15068132

The secondary rays are caused by the fact that a specular patch exists in the environment, and so extended formfactors are traced if this patch is hit. The effect of the number of sample points can be seen in the pictures. Because in picture 2 the sample points represent a smaller part of the patch, the shading is more subtle. This is for example seen in the lower left corner of the back patch of the room. In picture 1 the dark spot is larger. The used gradient test for picture 2 was very strict, so almost all elements on level 2 were further subdivided.

Adaptive sampling can reduce the number of needed sample points. An experiment with adaptive sampling for the environment of the pictures is done. The gradient threshold was less strict than the threshold used to get picture 2. For example, the number of used sample points at level 8 was 9666, instead of 792588, the number needed for regular sampling. The percentage of the number of sample points used by adaptive sampling compared with regular sampling is given in figure 8.

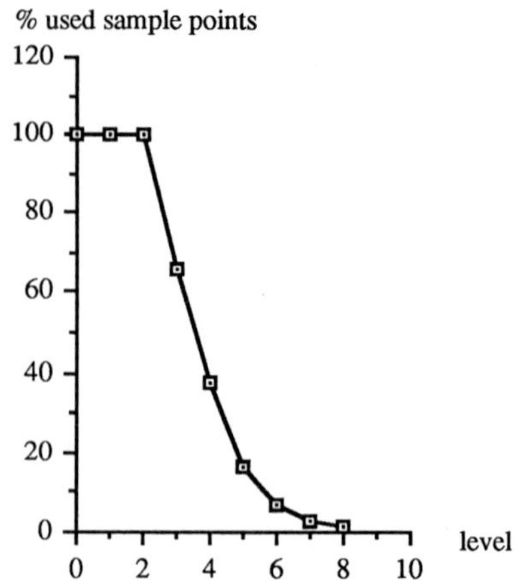

Fig. 8: Result adaptive sampling

One of the advantages of using Bézier patches directly instead of an approximation with polygons is the fact that there are less patches in the environment. Less patches in the environment means that less data storage capacity is needed, and that a smaller matrix is needed for the radiosity equations. Consequently the solution of the radiosity equations is easier. Also, for each patch in the environment a ray-patch intersection test has to be performed in order to find the first patch that is intersected by the ray. Because the number of patches in the environment is limited because of the use of the exact Bézier representation, the number of ray-patch intersection tests can be limited. Also an advantage is the fact, that if the subdivision level for intersection calculation is high enough, the intersection point is calculated more accurately than with a polygon approximation. Consequently the normal, needed for determining the reflection direction can be calculated more accurately. A disadvantage is the fact that a ray-polygon intersection test can be performed much faster than a ray-Bézier intersection test.

Another advantage is the fact that a patch does not need any information of neighbouring patches to insure a continuous shading. If a polygon approximation is used, discontinuities can arise at the edges between two polygons, because the normals in the vertices in the different polygons are not equal. To solve this problem, the polygons need to know what the neighbouring polygons are. This requires a special datastructure. If Bézier patches are used, continuous shading is guaranteed. As can be seen in the pictures, the shading of the vase is continuous, although it consists of seven different patches and there are no geometric relations indicating which patches are connected.

The use of corner points instead of the centres of the elements as sample points causes the following problem. Consider two patches (a light source and a diffuse patch) in the two dimensional case as shown in figure 9a. The sample point under the hemisphere will not receive any light energy from the light source, because there will be no hit between the hemisphere rays and the light source. That means that the formfactor from this sample point to the light source is zero. So the area on the patch near the light source will be dark, which is not correct. This artifact can be removed by giving an offset to the origin of the hemisphere in such cases, see figure 9b.

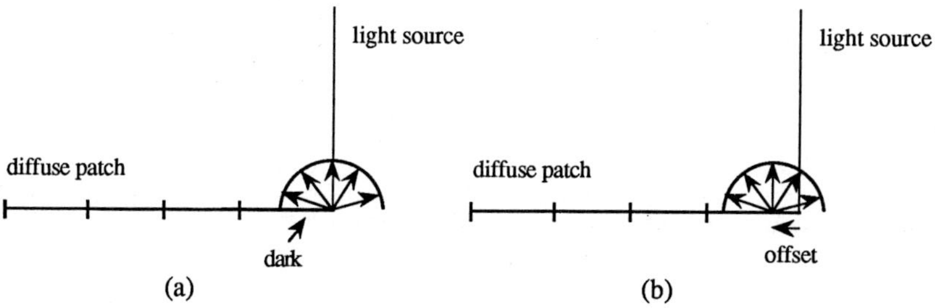

Fig. 9: a) Dark parts on edge of patch, b) Offset avoiding dark parts.

A major part of the performed calculations is the determination of the ray-patch intersections, and, most of all, the determination of the bounding boxes (as can be seen in the statistics) and the subdivision of the patches. A hardware implementation for the ray patch intersection will be useful to reduce the computation time [4,9]. For a hardware implementation the transport of data to the hardware should be minimized. The use of Bézier patches instead of an polygonal approximation reduces this data transport considerably.

In the proposed two-pass radiosity method only Bézier bicubic patches defined by 16 control points are used. This is no restriction. Other types of bicubic patches can be converted to or approximated by one or more of these Bézier patches.

5 Conclusion

To model a complex environment, curved surfaces like Bézier patches are necessary. To display this environment the correct intensities must be calculated. A two-pass radiosity method for Bézier surfaces is presented. It is based on ray tracing in both pre- and postprocess. It correctly computes the diffuse and specular intensities of the surfaces. Adaptive sampling of the patches results in pictures of high quality with a limited number of sample points. Using the actual Bézier patches instead of a polygonal approximation has different advantages. With the use of Bézier patches in the radiosity method, the applicability of the radiosity method becomes wider. This makes the use of the method more attractive.

Acknowledgements

This research is part of the project "A VLSI Radiosity Engine for Fast Realistic Image Synthesis". It is a cooperation of the Network Theory section of the faculty of Electrical Engineering and the Computer Graphics section of the faculty of Technical Mathematics and Informatics. We thank Professor F.W. Jansen (Computer Graphics section) and Dr. E. Deprettere (Network Theory section) for many valuable comments and ideas. We also thank all the people of the Network Theory section of the faculty of Electrical Engineering that contributed to the software.

References

1. Cohen, M.F., Greenberg, D.P.: The Hemi-Cube, A Radiosity Solution for Complex Environments. Computer Graphics 19(3), July 85, pp 31-40.
2. Cohen, M.F., Greenberg, D.P., Immel, D.S., Brock, P.J.: An Efficient Radiosity Approach for Realistic Image Synthesis. IEEE Computer Graphics and Applications 6(2), March 86, pp 26-35.
3. Goral, C.M., Torrance, K.E., Greenberg, D.P., Battaile, B.: Modelling the Interaction of Light Between Diffuse Surfaces. Computer Graphics 18(3), July 84, pp 213-222.
4. Pulleyblank, R.W., Kapenga, J.A.: The Feasibility of a VLSI Chip for Ray Tracing Bicubic Patches. IEEE Computer Graphics and Applications 7(2), March 87, pp 33-44.

5. Sillion, R., Puech, C.: A General Two-Pass Method Integrating Specular and Diffuse Reflection. Computer Graphics 23(3), July 89, pp 335-344.
6. Wallace, J.R., Cohen, M.F., Greenberg, D.P.: A Two-Pass Solution to the Rendering Equation: A Synthesis of Ray Tracing and Radiosity Methods. Computer Graphics 21(4), July 87, pp 311-320.
7. Wallace, J.R., Elmquist, K.A., Haines, E.A.: A Ray Tracing Algorithm for Progressive Radiosity. Computer Graphics 23(3), July 89, pp 315-324.
8. Whitted, T.: An Improved Illumination Model for Shaded Display. CACM 23(6), June 80, pp 343-349.
9. Yilmaz, A.C., Hagestein, S., Deprettere, E., Dewilde P.: A Hardware Solution to the Generalized Two-Pass Approach for Rendering of Artificial Scenes. Proceedings Eurographics Hardware Workshop, Hamburg, Sept 89.

Chapter 4

Form Factor Calculation

The Hemisphere Radiosity Method: A Tale of Two Algorithms

Stephen N. Spencer [1]

1 Introduction

The most important and most computationally–intensive operation within the radiosity illumination model is the calculation of *form–factors,* the geometric measure of the fraction of the radiant energy leaving one surface and received by another surface. This form-factor calculation must account for potential obstructions between the target surfaces yet be computationally efficient and accurate.

This paper presents two efficient variations on the "hemi–cube" form–factor calculation algorithm, using the hemisphere as the projection volume. These methods represent an evolution of the algorithm through continued research, in a search for improved accuracy and efficiency.

Methods from the field of thermal engineering describe how energy leaving a surface can be measured at a second surface. The measure, known as a form–factor, takes into account not only spatial displacement of the surfaces but also their rotational alignment with one another. [4] In 1928, Nusselt introduced his "unit–sphere" method of form–factor calculation, which used a unit hemisphere onto which a surface was projected spherically, then orthographically onto its base. The resulting form–factor was the ratio of the area covered on the base by the projection to the area of the hemisphere base.

The application of heat transfer theory to describe the interreflection of light energy in an environment was first presented by Goral in 1984. Her paper described the "contour edge" method of form–factor calculation. The contour edge method was limited to simple environments (environments without obstructed views) but was an elegant proof of the principles of radiosity and of the power of this method for producing highly realistic computer–rendered images. [3]

In 1985, Michael Cohen presented his hemi–cube method, extending the domain of environments from the empty room to general environments where obstructions are present. His algorithm calculates the form–factors between two surface elements by placing a hemi–cube over one of the surface elements, projecting the other surface element onto each of the hemi–cube faces, clipping the projection to the faces, and identifying the closest surface elements represented at each location on the discretized faces of the hemi–cube. [1]

2 The Hemisphere Radiosity Method

The hemisphere radiosity method uses a single hemisphere as projection surface for form–factor calculation as opposed to the five planar projection surfaces needed for the hemi–cube. This section will describe two variations on the hemisphere radiosity method, developed as efficient alternatives to the hemicube algorithm.

[1]The Advanced Computing Center for the Arts and Design, The Ohio State University, Columbus OH 43212-1154 U.S.A.

2.1 Rationale

Criteria for choosing a five–faced "hemicube" (or one–half of a unit cube placed at the center of a surface element), according to Cohen in his 1985 paper included "difficulty in creating equal–sized elements on [the] hemisphere, as well as creating a set of linear coordinates to uniquely describe locations on its surface." [1]

Selection of an appropriate coordinate system in which to work on the hemisphere is an important step: the chosen coordinate system must be sufficient for the task yet algorithmically simple. The rectangular coordinate system used in the hemi–cube algorithm, while well–understood, will not adapt easily to the hemisphere's surface. A discretization of the single surface of a hemisphere (one–half of a unit sphere placed at the center of a surface element) using the spherical coordinate system yields small finite areas which are of equal spherical area, and which are uniquely identifiable.

Using a spherical coordinate discretization will result in areas on the hemisphere not equal to each other in size, from the point of view of a rectangular coordinate system. This is not a major issue for several reasons: first, (given that one sample per discretized area is used) at a given resolution, more samples are taken closer to the apex of the hemisphere than at the base of the hemisphere, concentrating the *sampling* where it will make the most difference to the form–factor calculation. Second, each discretized area, as in the hemi–cube algorithm, can have its own individualized incremental form–factor value. This will effectively balance out the variations in sampling areas, assigning lower weights, proportionally, to smaller sample areas.

In the first hemisphere algorithm, shown in Figure 1, the discretization yields a two–dimensional array of locations on the hemisphere, referenced by Φ, a measure of a location's displacement "down" the side of the hemisphere from the apex, and Θ, a measure of a location's displacement "around" the hemisphere from some reference point.

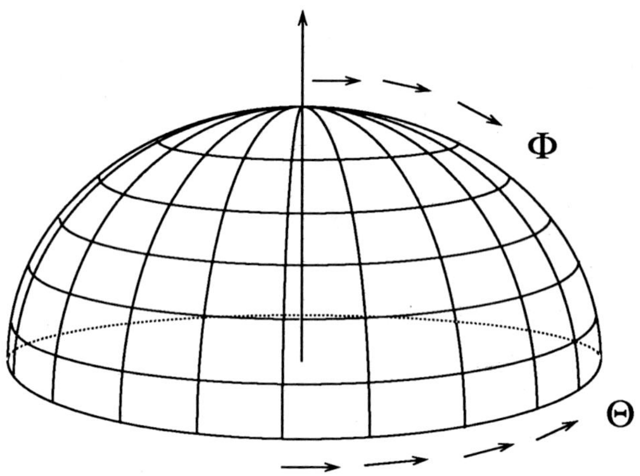

Fig. 1: Discretization of the hemisphere's surface.

In the second hemisphere algorithm, (see Figure 2 on page 6) this discretization is rendered unnecessary and is removed, in favor of more accurate spherical projection of surface elements onto the hemisphere, orthographic projection onto the base of the hemisphere, and a fine–grain discretization of the base.

2.2 Working on the Hemisphere

The "on the hemisphere" algorithm begins as does the hemi–cube algorithm, by the selection of the target surface elements, referred to here as the "base" element and "test" element. The base element is that surface element which has the hemisphere placed above it, while the test element is situated elsewhere in the environment. The hemisphere algorithm does require, in its present implementation, that all surface elements be triangular. This restriction makes subsequent rendering of a shaded image simpler and provides a more general base for data generation, as all polygonal data can be decomposed into a series of triangles. [5]

As in the hemi–cube algorithm, the projection surface discretization has a "depth buffer" associated with it. Each location on the surface of the hemisphere corresponds directly to a unique location in the depth buffer and stores identifying information about a surface element visible at that location and the distance from the base polygon to that element.

In addition, each discrete area on the hemisphere will yield a incremental form–factor, just as in the hemi–cube algorithm. These form–factor values can be pre–calculated and stored, and, due to the geometric nature of the hemisphere, only "n" form–factors will have to be pre–calculated and stored, where "n" is the Φ discretization factor of the hemisphere. For example, if the hemisphere were discretized into one–degree spherical areas, it would require ninety divisions in Φ and three hundred and sixty divisions in Θ. Due to similarity, only ninety unique form–factor values need to be calculated and stored.

After back–face testing has determined that the test element could indeed be visible to the base element, the vertices of the test element are projected onto the hemisphere. Because the hemisphere is of unit radius, this projection is nothing more than normalization of the vertices of the test element. One immediate advantage of this algorithm over the hemi–cube algorithm is seen here: projection must be done only once per test surface element, in comparison to up to five times per test surface element in the hemi–cube algorithm. At this point, Φ and Θ values are calculated for each projected vertex, and these values are sorted into ascending order.

Clipping of the projected surface element follows. Due to the geometric nature of the hemisphere there is only one clipping boundary: the base of the hemisphere. Each edge of the projected surface element is tested against the base plane of the hemisphere. If the edge crosses the base plane, the edge is shortened so that it lies completely above the base.

The projection and clipping accomplished, the projected element must be classified as to its spatial relationship to the hemisphere: a surface element either (a) covers the apex of the hemisphere, (b) covers the "Θ" reference line (also the place where the ends of the two–dimensional depth buffer meet), or (c) "ordinary" projection. This classification is important, as it determines the method by which the discrete areas which lie under the projected surface element are calculated.

Given this classification, the algorithm then determines the "bounding box," in terms of the hemisphere discretization areas, in which the projection must lie. Calculation of the minimum and maximum Θ values is straightforward since the Θ values are sorted. Care must be taken if the projected test polygon crosses the Θ reference line. Calculation of the minimum and maximum Φ values is more complicated: the endpoints of an edge may not necessarily be the closest point to, or the farthest from, the apex of the hemisphere. If this is the case, using the point's Φ value can cause error. To minimize this potential error, calculations are performed which compare an edge's perpendicular bisection point and its distance from the apex to the distances from the edge's endpoints. If the bisection point is closer (and in cases where the polygon is close to but not covering the apex of the hemisphere it often is) then a Φ value is calculated for it and used in forming the bounding box. If the test polygon covers the apex of the hemisphere, every Θ value is represented in the bounding box values.

The algorithm then tests each member of the bounding box, determining whether the test polygon covers the hemisphere at that location and if so, if it is closer than any polygon previously tested at that location. This is done in two steps: first, a "point-in-triangle" test, very similar to a ray–casting operation, is performed with the test polygon and a vector formed with the origin and a point in the center of the bounding box member currently being checked. If this is successful, the distance from the origin to the test polygon is calculated and compared against the entry in the depth buffer for this location. If the test polygon is closer the depth buffer is updated with ID and distance information from the test polygon.

This process of visibility testing, projecting, clipping, and comparison against the depth buffer continues for each surface element. When this process is finished, just as in the hemi–cube algorithm, the depth buffer holds a representation of the surface elements visible, partially visible and invisible to the base surface element.

The calculation of the form–factor between the base surface element and a test surface element is, as in the hemi–cube algorithm, the sum of the incremental form–factors of the set of areas on the hemisphere covered by the test surface.

2.2.1 Results

Comparison of the hemisphere algorithm to the hemicube algorithm can be made on several levels. The first and most important comparison is in the form factors computed by each algorithm: each should, given identical input, produce form factors close enough to each other as to be statistically equal. These form factors must also be compared to analytically derived form factors, to show the absolute accuracy of the algorithm. Table 1 compares form factors generated by the two algorithms as well as analytically derived form factors. The input to each algorithm consisted of two flat square surfaces, each subdivided into thirty-two (32) equal-sized triangular elements. The two squares share one edge, and an angle is formed between the two squares across this shared edge. The hemisphere algorithm had a resolution of 180 $\times$ 45 in Θ and Φ, respectively, while the hemicube algorithm had a resolution of 50 $\times$ 100 faces on each side and 100 $\times$ 100 faces on its top.

Table 1: Comparison of accuracy of hemisphere and hemicube algorithms.

Angle between surfaces	Analytic solution	Hemisphere solution	Percent Error	Hemicube solution	Percent Error
30.0	0.6190	0.6242	0.84	0.6308	1.91
60.0	0.3709	0.3691	0.48	0.3802	2.51
90.0	0.2000	0.1996	0.20	0.2048	2.40
120.0	0.0866	0.0857	1.04	0.0893	3.46

Comparing actual execution times of the algorithms is another important issue. While two algorithms may produce results very similar relative to each other and similar to some absolute measurement, a comparison of their execution times may point out algorithmic advantages of one algorithm over the other.

Two different environments were used as input to an implementation of the hemisphere algorithm and an implementation of the hemicube algorithm. The hemicube was configured as in the first example, while two different resolutions of the hemisphere were used: the first identical to the first example, and the second at a higher resolution of 360×90 in Θ and Φ. This resolution was used because the total number of "grid squares" closely approximates the number of "grid squares" used in the hemicube algorithm. Table 2 shows the execution times of each algorithm on each of two inputs.

A final test of the hemisphere algorithm was how its performance changed as the resolution of the hemisphere changed. For this test the input environment from the first test was used, with the angle between the two square surfaces being ninety (90) degrees and thirty-two (32) triangular elements per surface. Table 3 shows that as the resolution of the hemisphere decreased, both the execution time needed as well as the accuracy of the solution decreased. For reference, the analytically derived result for this input environment is 0.2000. [8]

Table 2: Comparison of execution times of the implemented algorithms.

number of surface elements	50 by 100 hemicube (CPU min)	360 by 90 hemisphere (CPU min)	180 by 45 hemisphere (CPU min)
216	18.11	5.45	1.47
2304	775.33	87.79	31.81

Table 3: Comparison of computation cost at varying hemisphere resolution.

resolution in degrees	number of grid squares	CPU time in seconds	form factor for test case	Percent error from analytic solution
1.0	32400	90.2	0.1998	0.10
2.0	8100	33.5	0.1996	0.20
5.0	1296	9.6	0.1987	0.65
10.0	324	6.6	0.1979	1.05

2.2.2 Advantages and Disadvantages

The hemisphere algorithm as presented above has some impressive advantages when compared to the hemi–cube algorithm. There is only a single surface onto which a surface element is projected, not the five surfaces of the hemi–cube algorithm. That projection is a very simple normalization process. Clipping against the hemisphere is simple as well, as there is only one clipping boundary against which to compare, and this clipping, as described previously, is very simple to implement.

The hemisphere algorithm also yields greater accuracy at lower memory costs. Van Wyk discusses the spherical area resolution or "solid angle view" of the hemisphere and hemi–cube algorithms. His results indicate that the hemisphere, discretized into 8100 discrete areas (a resolution of 180×45 in Θ and Φ respectively, or two–degree spherical area discretization), has a spherical area resolution of approximately 0.000776. The hemi–cube algorithm, discretized into "an orthogonal geometric grid of 50×100 on each of the four smaller faces of the hemicube (sic) and a 100×100 grid on the larger, top face, resulting in 30000 discrete points ..." [6] yields a spherical area resolution of approximately 0.003142 for the top face and 0.001571 for the side faces, a much coarser resolution at over three times the discretization and storage requirements.

The hemisphere algorithm, as described above, suffers from the same sampling problems of the hemi–cube algorithm: very small surface elements can be under–represented when projected onto the hemisphere and indeed may not be represented at all. Although increasing the resolution of the hemisphere in order to more accurately represent the environment comes at a much lower cost than with the hemi–cube, we cannot completely eliminate sampling aliasing artifacts.

2.3 Working on the Base

Dissatisfaction with sampling inadequacies of the first hemisphere method, including the odd–sized discretization and somewhat involved coverage calculations, led to further research into this matter, yielding the second hemisphere method, which will be described in this section. In brief, the second hemisphere algorithm does away with the discretization of the surface of the hemisphere in favor of a discretization of the base of the hemisphere and projection of the test surface elements from the surface of the hemisphere to the base orthographically.

As expected, the second hemisphere algorithm is similar to the first hemisphere algorithm and the hemi–cube algorithm except for the form–factor calculation. In this algorithm, the projection surface is not discretized at all. In its place, the base of the hemisphere is discretized with a regular grid, with an associated depth buffer. Each discrete area on the base of the hemisphere has the same incremental form–factor value: the ratio of any discrete area to the area of the base of the hemisphere will be the same. In Figure 2, the shaded area, the base of the hemisphere, is discretized. In this particular implementation the entire square base is discretized using the regular grid. The discrete areas which are not covered by the base of the hemisphere are not used in any calculation.

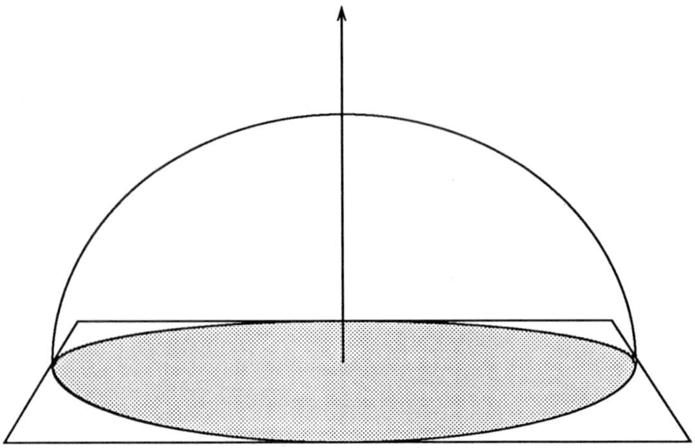

Fig. 2: Discretization of the hemisphere's base.

Once it has been determined that the test and base elements are visible to one another, calculation of the form–factor between them can begin. The spherical projection of the test element onto the surface of the hemisphere involves a translation from rectangular to spherical coordinate space. "Straight" lines in rectangular space do not always translate directly to "straight" lines in spherical space, so steps must be taken to ensure accurate representation of the test element on the hemisphere. Van Wyk [6] proposes calculation of the degree measure of the arc between pairs of points projected onto the hemisphere and using this degree measure in calculating a number of intermediate points along the test element's edge in rectangular space to ensure accurate projection.

In this implementation, the degree measure of the arc is multiplied by two, which will yield a set of intermediate points which should project onto the hemisphere at approximately two degree intervals. These intermediate points are calculated, then spherically projected onto the surface of the hemisphere, and all projected points are then orthographically projected onto the hemisphere's base. Clipping of the spherically projected element is also performed during this step.

Once the orthographic projection has been done, a standard edge list scan–conversion algorithm is used to determine the set of discrete areas on the base covered by the projected surface element.

The resolution of the base of the hemisphere can be arbitrarily fine. In testing, as would be expected, increased resolution decreased the sampling shortcomings, at a cost of increased computation time and allocated memory. When the base of the hemisphere is discretized into, for example, 1.0×10^3 by 1.0×10^3 units, the 1.0×10^6 individual locations of the depth buffer need to take up as little space as possible. In this implementation, the object number and surface element number are encoded into a single integer value, which is stored at a location in the depth buffer. Depth comparisons require decoding of this integer value then comparison of the depths of the stored and test surface elements. If the test surface element is closer, its object and surface element numbers are encoded and stored in the depth buffer. In this manner only a single integer value need be allocated for each depth buffer location.

2.3.1 *Results*

This algorithm, at varying resolutions, was executed using the same input as was used for Table 1. Table 4 shows form factor and execution time results.

Table 4: Accuracy of second hemisphere algorithm.

Angle between surfaces	Analytic solution	50 by 50 grid	500 by 500 grid	1000 by 1000 grid
30.0	0.6190	0.6603	0.6273	0.6258
90.0	0.2000	0.2205	0.2016	0.2006
120.0	0.0866	0.1053	0.0862	0.0863

2.3.2 *Advantages and Disadvantages*

When compared to the first hemisphere algorithm, the second hemisphere algorithm has several distinct advantages. Projection and clipping has become simpler, and a more standard algorithm utilized in calculation of the area covered by the projected surface element. The sampling inadequacies present in the first algorithm are greatly diminished, as the element can be projected with more accuracy onto the hemisphere and the base.

The increased resolution of the base of the hemisphere, as discussed above, increases the amount of memory used. It also requires that an average surface element depth be calculated for each test surface element. This is not as large a disadvantage as it may seem: applications which require the accuracy of the form–factor calculation will most likely require fine subdivision of the surfaces involved. This fine surface subdivision will yield surface elements with relatively little variation in distance to a base surface element across its surface area. Explicit depth testing is performed in the first hemisphere algorithm, and could be performed in the second algorithm, with increased accuracy but also increased computation.

3 Conclusion and Related Work

Accurate, efficient calculation of form–factors between surfaces will continue to be the most important aspect of any radiosity illumination model: its results are the heart of the algorithm. This paper has presented two similar algorithms, both of which improve upon the hemi–cube algorithm in efficiency and accuracy.

There has been recent work done which also shows great promise in this area of research: similar work performed by Goldfeather at the University of North Carolina at Chapel Hill utilizes a cartesian coordinate system on the hemisphere yielding projections which require the solution of quadratic equations. [2] Van Wyk has independently developed an algorithm very similar to the "on the base" hemisphere algorithm, using the QuickDraw[2] region set operation capabilities of the Apple Macintosh microcomputer[3] to determine the area of the base covered by the projection of a test element and to resolve occlusion of simple environments, for use in daylighting models. [6] The Wallace algorithm, presented at SIGGRAPH in 1989, uses a ray–tracing algorithm to calculate visibility between pairs of surface elements. This algorithm comes at some computational cost, although it reduces sampling problems through sampling of surface element vertices rather that the element's surface. [7]

A balance must be attained between accuracy and efficiency. Highly accurate algorithms often require far too much computation to be practical, and highly efficient

[2] QuickDraw is a trademark of Apple Computer, Inc.

[3] Apple and Macintosh are trademarks of Apple Computer, Inc.

algorithms often lack accuracy necessary for particular applications. Continued research in this area will, hopefully, produce algorithms with balance.

4 Acknowledgements

The author wishes to thank Dr. Charles Csuri, director of the Advanced Computing Center for the Arts and Design at The Ohio State University, for his continued support and encouragement, Dr. C. "Skip" Van Wyk for his knowledge of the subject matter, technical advice and intellectual companionship, and the staff and students of The Advanced Computing Center for the Arts and Design and the Ohio Supercomputer Graphics Project for their technical support.

A. Algorithms

Each of the following algorithms describes how to calculate the form factors from one polygon, denoted the "base" polygon, to the set of all other polygons in an environment, denoted the "test" polygons. A complete form factor solution would repeat the steps in this algorithm with each polygon in the environment taking its turn as "base" polygon.

A.1 The "on the hemisphere" Algorithm

```
- initialize form factor array and depth buffer
- for each polygon in the environment
- determine if the test polygon is visible to the base polygon
- if it is visible
    - project the vertices onto the hemisphere
    - calculate ''phi'' and ''theta'' values for each vertex
    - calculate radian measure of arc between adjacent vertices
       to determine whether apex of hemisphere is covered
    - sort ''phi'' values into ascending order
    - if apex is not covered
      - determine whether the depth buffer boundary is crossed
    - assign min and max theta bounding box values from sorted thetas
    - calculate min and max phi bounding box values:
      - (requires a table relating distance on base to phi value)
      - using projection of vertices onto base, build list of
         distances of vertices from origin and list of distances
         of edge perpendicular bisection points from origin
      - sort each list into ascending order
      - assign min and max phi bounding box values from sorted phi
         values and table values:
      - (if perpendicular distance is {less than, greater than}
         either edge endpoint distance, look up phi value for that
         distance and use it for {min, max} phi bounding box value)
    - calculate plane equations of edge planes
      (each edge plane contains the origin and
      two test polygon vertices)
    - for each member of the bounding box
      - convert ''phi'' and ''theta'' values for this member into
         rectangular coordinates for the center of this grid square.
      - plug rectangular coordinates into edgeplane equations
         to test for coverage of this grid square by the test polygon
```

```
    - if this grid square is covered
      - calculate distance from origin to test polygon along vector
        from origin through center of grid square
      - if distance is less than what is stored in the depth buffer
        location corresponding to this grid square
        - update the item buffer with the test polygon ID
```

A.2 The "on the base" Algorithm

```
- initialize form factor array and depth buffer
- for each polygon in the environment
  - determine if the test polygon is visible to the base polygon
  - if it is visible
    - project the vertices onto the hemisphere
    - calculate the angle between each pair of vertices
    - calculate the level of subdivision for each edge
    - calculate the intermediate edge points
    - project (and clip if necessary) all points onto the base
    - create an edge list, on the base, using the projected points
    - work the edge list, testing each area as follows:
    - if the depth buffer at this area is empty,
      - encode the polygon ID and store at this location
      ELSE
      - decode the polygon ID stored at this location
        - compare distance to stored polygon and
          distance to test polygon
          - if the test polygon is closer
            - encode the test polygon ID and store at this location
```

References

[1] Cohen, M. E., Greenberg, D. P.: The hemi-cube: A radiosity solution for complex environments. Proceedings of SIGGRAPH 1985 (ACM Computer Graphics), 19(3):31–40, July 1985.

[2] Goldfeather, J.: Progressive radiosity using hemispheres. Technical Report TR89–002, University of North Carolina at Chapel Hill, 1989.

[3] Goral, C. M., Torrance, K. E., Greenberg, D. P., Battaile, B.: Modeling the Interaction of Light Between Diffuse Surfaces. Proceedings of SIGGRAPH 1984 (ACM Computer Graphics), 18(3):213–222, July 1984.

[4] Siegel, R., Howell, J. R.: Thermal Radiation Heat Transfer. Hemisphere Publishing Corporation, 1981.

[5] Spencer, S. N.: The Hemisphere Radiosity Method for Computer–Generated Images. Master's thesis, The Ohio State University, August 1988.

[6] Van Wyk, Jr., Christopher G.: A Geometry–Based Insolation Model for Computer–Aided Design. PhD thesis, The University of Michigan, 1988.

[7] Wallace, J. R., Elmquist, K. A., Haines, E. A.: A Ray Tracing Algorithm for Progressive Radiosity. Proceedings of SIGGRAPH 1989 (ACM Computer Graphics), 23(3):315–324, August 1989.

[8] Weibelt, J. A.: Engineering Radiative Heat Transfer. Holt, Rinehart, and Winston, 1966.

Exploiting Coherence for Clipping and View Transformations in Radiosity Algorithms

Joseppe Vilaplana,* Xavier Pueyo †‡

Abstract

In radiosity techniques, a visibility computation process is repeatedly applied for different "view points". Because of the close relationship between these "view points", we can take advantage of several kinds of coherence in order to speed up the different steps of the rendering pipeline. In this paper we focus on the clipping and the view transformation steps.

1 Introduction

As well known [9, 10], *radiosity* was introduced in 1984 [7] as a new powerfull method to model the behavior of light interacting between diffuse reflecting surfaces. This new technique dealt with a problem of illumination models not studied in depth up to this moment.

Radiosity was borrowed from thermal engineering [14] and its application to image synthesis has evolved very quickly. The bursting of the new technique into computer graphics has also activated the development of *direct and inverse ray tracing* techniques to compute diffuse reflections and to obtain global illumination models with suitable implementation techniques [11, 1]. On the other hand, instead of rivaling, radiosity has collaborated with both types of ray tracing in search for a good implementation technique for *global illumination models* [15].

After analysing [13] different strategies proposed for the implementation of radiosity [2, 4, 5, 6, 7, 12, 16, 19] we observe that the visibility computation is repeated for every sample of the environment. Neverthless, the piece of environment seen from a given sample point is, often, very similar to the piece of environment which is visible for other points neighbouring the current sample. From this, we can derive that different types of coherence could be applied to improve radiosity's efficiency.

In this paper we propose some solutions to take advantage of this coherence in the first steps of the rendering pipeline. This coherence is going to be used in a hierarchical way. First we have to analyse the coherence inherent in the fact that different patches belong to a same surface. After that, we can take advantage of the similarity between visibility of neighbour patches. Finally, coherence will be used for computation in different frustrums of a sample point.

*Secció d'Informàtica Gràfica. Dept. Llenguatges i Sistemes Informàtics. UPC. Av.Diagonal 647 pl.8. E-08028 BARCELONA

†INRIA - IRISA. Projet SIAMES. Campus de Beaulieu. F-35042 RENNES.

‡Secció d'Informàtica Gràfica. Dept. Llenguatges i Sistemes Informàtics. UPC. Av.Diagonal 647 pl.8. E-08028 BARCELONA

2 The Hemi-Cube Technique

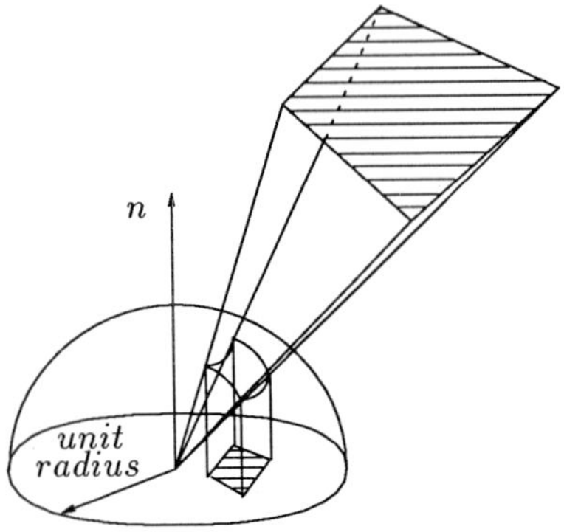

Fig. 1: Nusselt's analog

Cohen and Greenberg [5] introduced the hemi-cube technique for form factor calculation taking advantage of the Nusselt's geometric analog. This analog allows to map all the surfaces of the environment (seen from the patch center) on a unit hemisphere surrounding the patch normal (figure 1), then discretizing the hemisphere and preprocessing it to compute form factors (delta form factors) of each hemisphere piece (called pixels). Geometric problems of this approximation are solved by replacing the hemisphere by a hemi-cube (figure 2) which, moreover, provides a good way to treat occlusions. So, each

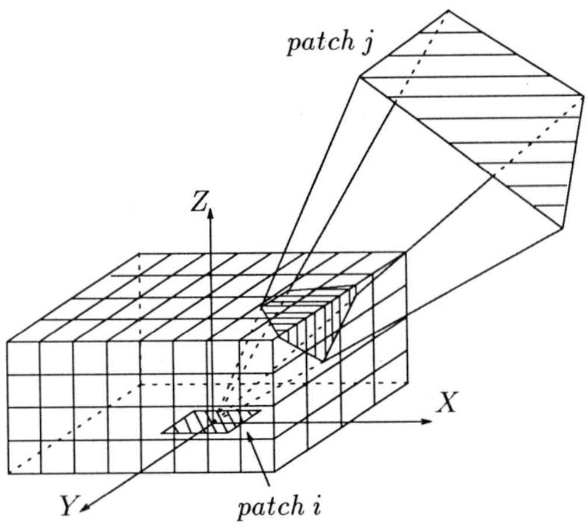

Fig. 2: The hemicube

of the five faces of the hemi-cube is subdivided into pixels. The whole environmemnt is projected onto each face and a z-buffering process is applied in order to perform visibility calculation. At the end, the form factor between patch i and patch j is given by,

$$F_{ij} = \sum_{q=1}^{p} \Delta F_q$$

where, ΔF_q is the delta form factor associated with pixel q on the hemi-cube and p is the number of hemi-cube pixels covered by the projection of patch j onto the hemi-cube of patch i.

With this technique we estimate the ith row of form factor matrix extending a hemi-cube at *ith* patch center. We next give a sketch of the algorithm form factor calculation:

```
procedure form_factor_calculation()

    form_factor_matrix_to_zero;
    foreach patch i in environment do
       place hemi-cube at center of patch i;
       foreach face in hemi-cube do
          visible_surface(face_view, environment, itembuffer)
          {update row with delta form factor of the current face}
          foreach sample s of the current face do
             j:= itembuffer[s]; {j points to patch j}
             if j=0
                then
                   ff[i,j]:=ff[i,j]+delta[s]
             endif
          endfor
       endfor
    endfor
endprocedure
```

For clarity, we don't word in this algorithm some details like difference between the treatment of the top face of hemi-cube and the treatment of lateral faces. Details can be found in [5].

2.1 Cost Analysis

In the worst case, the previous algorithm has a cost in time

$$T = i + N \cdot (p + 5 \cdot v + 3 \cdot R^2 \cdot s) \tag{1}$$

Where:
i is the initialization cost,
p is the cost of placing a hemi-cube at center of patch i,
v is the cost of determining the visible surfaces for one face of the hemi-cube at patch i,
s is the cost of a single summation of delta form factor to an element of the matrix,
R is the resolution of the hemi-cube, and
N is the number of patches in the environment.

The z-buffer based determination of visible surface is done by the classical graphic pipeline which is hardware implemented in current workstation's technology [8, 18, 3]. After initializing a view from the current patch center for the current face of hemi-cube, we must do the following stages of the pipeline for each patch:

- Transform it from the world coordinates system to view coordinates system, applying perspective transformation;

- Clip it against viewing frustrum;

- Patch scan conversion and mapping the patch identifier in the current face's depth buffer.

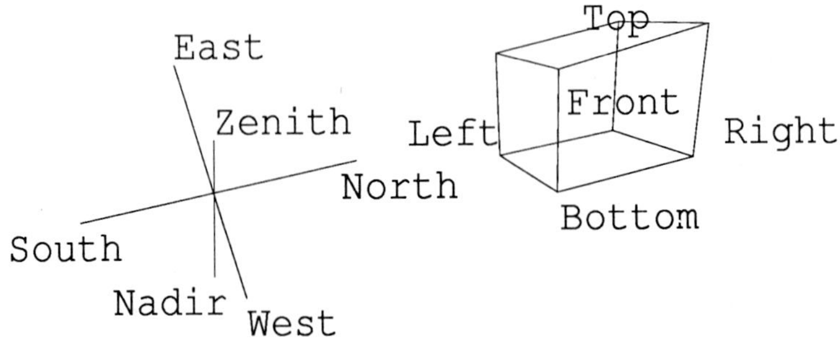

Fig. 3: Astronomy horizon agreement and face naming

The cost in time of this process can be stated as

$$v = i' + (N-1) \cdot v' \tag{2}$$

where i' is the cost of the initial view transformation matrix evaluation, and v' is the cost for a patch to traverse the pipeline.

This cost is very hard to evaluate because it depends on many factors. For example, the patch can be outside of the viewing frustrum and doesn't need to continue the pipe, the patch scan conversion cost depends on the hemi-cube's resolution and the patch's area "seen" from the current face, ...

Substituting equation (2) in (1) gives an idea of the basic cost parameters of the form factor calculation.

$$T = i + N \cdot (p + 5 \cdot (i' + (N-1) \cdot v') + 3 \cdot R^2 \cdot s) \tag{3}$$

3 Improving the Algorithm by Means of Frustrum's Coherence

In equation (3) we can see that form factor computations is $O(n^2)$. We must notice that the algorithm traverses the environment's database five times for a single full hemi-cube calculation (i.e. one row of the form factor matrix computation). We discuss below two aspects of the process in order to improve its performance. The proposed algorithm goes through the database only one time for a single hemi-cube full calculation. This strategy is specially suited for applications with complex environments whose database doesn't fit in a host memory involving the access to database's portions, as well as in implementations with the environment's database mapped on distributed memory parallel architectures with local communication between processors.

Our study towards an improvement in which the algorithm goes through the environment's database only once for a full hemi-cube calculation is based on the two following observations.

First, the viewing transformation, without perspective, can be done only one time for a single hemi-cube and for each patch to be mapped onto the hemi-cube. If a patch is seen from more than one face, the viewing transformations for other faces can be obtained from the first patch's viewing coordinates. For example, if we have the patch's viewing coordinates associated with the top view, the patch viewing coordinates associated with any lateral face is obtained by exchanging the top viewing coordinates and likely some changes of sign. No floating point operations as sum or product is involved. In our case, these transformations are:

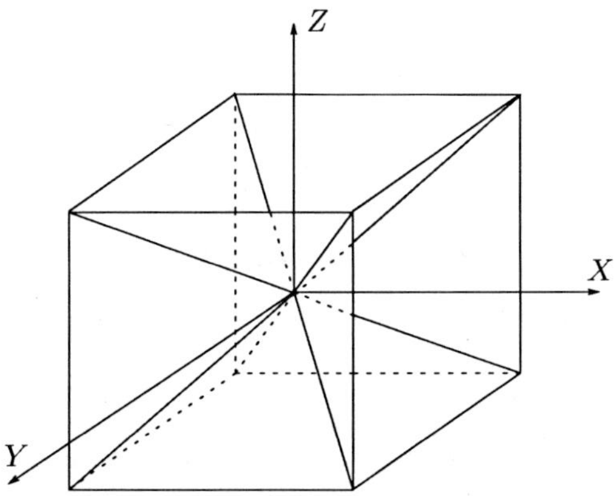

Fig. 4: The clipping planes of the cube

TABLE 1

From top view to:

Left	:	$(x', y', z') = (y, z, x)$
Right	:	$(x', y', z') = (-y, z, x)$
Front	:	$(x', y', z') = (x, z, -y)$
Back	:	$(x', y', z') = (-x, z, y)$
Bottom	:	$(x', y', z') = (x, -y, -z)$

The other observation is that clipping can be done at the same time for multiple views. This was suggested by Sutherland and Hodgman [17]. As they noted, a few modifications in their reentrant polygon clipper allows a simultaneous clipping for multiple views. Instead of rejecting vertices outside the view clipping plane, they are supplied to clipping against planes of another adjacent view frustrum. On the other hand, the calculated intersections of a clipping plane are used for the two adjacent views sharing the plane. The last avoids repeating the same intersection calculation twice. Comparisons are also saved.

3.1 Clipping against a Cube

In this section we deal with the clipping process against a full cube view because of its generality. In fact, the use of a full cube allows to handle transmission of light in all directions instead of limiting it to reflections. After this, we will extend the conclusions to the clipping process against a hemi-cube which is a reduced case of the former.

For clarity, we introduce the following notation as reference of the clipping planes that take part in the process (see figure 3). For each face, we have an infinite viewing pyramid with apex at the center of a cube which is bounded by four planes. This planes are shared by other infinite viewing pyramids of the other faces. We use the astronomy horizon agreement to denote the planes normals using only the first letter of the cardinal orientation. The normal orientation points out the inner half-space of the corresponding plane. For example (figure 4), if a point is in the visible half-space of the planes ZE and ZN, it is only in the top view of the cube. If the point is on the ZW plane and is in the visible half-space of the planes ZS, ZE and ZN, the point shares the top view and the front view. Sutherland-Hodgman's clipping algorithm for a single view tests a patch vertex with a bounding plane of the view. If the test indicates that the vertex is in the hidden half-space bounded by the plane, the vertex is rejected. If the vertex is in the visible half-space, the algorithm continues testing it against the remaining view bounding planes. If the vertex is inside all the bounding planes, it is included in a list of passed vertices. Two specific cases must be considered. When a vertex is in the hidden (visible) half-space and the next vertex is in the visible (hidden) half-space an intersection calculation is done. The new resulting point must then be tested against the remaining view bounding planes as for vertices.

To clip in a multiple view at a time we must test a "rejected" (not more rejected) vertex against other view bounding planes than the initial view bounding planes to decide in which view it must be included. For this purpose, one vertex list for each view must be maintained.

In table 2 we present the required relationships, between a point and the view bounding planes, to decide which view the point belongs to. *in* means inside the visible half-space, *out* means inside the hidden half-space and *i/o* means that the plane does'nt decide for the current view. Clearly, for each view there are four deciding planes.

TABLE 2

	NW	*NE*	*ZW*	*ZS*	*ZE*	*ZN*
Right	*in*	*in*	*i/o*	*out*	*i/o*	*in*
Back	*in*	*out*	*in*	*i/o*	*out*	*i/o*
Front	*out*	*in*	*out*	*i/o*	*in*	*i/o*
Left	*out*	*out*	*i/o*	*in*	*i/o*	*out*
Top	*i/o*	*i/o*	*in*	*in*	*in*	*in*
Bottom	*i/o*	*i/o*	*out*	*out*	*out*	*out*

Given the relationship between a point and a plane, we must decide which is the next clipping plane. We must also store the relationship between the point and each treated clipping plane. Finally, this information will be used to determine the frustrum containing the point. This can be accomplished with a decision binary tree (see figure 5) implemented in the following *clip* algorithm:

```
var
    former, first_point:  array [clipping_planes] OF vertex3D;
    new_edge:  array [clipping_planes] OF boolean;
    first_node:  array [clipping_planes] OF tree_pointer;
    ...   ...   ...

procedure clip(current:  vertex3D; tree_node:  tree) is

    p:= plane_or_face(tree_node);
    if p indicates a plane
       then
          if new_edge[p]
             then
                first_point[p]:= current; new_edge[p]:= false;
                first_node[p]:= node
             else
                if cross(current,former[p],p)
                   then
                      intersect(current,former[p],p,interspoint);
                      clip(interspoint,left_son(node));
                      clip(interspoint,right_son(node))
                endif
```

```
            endif;
            former[p]:= current;
            if inside(current,p)
               then clip(current, left_son(node))
               else clip(current, right_son(node))
            endif
         else
            clip_depth(current,front,p) {here p is a face}
      endif
endprocedure ;
```

Each tree's internal node represents a clipping plane, the leaves represent the frustrums and the path followed by a point from the root to a leave represents it's relationship with the visited planes (nodes). In four stages the algorithm will deduce in which view is a

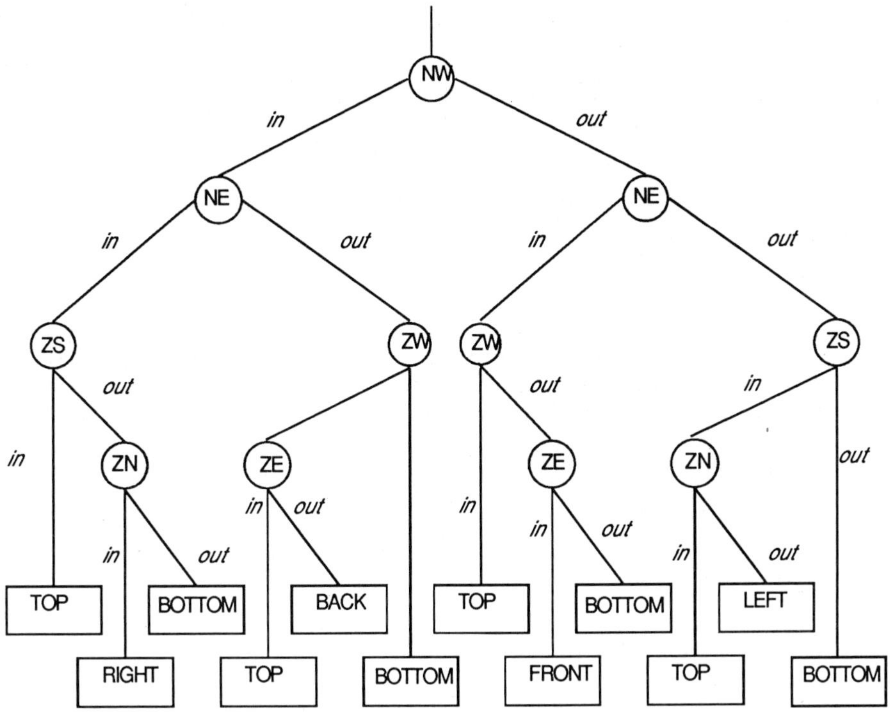

Fig. 5: Decision tree for cube clipping planes

vertex. We can add a hither and yon plane (not included in the tree) for each view with a few modifications in the clipping algorithm. When the procedure *clip* has found the view for the vertex, this view will indicate the hither and yon planes for the procedure $clip - depth$.

After the clipping process, the vertex is inserted in the list of vertices of the corresponding view. So, six lists must be maintained in the cube case. After clipping, each list is transformed according to table 1. Then, we apply, for each view, a perspective transformation and a patch scan convertion. This implies to save a buffer for each view. For a hemi-cube resolution R, the complete set of buffers needs a $6 \cdot R^2$ object identifiers. The trade-off between time and space appears also here (the algorithm without improvement

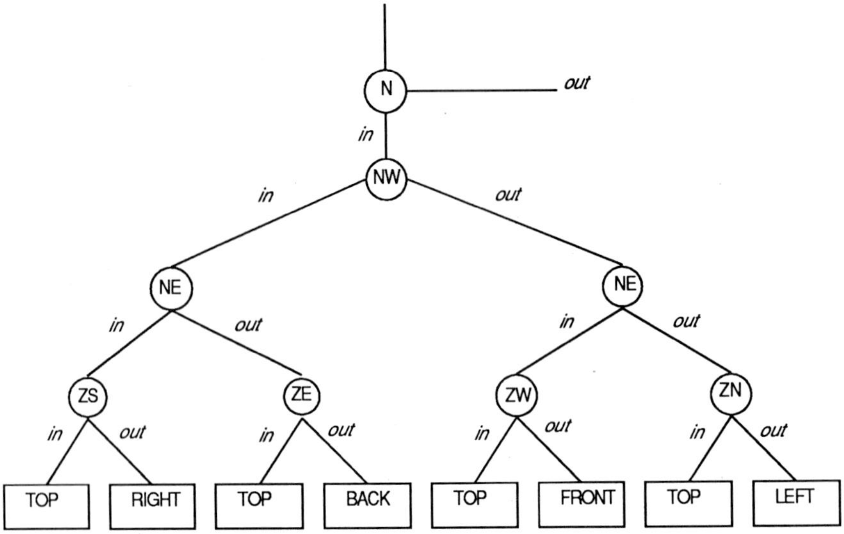

Fig. 6: Decision tree for hemicube clipping planes

in time only needs a R^2 object identifiers).

In the proposed algorithm, a perspective transformation must be applied after clipping and view coordinate exchange because we don't know a priori the depth coordinate (i.e. we don't know, before clipping, in which face(s) must be projected the patch). This differs from other proposed graphic pipelines which perform the clipping process after view and perspective transformation in homogeneous coordinates [17]. The homogeneous coordinates are used to delay the perspective division at the end of the graphic pipeline.

On the other hand, the fourth homogeneous coordinate, w, is related to the clipping plane equations ($-w \leq x \leq +w, -w \leq y \leq +w$). This is useful for perspective transformations with general clipping planes ($w = k \cdot z$, where k is related to the plane's slope); but for a 45° (as in our case study) oriented plane, $w = z$, the clipping process may be done before or after perspective transformation without affecting the pipeline efficiency.

3.2 Clipping againts a Hemi-Cube

The hemi-cube is a reduced case of a cube. We must add a new clipping plane $z = 0$ with visible half-space $z > 0$. Putting it as a root of the decision tree, major changes in the clipping algorithm are not necessary (Now it needs to treat rejected vertices). Figure 6 shows the resulting decision tree. All the vertices with $z \leq 0$ are rejected. The resulting algorithm needs $3 \cdot R^2$ (as stated above, R is the hemi-cube's resolution) object identifiers for all the z-buffers.

4 Surface and Patch-to-Patch Coherence

In this section we discuss two other kinds of coherence:

- **Surface coherence** takes advantage of the fact that a set of patches belongs to a same surface.

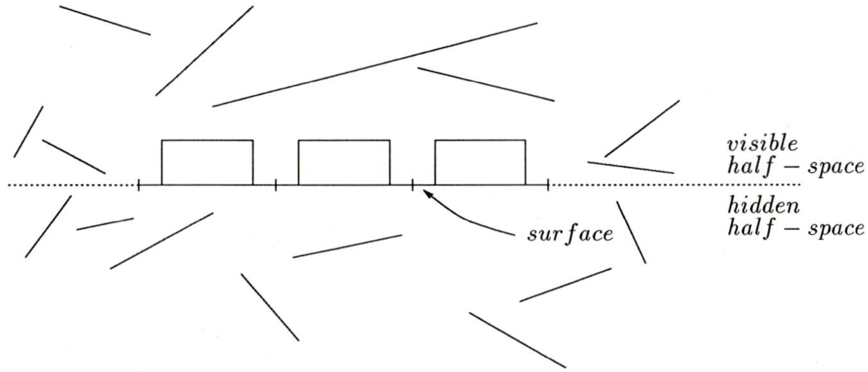

Fig. 7: Selecting potentially visible patches

- **Patch-to-pach** coherence is based on similarity between neighbour patches of a same surface.

For a planar surface, the hemicubes of their patches share a same half-space of the environment in the direction of the surface's normal (figure 7). This implies that, in a first step we can select the elements of this half space as patches potentially visible from the surface, i.e. from the hemi-cubes of its patches.

For geometric transformations we can also take advantage of the surface coherence. The view rotation matrix, for exemple, will be the same for all the patches of the surface; only translation changes from one patch to the other.

We define an hemicube system as three normalized ortogonal vectors $(\vec{x}_v, \vec{y}_v, \vec{z}_v)$ with one of them matching the surface's normal direction. If the vector components are

$$\vec{x}_v = (x_{hx}, x_{hy}, x_{hz})$$
$$\vec{y}_v = (y_{hx}, y_{hy}, y_{hz})$$
$$\vec{z}_v = (z_{hx}, z_{hy}, z_{hz})$$

and the hemicube center is (c_x, c_y, c_z), the view transformation matrix T_v can be easily computed.

Given the view transformed coordinates for an hemicube 1, centered at point $c1$, we may obtain the transformed coordinates for an hemicube 2 centered at point $c2$, with

$$\begin{aligned} x_{v2} - x_{v1} &= (c1_x - c2_x) \cdot x_{hx} + (c1_y - c2_y) \cdot x_{hy} - (c1_z - c2_z) \cdot x_{hz} \\ y_{v2} - y_{v1} &= (c1_x - c2_x) \cdot y_{hx} + (c1_y - c2_y) \cdot y_{hy} - (c1_z - c2_z) \cdot y_{hz} \\ z_{v2} - z_{v1} &= (c1_x - c2_x) \cdot z_{hx} + (c1_y - c2_y) \cdot z_{hy} - (c1_z - c2_z) \cdot z_{hz}. \end{aligned} \tag{5}$$

Equations (5) are constant for all the points to be transformed.
A first algorithm can be stated as:

```
procedure form_factor_calculation is

    form_factor_matrix_to_zero;
    foreach surface in environment do
       place_hemi-cube_at_a_single_patch_of_current_surface;
       create_view_transformation(hemi-cube_view);
       foreachz patch in environment do
```

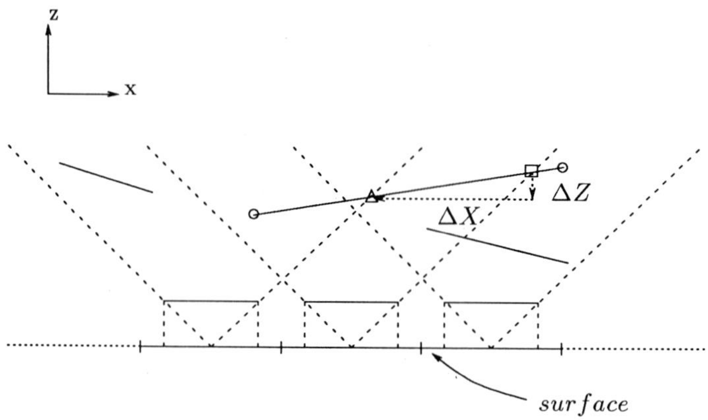

Fig. 8: Incremental clipping using patch-to-patch coherence

```
          hemi-cube_view_transform(patch);
          if patch in half-space
             then
                foreach hemi-cube in current surface do
                   adapt_view_transform(hemi-cube_view, patch);
                   hemi-cube_clip(patch, lists)
                   foreach face of hemi-cube do
                      adapt_face_view_coordinates(face,lists[face]);
                      perspective_transformation(lists[face]);
                      z-buffer(face,lists[face]);
                   endfor
                endfor
          endif
          foreach patch p in current surface do
             update_form_factor_row(p)
          endfor
       endfor
    endfor
endprocedure
```

As stated above, patch-to-patch coherence may also be used in the clipping process for both: *vertex classification* and *intersection points computation.*

We next describe the use of this type of coherence on the basis of a uniform distribution of surface's patches. Similar techniques could be derived for some kind of non uniform patch distribution.

Because of the sorted (in x and y) characteristics of surface's patches, we can proceed in the folowing way (see figure 8):

- Compute segment's vertices location; i.e. the frustra containing them.
- Derive, from the results of the previous step, which frustra are crossed by the segment.

– Clipp againts first frustrum (compute intersection point).

– Clipp againts other crossed frustra using an incremental technique.

In fact, the above is only a possible strategy ; but this type of coherence can be exploited in other algorithms. For exemple, given a point P in the visible half-space, and H hemi-cubes, we can know in which faces it is projected.

Let's first remember that view bounding planes for an hemi-cube are $x = z$, $x = -z$, $y = z$ and $y = -z$. In figure 9 we have a 2-D exemple of a surface with 3 hemi-cubes. The straight lines from the point to the centre of each hemi-cube give us the answer directly. In order to know which top faces will contain a point projection, we use the relations

$$abs(C1_x - P_x) \leq P_z \qquad abs(C1_y - P_y) \leq P_z$$

which are true for a point projected in the top face of hemicube 1.

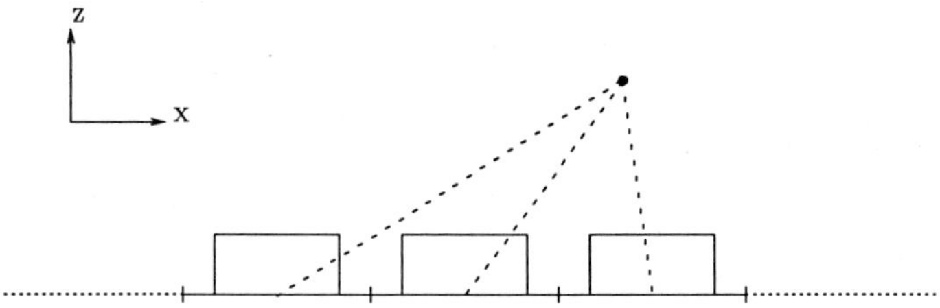

Fig. 9: Projection of a point onto three hemicubes

5 Conclusions and Future Work

We have proposed the use of a hierarchy of coherence techniques to improve the performances of the first steps of the rendering pipeline. In this way, instead of applying transformation and clipping operations to the whole environment for each frustrum of each patch, we use different transformation and clipping operations suitable to each level of the scene decomposition; i.e. surface, patch and frustrum.

In fact, the strategies proposed in section 4, as they have been exposed, cannot be directly applied along with the technique described in section 3. So, further work must be done in order to make cooperated the three levels of coherence in the best way.

On going work is the design of a scene's data structure well suited to the implementation of an integrated solution of the different proposed techniques, as well as to other aspects of radiosity algorithms.

The results of this paper arise from the research of parallel techniques for radiosity algorithms. Let's take an exemple to present the kind of problems to deal with and its relationship with the presented work.

Mapping the algorithm of form factor calculation in a ring of computers, perhaps allocating a subset of rows of the form factor matrix to each processor could be a solution. Each processor would work with its subset of rows, say, with its subset of hemi-cubes. Full hemi-cube calculation needs the full environment. Replicating it on all local memories is an expensive solution and leads to an inefficient use of resources. An alternative is a host connected to the ring of computers sending the patches (or patch packets) of the environment to the computers requesting them. In our algorithm, the message flow is reduced five times.

The study of different possible kinds of coherence will give other strategies for the distribution of the environment in local memories as well as other possible mappings accelerating the form factor calculation. Of course, the use of coherence will entail load balancing problems that have to be solved.

To deal with these problems a good knowledge of some characteristics of the environment's complexity (related to the data base organization) could be exploited. For example, the number of patches in the visible half-space of a surface near the environment's boundary with normal pointing to the boundary will usually be small, for surfaces in the "center" of the environment whose number will be (on average) near half the number of elements in the environment, ...

References

[1] ARVO, J. Backward ray tracing. In *Developments in Ray Tracing: Course Notes*, ACM SIGGRAPH, 1986.

[2] BAUM, D. R., RUSHMEIER, H. E., AND WINGET, J. M. Imrpoving radiosity solutions through the use of anallytically determined form-factors. In *ACM SIGGRAPH Conf. Proc.* (july 1989), pp. 325–334. Computer Graphics vol.23 num.3.

[3] CLARK, J. H. The geometry engine: a vlsi geometry system for graphics. In *ACM SIGGRAPH Conf. Proc.* (july 1982), pp. 127–133.

[4] COHEN, M. F., CHEN, S. E., WALLACE, J. R., AND GREENBERG, D. P. A progessive refinement approach to fast radiosity image generation. In *ACM SIGGRAPH Conf. Proc.* (august 1988), pp. 75–84. Computer Graphics vol.22 num.4.

[5] COHEN, M. F., AND GREENBERG, D. P. The hemi-cube. a radiosity solution for complex environments. In *ACM SIGGRAPH Conf. Proc.* (july 1985), pp. 31–40. Computer Graphics vol.19 num.3.

[6] COHEN, M. F., GREENBERG, D. P., IMMEL, D. S., AND BROCK, P. J. An efficient radiosity approach for realistic image synthesis. *IEEE Computer Graphics and Applications 6*, 3 (1986), 26–35.

[7] GORAL, C. M., TORRANCE, K. E., GREENBERG, D. P., AND BATTAILE, B. Modeling the interaction of light between diffuse surfaces. In *ACM SIGGRAPH Conf. Proc.* (july 1984), pp. 213–222. Computer Graphics vol.18 num.3.

[8] GORIS, A., FFREDRICKSON, B., AND BAEVERSTAD, H. L. A configurable pixel cache for fast image generation. *IEEE Computer Graphics and Applications* (march 1987), 24–32.

[9] GREENBERG, D., Ed. *Radiosity: Course Notes.* ACM SIGGRAPH, 31 july - 4 august 1989.

[10] HALL, R. *Illumination and Color in Computer Generated Imagery.* Springer-Verlag, New York, 1988. ISBN 0-387-96774-5.

[11] KAJIYA, J. T. The rendering equation. In *ACM SIGGRAPH Conf. Proc.* (august 1986), pp. 143–150. Computer Graphics vol.20 num.4.

[12] NISHITA, T., AND NAKAMAE, E. Continuous tone representation of three-dimensional objects taking account of shadows and interreflection. In *ACM SIGGRAPH Conf. Proc.* (july 1985), pp. 23–30. Computer Graphics vol.19 num.3.

[13] PUEYO, X. Diffuse interreflections. techniques for form factor computation. *Submitted* (may 1990).

[14] SEIGEL, R., AND HOWELL, J. R. *Termal Radiation. Heat Transfer.* Hemisphre Publishing Corp., 1978.

[15] SHAO, M., PENG, Q., AND LIANG, Y. A new radiosity approach by procedural refinements for realistic image synthesis. In *ACM SIGGRAPH Conf. Proc.* (august 1988), pp. 93–101. Computer Graphics vol.22 num.4.

[16] SILLION, F., AND PUECH, C. A general two-pass method integrating specular and diffuse reflection. In *ACM SIGGRAPH Conf. Proc.* (july 1989), pp. 335–344. Computer Graphics vol.23 num.3.

[17] SUTHERLAND, I. E., AND HODGMAN, G. W. Reentrant polygon clipping. *Com. ACM 17*, 1 (january 1974), 32–42.

[18] SWANSON, R. W., AND THAYER, L. A fast shaded polygon renderer. In *ACM SIGGRAPH Conf. Proc.* (august 1986), pp. 95–101.

[19] WALLACE, J. R., ELMQUIST, K. A., AND HAINES, E. A. A ray tracing algorithm for progressive radiosity. In *ACM SIGGRAPH Conf. Proc.* (july 1989), pp. 315–324. Computer Graphics vol.23 num.3.

A Rapid Hierarchical Radiosity Algorithm for Unoccluded Environments

Pat Hanrahan*and David Salzman†

Abstract

This paper presents a linear-time radiosity algorithm for scenes containing large mutually unoccluded polygonal patches. It subdivides pairs of patches adaptively to build a hierarchical data structure with n elements at the leaves, and it encodes all the light transport between component polygonal elements. Given a required numerical precision, determined by the specified bounds for maximum solid angle F_ϵ and minimum area A_ϵ, our algorithm reduces the number of form factor calculations and interactions to $O(n)$ in the worst case and $\sqrt{O(n)}$ in the best case. Standard techniques for shooting and gathering can then be used with the data structure. The best previous radiosity algorithms represented the element-to-element transport interactions with n^2 form factors.

1 Introduction

Methods for producing realistic images from geometric descriptions of a scene have always been one of the central themes of research in computer graphics. The earliest "local illumination" algorithms considered only geometric and material properties of objets in isolation, and measured the amount of light reflected from a surface to the viewer without considering objets that might shadow or obscure the surface. More modern "global illumination" algorithms, however, consider the the entire environment and produce pictures with shadows, reflections, refractions, diffuse inter-reflections and color bleeding, and light focusing or caustics. Although the physics of global illumination can be formulated as an integral rendering equation describing the transport of light within an environment [14], fully general solutions are computationally intractable in practice.

Radiosity offers the best case today in which the general rendering equation can be solved [11]. Radiosity makes the simplifying assumption that all surfaces scatter light isotropically, so the intensity of outgoing energy has no directional dependence, and the directional distribution of light at any point on surface can be represented as a single number. There are two major steps in solving for radiosities. First, geometric form factors are computed between all pairs of surfaces. These form factors give the proportion of light leaving one surface that is incident on another. Second, a large system of simultaneous linear equations involving form factors and brightnesses must be solved to yield the light energy transported to each surface. Researchers have devised better methods in recent years both for computing form factors and calculating brightnesses.

This paper describes a method for applying techniques recently developed for efficiently solving the N-body problem [1, 2, 12] to the radiosity problem. We concentrate on the case of k large unoccluded polygonal patches, discretized into n finer polygonal elements. We show that the form factor matrix can always be approximated to within

*Departement of Computer Science, Princeton University, Princeton, NJ 08540, hanrahan@princeton.edu

†John von Neumann National Supercomputer Center, Princeton, NJ 08540, salzman@princeton.edu

some preset numerical tolerance with $O(n)$ terms. Each term corresponds to coalescing a $n_1 \times n_2$ rectangular block in the form factor matrix, and representing the sum of the entries with a single number. Significantly fewer than n^2 independent form factors need to be computed, speeding up the first step in the radiosity algorithm. The successive matrix iterations needed to compute the brightnesses also run faster, since the multiplication of the $O(n)$ blocks in the form factor matrix by the column vector of brightnesses can be done in $O(n)$ time.

2 Review of the Basic Radiosity Formulation

This section briefly describes the matrix formulation of the radiosity problem. More details are contained in standard textbooks on radiative heat transfer [16, 18].

Radiosity algorithms assume that all surfaces in the environment are perfect Lambertian reflectors, and hence scatter light equally in all directions. The energy distribution per unit area per unit solid angle is called *radiosity*, which we will also refer to as *brightness*. The radiosity of a diffuse material has no directional dependence, and can be denoted by a single number. We assume that a scene description has been discretized into n elements, where each element is small enough that the brightness does not vary significantly across its surface. The energy leaving each element i is given by

$$B_i A_i = E_i A_i + \rho_i \sum_j^n F_{ji} B_j A_j \tag{1}$$

where :

- B_i is brightness of element i,
- E_i is the emissivity of element i,
- A_i is the area of element i,
- ρ_i is the diffuse reflectivity of element i,
- F_{ij} is the form factor from element i to element j.

Equation (1) represents an energy equilibrium. It states that the radiosity (light energy) leaving element i consists of the light it emits directly plus the sum of all the diffusely scattered light energy incident on it and retransmitted. The contribution of element i to the brightness of element j is equal to its own brightness times a form factor, giving the proportion of light leaving element i which reaches,j, times the the diffuse scattering coefficient of j.

The radiosity algorithm involves two steps. First, one calculates the form factors. The form factor is purely geometric, and is proportional to the solid angle subtended by the emitter from the vantage point of the element receiving the light, assuming all points on the emitter are visible from the receiver. The differential form between two infinitesimal areas is given by

$$F_{ij} = \frac{\cos\theta_i \cos\theta_j}{\pi r_{ij}^2} dA_j. \tag{2}$$

This is illustrated in Figure (1). The angle θ_i (or θ_j) relates the normal vector of element i (or j) to the vector joining the two elements. The cosine factors arise because the brightness is measured per unit area in the direction in which light is transported. The form factor from an infinitesimal area to a finite area is

$$F_{ij} = \int_{A_j} \frac{\cos\theta_i \cos\theta_j}{\pi r_{ij}^2} dA_j, \tag{3}$$

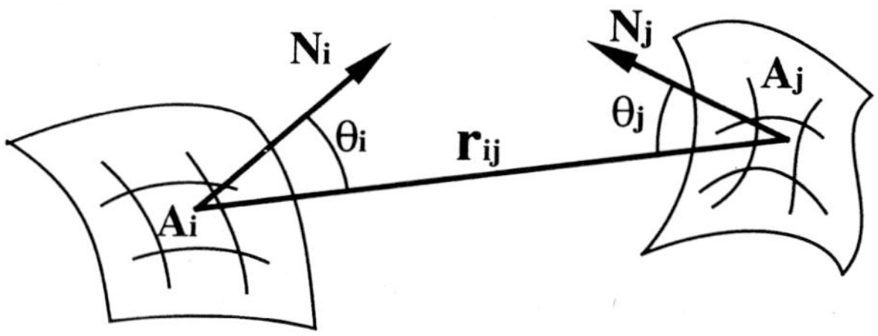

Fig. 1: Differential Form Factor Geometry

and the form factor between two finite areas is

$$F_{ij} = \frac{1}{A_i} \int_{A_i} \int_{A_j} \frac{\cos\theta_i \cos\theta_j}{\pi r_{ij}^2} dA_j dA_i.$$

For an enclosed environment, where all energy leaving a surface eventually falls on another surface, the form factors sum to 1,

$$\sum_{i}^{n} F_{ij} = \sum_{j}^{n} F_{ij} = 1 \tag{4}$$

Moreover, the *reciprocity principle* states that the amount of light exchanged between emitter and receiver is unchanged if they are swapped, so

$$A_i F_{ij} = A_j F_{ji}. \tag{5}$$

Form factors must be approximated numerically, since the integrals in Equation (3) do not yield closed-form solutions for the geometries commonly encountered in computer graphics. For example, there appears to be no closed-form expression for the form factor between a differential area and a polygon [13, 3]. The calculation of a form factor between two surfaces is further complicated by the need to determine the mutual visibility of all pairs of points on the two surfaces. A surface may hide a portion of itself, or be partially eclipsed from another element by intervening objets.

A number of researchers have invented projection methods for computing the differential form factor to any arbitrary shape. Nusselt projected a shape onto a sphere and measured its cross sectional area when viewed from the top of the sphere [16, 15]. Cohen modified this method by projecting shapes onto a hemi-cube [5], since the hemi-cube projection is easier to compute with traditional computer graphics techniques. Each pixel on the hemi-cube stores information about the visibility of objets within the solid angle which projects onto that pixel's area. Associated with each pixel is a delta form factor. The total form for an element is equal to the sum of the delta form factors from each pixel which it covers on the hemi-cube. Sillion improved on this further by projecting onto a single plane positioned close to the differential area [17], which entailed only a single projection where the hemi-cube used five.

Several sources of error arise when computing form factors using a hemi-cube. Most notable is the aliasing, or beating, that occurs between the sampled elements and the sampled solid angles corresponding to pixels on the hemi-cube. Another source of error arises because projection methods compute form factors from source to receiver, whereas the form factor from receiver to source is needed. The reverse form factors can be computed using the reciprocity principle, but this will be inaccurate when the source is larger than the receiver or when parts of the source are not visible from the receiver. The other major source of error arises when two areas are large relative to their separation. When this occurs, equation (2) cannot be used to estimate the form factor between them [3].

Ray tracing offers an alternative to projection methods for computing form factors [15, 20, 19]. The simplest method is to break a patch uniformly into small elements, and trace rays between the elements to determine mutual visibility. If the elements are small, the form factor between two elements can be approximated by the equation for the differential form factor. A better method, however, is to approximate the element-element form factor with the simple (closed-form) differential form factor for a point to a disk; this allows the form factor to be estimated with fewer larger samples. The accuracy of the form factor can be improved further by jittering sample positions on the source to prevent aliasing of shadow boundaries, by supersampling until the form factor converges, and by adaptively subdividing the source based on the amount of energy received [19]. These methods address many of the sources of error described in the preceding paragraph.

The second step in a radiosity algorithm is the calculation of the brightnesses. This requires solving a linear system of equations.

Using the reciprocity principle, the basic radiosity Equation (1) can be divided through by A_i, and then rewritten in the following form

$$B_i = E_i + \rho_i \sum_j^n F_{ij} B_j. \tag{6}$$

A similar equation can be written for every element. All these equations hold simultaneously, so the solution to the radiosity transport equation is the solution of the following matrix equation.

$$\begin{bmatrix} 1 & -\rho_1 F_{1,2} & \cdots & -\rho_1 F_{1,n-1} & -\rho_1 F_{1,n} \\ -\rho_2 F_{2,1} & 1 & \cdots & \rho_2 F_{2,n-1} & \rho_2 F_{2,n} \\ \vdots & \vdots & \ddots & \vdots & \vdots \\ -\rho_{n-1} F_{n-1,1} & -\rho_{n-1} F_{n-1,2} & \cdots & 1 & -\rho_{n-1} F_{n-1,n} \\ -\rho_n F_{n,1} & -\rho_n F_{n,2} & \cdots & -\rho_n F_{n,n} & 1 \end{bmatrix} \begin{bmatrix} B_1 \\ B_2 \\ \vdots \\ B_{n-1} \\ B_n \end{bmatrix} = \begin{bmatrix} E_1 \\ E_2 \\ \vdots \\ E_{n-1} \\ E_n \end{bmatrix} \tag{7}$$

Several methods have been used to solve this system of equations. Direct matrix inversion (e.g. Gauss's method with partial pivoting) can solve the linear radiosity system in $O(n^3)$ steps. This is the method used in the original radiosity paper [10]. The matrix can also be inverted using iterative methods such as the Gauss-Seidel algorithm [5]. Each iteration requires multiplying a matrix times a vector, which requires only $O(n^2)$ operations. Moreover, because the form factor matrix is strictly diagonally dominant, iterative methods are guaranteed to converge to a solution [9], often after only a few steps. Iterative methods also have the advantage that form factors can be computed one row at a time, as needed. Thus, they need not be precomputed and stored, which becomes desirable when the number of elements is large. On the other hand, when many iterations will be required before the brightness values converge, it remains preferable to save the form factors rather than recompute them. Physically, each iteration of the Gauss-Seidel algorithm means that the new brightness of a patch is computed by gathering the incoming energy from all the other pathes. This is illustrated in Figure (2).

A competing way to organize the iteration is to shoot radiosity from one element at a time to all the other elements in the environment as shown in Figure (2B) [7]. This entails multiplying a column of the form factor matrix by one brightness value at a time:

$$\begin{bmatrix} B_1^{l+1} \\ \vdots \\ B_i^{l+1} \\ \vdots \\ B_n^{l+1} \end{bmatrix} = \begin{bmatrix} F_{1j} B_j^l \\ \vdots \\ F_{ij} B_j^l \\ \vdots \\ F_{nj} B_j^l \end{bmatrix} \tag{8}$$

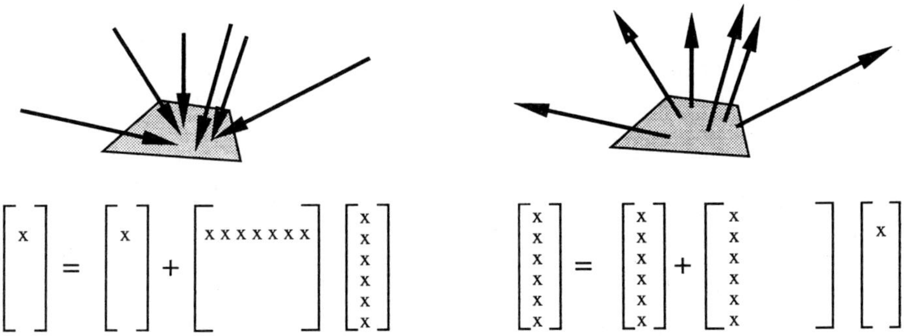

Fig. 2: Gathering vs. Shooting

Most of light energy is initially concentrated in a small number of patches: the light sources. To take advantage of this, the patches can be sorted by brightness and the brightest ones shot first. Then, only patches with unshot brightness need be used during the iteration and dark patches can be skipped, resulting in faster convergence. Another advantage of shooting over gathering is that each iteration transfers light from a bright patch to the many patches in the environment, so as calculation proceeds the image is "progressively refined".

The matrix iteration can be written using changes in brightness rather than absolute brightness:

$$\Delta B_i^{l+1} = \rho_i \sum_{j \neq i}^{n} F_{ij} \Delta B_j^l, \tag{9}$$

where $\Delta B_i^l = B_i^l - B_i^{l-1}$ and $B_i^l = \sum_j^l \Delta B_i^j$. This way of organizing the iteration simplifies testing for convergence. It also makes it convenient to sort patches based on unshot brightness.

3 Review of N-Body Formulations

The radiosity subdivision algorithm proposed in this paper is inspired by methods recently developed for solving the N-body problem. In the N-body problem, each of n particles exerts a force on all $n-1$ other particles. The straightforward solution entails calculating all $n(n-1)/2$ pairwise interactions. Appel [1], Barnes & Hut [2], and Greengard & Rokhlin [12] have each devised algorithms that compute all the forces on a particle to within a given precision in less than quadratic time. All three methods recognize the importance of hierarchical data structures for clustering particles.

Appel was the first to recognize that the forces acting on a particle need only be computed to within some numerical tolerance, and that the interaction between two clusters whose separation significantly exceeded their sizes could be reduced to a single resultant force within the allowable error. If two clusters with m particles interact directly, then the force between the two clusters can be computed in constant time rather than in $m(m-1)/2$ time. He devised a simple top-down divide and conquer algorithm for computing these forces in $O(N \log n)$ time [1]. Barnes and Hut developed an adaptive N-body algorithm that formed clusters by building an octtree from the bottom up. The leaf nodes contained single particles and the interior nodes were formed by merging eight-child clusters [2]. The algorithm makes two passes, computing total mass and center of mass while sweeping upwards, and distributing forces in a downwards traversal of the tree. Greengard and Roklin devised an $O(n)$ algorithm, using a p-term multipole expansion for the potential due to any cluster, along with algorithms for splitting, merging, and translating the resulting multipole expansions [12]. The algorithm achieves linear time by estimating the potential for each particle in some constant number of terms. There exist terms for each of the particle's nearest neighbors plus a p-term multipole expansion of the potential from the remaining particles in the system.

Both Appel and Barnes & Hut claimed, but did not prove, that their algorithms ran in $O(n \log n)$ time. More recently, Esselink has analyzed Appel's algorithm showing that time needed to calculate the forces takes $O(n)$ time [8]. The observed $O(n \log n)$ running time is a consequence of the preprocessing time required to build the hierarchical data structures.

4 Relationship Between the N-Body and Radiosity Problem

The radiosity problem shares many similarities with the N-body problem. In the N-body problem each body exerts a force on every other body resulting in $n(n-1)/2$ pairs of interactions. Similarly, in the radiosity problem each patch may scatter light to every other patch resulting in n^2 interactions. In the N-body problem, the forces obey Newton's third law and are therefore equal but opposite; in the radiosity problem, there is no requirement that the amount of light transferred between two surfaces is the same in both directions. However, the reciprocity principle does relate the form factors in both directions. Moreover, just as gravitational or electromagnetic forces fall off as $1/r^2$, the magnitude of the form factor between two patches also falls off as $1/r^2$. For this reason, the hierarchical clustering ideas like those used for the N-body problem apply to the radiosity problem.

There are differences, however. The N-body algorithms begin with n particles and must cluster them into larger groups. The radiosity algorithm usually begins with a few large patches and must subdivide them into elements. In the classical approach, the minimum size of elements needed to subdivide a patch is normally given as an input parameter A_ϵ, and all patches are divided uniformly into elements with the given area. As will be seen here, an adaptive algorithm can be used to subdivide large polygons into n smaller elements. This is done by recursively dividing the large polygon. The resulting tree decomposition is very similar to the hierarchical clusters used in the N-body algorithms. Thus, the subdivision requirement provides a convenient way to build the hierarchy needed for the clustering algorithm to work. The separate problem of building clusters out of individual patches is more difficult, and not dealt with in this paper.

Another difference is whereas the N-body problem is based on a differential equation, the radiosity problem requires the solution of an integral equation. However, as has been described, the integral equation arising from the radiosity problem can be solved efficiently using iterative techniques. Each iteration is similar to one time step of the force calculation in the N-body problem, but multiple iterations need to be performed before the solution converges. Performing this iteration efficiently requires a slightly more complicated data structure than typically is used with the N-body problem. It should also be mentioned that while the N-body problem requires the calculations of forces over time because the bodies accelerate and move to new positions, radiosity calculations are normally done for static environments with constant form factors (although see [4]).

Finally, the N-body algorithms mentioned above all take advantage of linear superposition, which states that the potential due to a cluster of particles is the sum of the potentials of the individual particles. The physics of radiosity differs. In radiosity problems, an intervening opaque surface can block the transport of light between two other surfaces, which makes the system non-linear. There is no such shielding of gravitational or electromagnetic interactions in the N-body problem precisely because superposition applies. Occlusion thereby introduces an additional cost to the radiosity problem. Nevertheless, since occlusion never increases the amount of light transported between two patches, the form factors between two patches can still be bounded from above in spite of occlusion. Although in this paper we ignore the problems caused by occlusion, the basic ideas reported here can be extended to handle this case.

5 Outline of the Hierarchical Radiosity Algorithm

Our algorithm for each step in the radiosity problem is summarized below.

- Step 1: Form Factor Computation.

For all pairwise combinations of the k input patches, simultaneously subdivide each patch recursively with respect to the other patch and build a hierarchical representation of each patch's subdivision. During the subdivision process record the interactions between patches and build the form factor matrix. The hierarchical data structure corresponding to each patch subdivision occupies $O(n)$ space. Also, as will be shown, the number of interactions between two patches is $O(n)$, so the total running time of this step is $O(n)$ and the total storage needed for the trees and the interactions lists is also $O(n)$.

- Step 2: Transport of Radiosities.

Solve the simultaneous linear equations for the patch brightnesses. This is done using iterative methods just like shooting or gathering. Since the matrix of form factors has $O(n)$ terms, each complete iteration takes only $O(n)$ time.

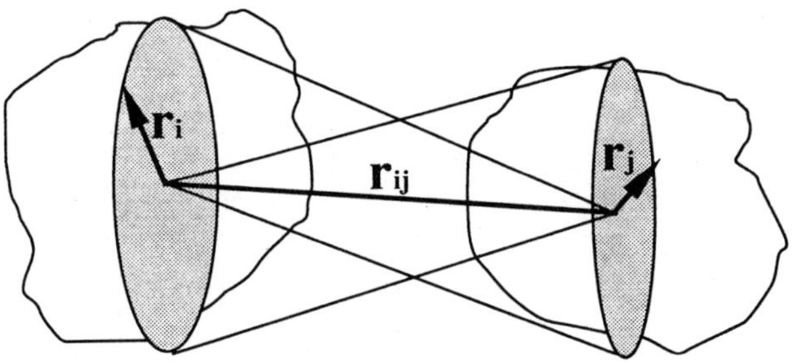

Fig. 3: Method used to Estimate Form Factor

6 Hierarchical Subdivision

The first step in a radiosity algorithm builds the hierarchies and computes the form factor matrix. This is done recursively using `Refine` that has as inputs two patches and error tolerances.

```
Refine( Patch *p, Patch *q, float Feps, float Aeps)
{
   float Fpq, Fqp;
   Fpq = FormFactorEstimate( p, q );
   Fqp = FormFactorEstimate( q, p );
   if( Fpq < Feps && Fqp < Feps )
      Link( p, q );
   else {
      if( Fpq < Fqp ) {
         if( Subdiv( q, Aeps ) ) {
```

```
                Refine( p, q->ne, Feps, Aeps );
                Refine( p, q->nw, Feps, Aeps );
                Refine( p, q->se, Feps, Aeps );
                Refine( p, q->sw, Feps, Aeps );
            }
            else
                Link( p, q );
        }
        else {
            if( Subdiv( p, Aeps ) ) {
                Refine( q, p->ne, Feps, Aeps );
                Refine( q, p->nw, Feps, Aeps );
                Refine( q, p->se, Feps, Aeps );
                Refine( q, p->sw, Feps, Aeps );
            }
            else
                Link( p, q );
        }
    }
}
```

`Refine` says that whenever the estimated form factors between two patches turn out to be smaller than some predefined F_ϵ, (`Feps` in the program), then allow the two patches to interact directly and terminate the subdivision. Link records the fact that two patches interact at a particular level in the tree. Howerer, if either of the form factors is larger than F, then split whichever patch has the larger form factor, and recursively refine the new patches. It should be mentioned that if F_ϵ is set equal to 0. Then each node will always be subdivided until its area is less than the area limit A_ϵ (`Aeps` in the program). The resulting set of interactions will be equivalent to the classical $O(n^2)$ subdivision method.

`FormFactorEstimate` returns an upper bound on the form factor from the first patch to the second patch, assuming the first patch has infinitesimal size and the second patch has finite size. The differential form factor is defined to be the solid angle that a patch subtends with respect to a point. This can be estimated by calculating the solid angle subtended by a disk with cross sectional area equal to the surface area of the patch [19]. If the patches were not planar, then the solid angle could be estimated by circumscribing a bounding sphere around each patch and estimating the solid angle subtended by each sphere with respect to the centers as shown in Figure (3).

`Subdiv` subdivides a patch into subpatches. In our implementation a patch is a planar quadrilateral, and it is subdivided equally into four new quadrilaterals by splitting it at its center. The subdivision hierarchy is stored in a quadtree; the pointers to the four children are stored in the parent fields `nw`, `ne`, `sw`, and `se`. `Subdiv` returns *false* if the patch cannot be split, which occurs if the area of the patch is smaller than some absolute predetermined area A_ϵ. If subdivision is not possible, we force the two patches to interact and use `Link` to record this information. Note that the `Refine` procedure is invoked for all pairs of input patches, therefore each patch is refined multiple times-once for every other input patch. Thus, the actual subdivision of a patch may have been performed previously when it was refined versus another patch. It the actual subdivision has already occurred, `Subdiv` simply returns *true* and need do no other work.

This subdivision technique will work in principle for any surface that can be subdivided into smaller pieces. Our decision to use planar quadrilaterals and subdivide them into fourths is not crucial to the algorithm; other patch geometries (e;g; triangles or bicubic patches) or subdivision techniques (e.g. halving with a k-D-tree) would also work.

The combination of all the interactions between nodes in the trees built by `Refine` represents the part of the form factor matrix corresponding to the interactions between

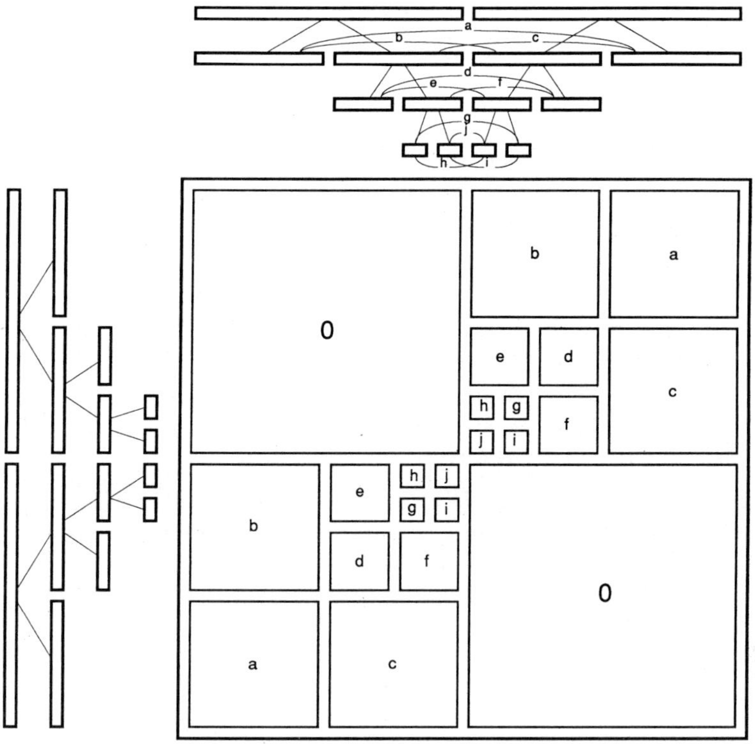

Fig. 4: The Block Form Matrix for a Particular Binary Tree Example

the two original parent patches. The number of rows and columns in the form factor matrix is equal to the number of leaves in the trees. The proper union of all the leaf nodes from a given tree exactly covers the original patch represented by the root of the tree. Interactions between leaf nodes in the tree would correspond to single entries in the standard form factor matrix. Interactions between nodes at higher levels correspond to a rectangular block of entries in the form factor matrix. Thus, the interactions between nodes in the tree can be interpreted as a coalescing of the standard form factor matrix into a set of disjoint rectangular blocks.

An example of a tree that might be produced by `Refine` and its associated form factor matrix is shown in Figure (4). For simplicity, the example illustrates the interactions between two hypothetical 1D patches. Since the patches are 1D, the subdivision is represented by a binary tree instead of quadtree. These two binary trees are drawn on the edges of the form factor matrix. Labelled arcs that connect nodes in the two trees correspond to interactions represented by blocks in the form factor matrix with the same label. The figure is drawn so that the left side and top side of each block has the same size and position as the two patches in the binary tree connected by the arc corresponding to that block. The diagonal blocks are all zero because patches are assumed not to interact with themselves. Other blocks are non-zero and contain a single number which is the form factor between the patches at that level in the tree. Notice that the size of the block depends on what level the patches reside in the tree.

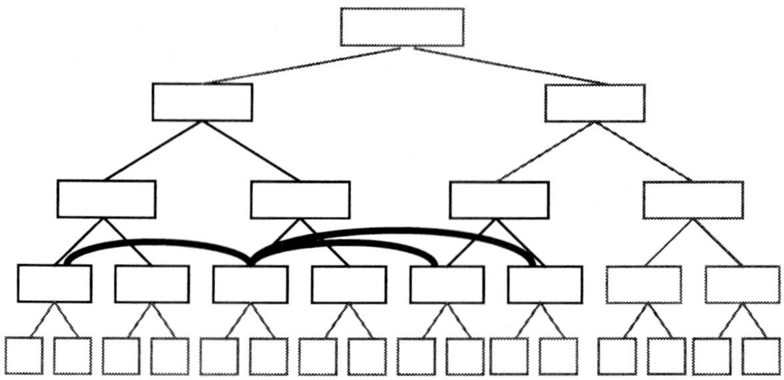

Fig. 5: Interactions Within a Binary Tree

7 Analysis of the Hierarchical Subdivision

The key result of this preprocessing is that each block in the form factor matrix has approximately the same value and error, and that there are at most a linear number of blocks.

To see that each interaction has the same error we show that the termination criteria also place an upper bound on the error associated with the form factor between the two interacting patches. In the N-body problem, the error in treating the potential of a cluster as a single particle varies as $(r/R)^2$, where r is the radius of the cluster, and R is the distance between the two clusters. This error analysis is based on the multipole expansion of the force due to a cluster [1, 12]. In the radiosity problem, the error introduced by using a single differential form factor to approximate the interaction between the two patches also varies as $(r/R)^2$. This can be verified by comparing the differential form factor to the form factor from a point to a disk of radius r, where the distance from the point to the center is R. The form factor to a disk is equal to

$$F_{disk} \approx \frac{r^2}{R^2 + r^2} = \left(\frac{r}{R}\right)^2 \left(1 - \left(\frac{r}{R}\right)^2 + \left(\frac{r}{R}\right)^4 + \cdots\right) \tag{10}$$

This differs from differential form factor only in the higher order terms. Thus, the magnitude of the form factor, as well as the error due to the finiteness of the geometry, have both been bounded by $(r/R)^2$. When $F \approx (r/R)^2$ is small, that is, the sizes of the patches are small compared to the distance separating them, then the differential form factor is a good estimate of the true form to within the error bound. Note that the size here is relative. Two large patches may interact if they are separated by a large distance, whereas two small patches may interact if separated by small distances. F_ϵ acts as the error bound in `Refine`.

The second key result of this preprocessing is the construction of a form factor matrix with fewer than n^2 blocks. Recall that for any leaf element, all its interactions with other patches is represented by a row in the form factor matrix. This row slices through rectangular blocks some of whose size may be greater than 1 and which represent interactions between interior nodes higher in the tree. Recall also that the form factor associated with each interaction is approximately F_ϵ. If it had been larger, Refine would already have split that node. As stated by Equation (4), the sum of all the form factors from a leaf node must equal 1. Thus, the total number of interactions from a leaf node including all its parents is roughly equal to $1/F_\epsilon$, which is constant. It depends on the precision required, but not on the total number of elements in the system. In effect, $1/F_\epsilon$ sets the resolution of the hemisphere above each patch. It then follows that the total number of blocks in the form factor matrix varies as $O(n)$ and not n^2, since each patch interacts with at most a constant number of other patches. This saving is the essential contribution of our method.

The above analysis slightly overestimates the number of independent form factors because interactions of interior nodes are counted more than once . A more precise argument for the number of form factors scaling linearly is based on simple counting. For simplicity, consider the 1D problem of n equally spaced patches along a line. Let us construct a binary tree (not a quadtree) above the patches by merging adjacent contiguous patches recursively. This is shown in Figure (5). The error criterion says that two patches can interact directly only if $(r/R)^2 < F_\epsilon$. In other words, two patches of size r can interact only if the distance R between them is greater than $r/\sqrt{F_\epsilon}$. For concreteness, let us fix F_ϵ so that this criterion is equivalent to saying that two patches at the same level in the binary tree can interact only if at least one other patch at that level is between them. Now consider the interactions of a patch p in the interior of the tree. At any level in the tree, the above rule forbids the patch p from interacting with its immediate sibling or with the closest of its two first cousins, since they occupy positions adjacent to it. Potentially p may need to interact with all the other patches at its level, but most of these interactions are handled by p's ancestors. p's parent is forbidden from interacting with its immediate neighbors by the same criterion, but it may interact with neighbors further away. Thus, p's parent and ancestors handle all the interactions except those to $p's$ parent's immediate neighbors. So p must connect to the children of its parent's immediate neighbors unless they are too close to it. Figure (5) shows a node p and part of a binary tree containing p. p makes three connections to nodes at its level. These are the 4 children of the two patches that its parent could not connect to, minus the cousin which is directly next to it. Interactions with any patches further aways will have been handled by ancestors.

This argument applies to all levels of the tree, except the top, the bottom, and the sides. There are not direct interactions at the top two levels because every patch is too close to the other patches; at the lowest level there are interactions with nearest neighbors, since there are no children to handle the interactions otherwise. This yields 5 direct interactions on the bottom level of the tree in our example. There are also boundary effects at the sides of the tree, which decrease the total number of interactions and can be ignored for our purposes. The final result is that each node in the tree connects to a constant number of other nodes. Thus, the total number of interactions is proportional to the number of nodes in the tree, which is $O(n)$. A similar analysis has been derived independently by [8].

Similar arguments can be made with quadtrees or octtrees. For quadtrees, the number of interactions at the leaf nodes is $6^2 - 1 = 35$, and the number at an interior node is $6^2 - (3^2 - 1) = 28$. The quadtree case is similar to the interaction of two parallel quadrilaterals.

Figure (6) shows the quadtree subdivision of a pair of perpendicular polygons computed by `Refine`. Also shown in this figure are the actual interactions at each level in the subdivision. This figure shows that each interior patch undergoes a constant number of interactions with other patches regardless of their level in the tree. Large patches that are far apart interact directly, in the same way that small patches near each other in the corner interact directly.

In summary, our hierarchical subdivision method computes the form factor matrix to within a fixed error tolerance automatically. In the process it reorganizes the form factor matrix into blocks; the estimated form factor associated with each block has the same value and error as other blocks. Furthermore, the total number of blocks grows at most linearly in the number of elements.

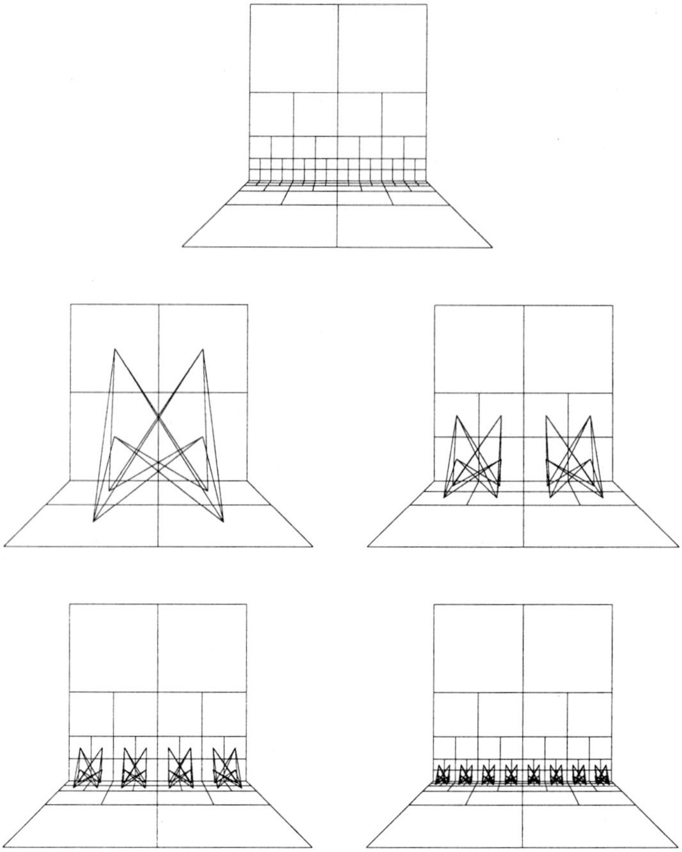

Fig. 6: Interactions Between Two Perpendicular Polygons

8 Iterative Solution

Once the form factors have been determined, the next step is to solve for the radiosities. As seen in the introduction the most efficient way to do this is to invert the matrix iteratively. Each iteration involves multiplying a matrix times a vector, which normally takes $O(n^2)$ operations. However, because the form factor matrix produced by our algorithm is represented with $O(n)$ blocks, each matrix multiplication can be done in linear time. In this section we will show how this is done, and give program fragments that implement the techniques of gathering and shooting.

The block matrix multiply can be made efficient because the blocks representing the matrix connect nodes in a tree representing the vector. The leaves of the tree represent elements of the vector, and the interior nodes in the tree correspond to recursively merging elements of the vector together.

The matrix multiplication proceeds in three steps. The first step computes a value for each interior node in the tree. This value is equal to the average value of all the elements of the vector comprising that node. This calculation can be done in a single depth-first traversal of the tree propagating averages upward. To compute the average for each node, the averages of its children are computed, and then the average of the node is set to the average of its children's values. The second step multiplies the value of each block times the appropriate average value of the source node and adds the result to the appropriate destination node in the tree. For each block this takes constant time. Finally, the third step distributes the results from the interior nodes to the elements of the vector. This is done by another depth first traversal of the tree which propagates values down to the leaf nodes. Each interior node adds its accumulated value to its children's values, recursively. The running time of this algorithm is easy to analyze. The upwards and downwards traversals of the trees can be done in n time. It also only takes $O(n)$ time to perform the block multiplies because there are $O(n)$ blocks. By using this algorithm, the result is that each iteration can be done in linear time.

There is one caveat to this method when used to perform an iterative matrix inversion. The broadcasting of the output must be deferred until the entire matrix multiplication has been completed, which requires allocating storage for two vectors. Also, iterations often converge faster when updated in place. Our method would permit this if additional passes were made through the tree to update the vector and recompute its averages, but we have not found this necessary.

It may be instructive to consider the physics of radiosity instead of the mathematics of general matrix iteration. The first step computes the brightness of the interior patches by averaging the brightnesses of their children weighted by their relative areas, and the second step multiplies individual blocks. Each block represents a form factor, and multiplying the form factor by the average patch brightness corresponds to shooting the energy of that patch to another patch. Finally, after the energy from some number of patches has been transported, each patch contains all the incoming energy which it has gathered. The new brightness of the leaf patches are then computed by summing the incoming energy of all their parents.

9 Gathering

The classic Jacobi iteration can be implemented using the following simple recursive procedure. For convenience the iteration is organized around ΔB's.

```
Gather( Patch *p )
{
   patch *q;
   float Fpq;
   if( p ) {
```

```
        p->dBg = 0.0;
        ForAllElements( q, p->arcs ) {
            Fpq = FormFactor( p, q );
            p->dBg += Fpq * p->rho * q->dBs;
        }
        Gather( p->sw );
        Gather( p->se );
        Gather( p->nw );
        Gather( p->ne );
    }
}
```

This procedure assumes the average brightness of each patch is stored in `dBs`, the delta brightness that needs to be shot. For leaf patches this is initially set to the amount of emitted light; for interior patches this is set to the average values, as discussed in the last section. Each patch also has diffuse color stored in `rho`. The delta brightness gathered is stored in `dBg`, and is computed by receiving energy from all the patches which interact with this patch. This process can then be applied recursively to the subpatches.

At this point, the form factor between the two patches needs to be computed. If the patches are completely visible to each other, then the form factor can be estimated within the allowable error using Equation (2).

10 Shooting

The radiosity equation can also be solved by shooting instead of gathering. The first step initializes patch brightnesses. After this, however, all the patches are sorted into a priority queue based on their brightness. Then a patch at a time is taken off the queue, and its energy shot to the other patches with this procedure.

```
Shoot( Patch *p )
{
    patch *q;
    float Fpq;
    ForAllElements( q, p->arcs ) {
        Fqp = FormFactor( q, p );
        q->dBg += Fqp * q->rho * p->dBs;
    }
    p->dBs = 0.0;
    ReSort( p );
}
```

`Shoot` distributes the unshot radiosity from a given patch to all other patches it interacts with directly. Once all the energy has been shot from the given node, that node is placed at the end of the queue with `ReSort`. This procedure is called repeatedly until the amount of unshot energy in the patch at the head of the queue is below some threshold.

11 Results

Figure (7) plots the number of interactions calculated by Refine for two simple geometries: two parallel and two perpendicular polygons. The graphs show the actual number of interactions versus the number of potential interactions at a fixed uniform level of discretization. These plots verify the $O(n)$ behavior for parallel polygons. The number of interactions for perpendicular polygons surprisingly, however, goes as $O(\sqrt{n})$. The reason for this is that the subdivision induced between two perpendicular polygons is comparable

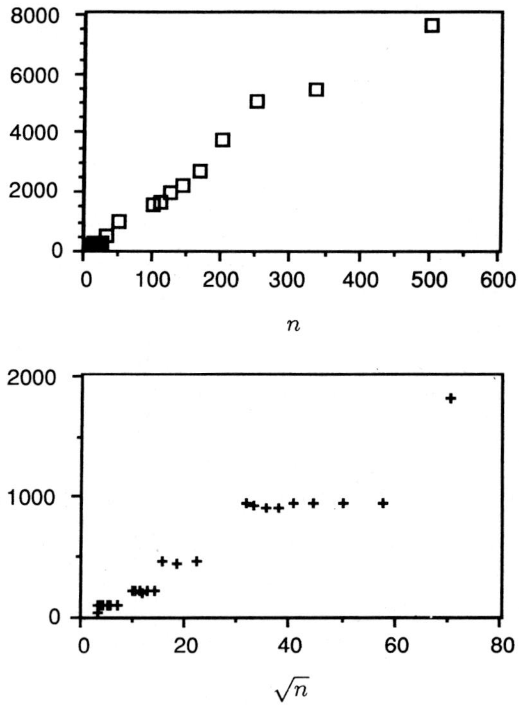

Fig. 7: Number of interactions between parallel (above) and perpendicular (below) polygons

to a binary tree turned on its side with its leaf nodes along the common edge, as in Figure (4). The total number of nodes in such a sideways binary tree will be $O(\sqrt{n})$. In general, the worst case occurs when two equal-sized polygons are near each other and directly facing; fewer form factors will be needed in all other cases. Note that in Figure 7 there are several plateaus; these result because of the all-or-none decision to subdivide or not subdivide.

To verify the accuracy of the form factors generated by our method, we compared the computed form factors with the analytical form factors which are available, for the same geometries shown in Figure (7) (see, for example, [16]). To compute the form factor between two finite areas, `Refine` can be modified to return the sum of the form factors of a patch's children or, if the patch is a leaf, the product of the patch's area and the differential form factor to the other patch. Figure (8) shows the measured relative error between the computed and the analytical form factors as a function of F_ϵ. As expected, the actual error in the form factor is proportional to the F_ϵ given to `Refine` as predicted by the theory.

As a final test of these ideas we modeled the interior of a barren room with 6 polygons of different diffuse colors, following [10]. For simplicity, the scene was illuminated with a single point light source at the center of the room. Figure (9) shows the hierarchical subdivision produced by `Refine` with a $F_\epsilon = 0.05$ and a $A_\epsilon = (1/16)^2$. The top figure is the quadtree subdivision; each subsequent row shows all interactions of the rear wall at that level of the hierarchy with all walls except the front wall, which is

not shown. A_ϵ was chosen so that each wall was divided into a grid of 16×16 elements. The additional refinement near the walls is a consequence of `Refine` improving the error bounds. Using the uniform subdivision, 983040 form factors were computed (6 walls interacting pairwise, with $16^2 \times 16^2$ elements interacting for each of the 15 pairs). Using hierarchical subdivision, only 2940 were computed. Of the 15 interactions between

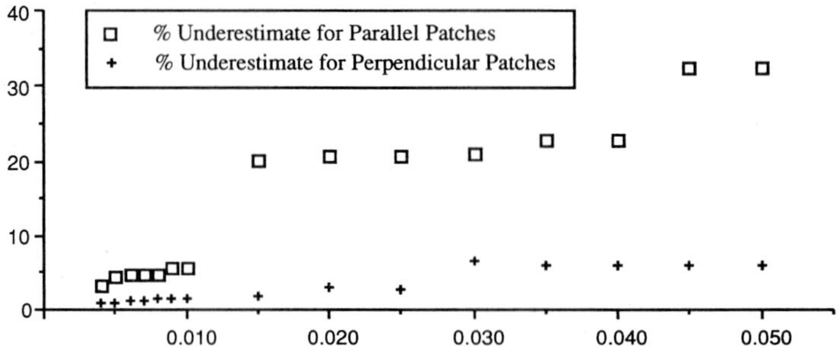

Fig. 8: Measured Relative Percentage Error vs. F_ϵ

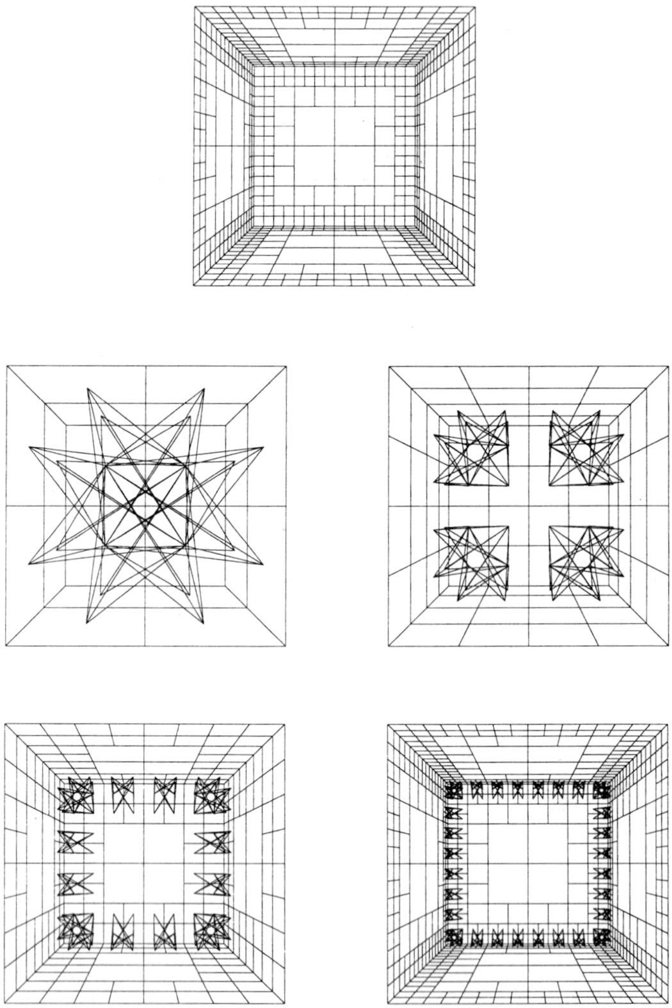

Fig. 9: Hierarchical Subdivision of a Room

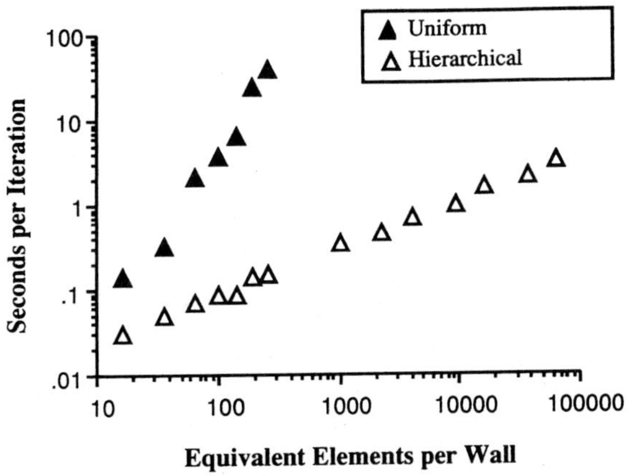

Fig. 10: Comparison of Hierarchical and Uniform Speeds

walls of the room, 12 are between perpendicular polygons and 3 are between parallel polygons. Thus the number of interactions in this example is dominated by terms that vary as $O(\sqrt{n})$. Figure (11) shows the solution converging after each iteration for both the hierarchical and uniform subdivisions. To emphasize the brightnesses of individual patches, we draw them here with constant brightness, although in practice patches would be drawn by interpolating brightnesses smoothly between vertices and by averaging the brightnesses of adjacent patches. Each iteration using our hierarchical method took approximately 0.15 seconds, versus 40 seconds for the uniform case. If we merely increased the subdivision to 64×64 subdivision, our method would run more than thirty thousand times faster than uniform subdivision. Figure (10) show relative timings for the uniform and hierarchical methods as a function of the desired precision. As previously mentioned, the time spent per iteration is varying as n^2 using the uniform method and as $\sqrt{n}$ using the hierarchical method.

12 Discussion

We have presented a new algorithm and data structure for radiosity calculations. It is based on an adaptive subdivision algorithm which automatically estimates form factors to a fixed error tolerance. More importantly, this algorithm allows patches in the subdivision to interact at different levels of detail. Large patches which are far away from each other are allowed to interact directly, whereas nearby patches are subdivided to the appropriate size based on their separating distance. This technique reduces the number of interactions from n^2 to $O(n)$ and in some cases $O(\sqrt{n})$. This work illustrates the importance of numerical analysis in the design of graphics algorithms. The algorithm is also easy to implement and we think will make global illumination calculations more practical for both realism and interactive applications.

Currently, the most common method for reducing the size of the form factor matrix involves breaking it into two levels [6]. The first level contains the patches, and the second level contains the elements into which each patch is broken. The number of elements that a patch is broken is normally fixed *a priori*, but could be determined adaptively. In the patch-element method, radiosity is always shot from patches to elements, even if they are far aways, and the new radiosity of a patch is computed by averaging the brightness of its elements. In our algorithm, radiosity from a patch is shot to patches at the appropriate resolution. Only if the receiving patch is very close will that patch be an element. Also, the patch-element method always treats sources as patches. This may lead to errors when the source is large, both because its brightness is proportional to its area, and because the form factor to a large source may have a large error when it is near to the receiver. In these cases, our algorithm automatically causes the source to be broken into smaller pieces.

The ideas developed in this paper can be used to speed up conventional hemi-cube algorithms. Remember that one way of explaining why our algorithm is linear is that each element subdivides the hemisphere above it into a fixed number of subdivisions independent of the number of other elements, but dependent on the precision required. Once the precision is fixed, the patch size of other patches in the environment should be chosen so that their projection covers approximately one pixel on the hemi-cube. There is no need to subdivide them further, since all the subdivided pieces would all project onto the same pixel and no new information would be gained.

As described in this paper, we subdivide patches first and then solve the equations for the radiosities. A better implementation would be to perform subdivision on demand using lazy evaluation. One application of this capability would be to successively solve for radiosities by gradually decreasing F_ϵ. Each time F_ϵ decreases, the patches would be subdivided further. This type of refinement algorithm would allow coarse solutions to be computed very quickly, with few elements, and gradually patches would be adaptively subdivided into finer pieces as the picture was refined. This idea is similar to the multi-grid method.

Another variation that would work effectively with lazy evaluation would be to subdivide based on brightness and angle instead of angle alone. During each iteration, the brightness of each patch increases, so its chances of being subdivided do too. Initially, when the brightness is low, a patch need not be subdivided much. As its brightness increases, so do its interactions with neighbors, so it needs to be computed more accurately and further subdivision should occur. Many of the interactions occur between pairs of patches in corners and along edges. However, these patches tend to be darker than large central areas near the light sources, so subdividing these based on brightness would avoid the needless calculations of their interactions until light was actually transported onto them.

We have begun to extend the algorithm described here to handle environments with occlusion. Occlusion exists in all systems of useful complexity, but violates the principle of linear superposition. The first fact to note is that the true form factor between two patches in the presence of occlusion can never be greater than the form factor estimate used in this paper. This is because intervening occluding surfaces can only decrease the percentage of light that is transported between two surfaces. Thus, the form factor estimate sets an upper bound on the form factor; the true form factor lies between 0 and this bound. This means that the methods used in this paper can still be used to estimate the appropriate resolution of two interacting patches. Once this is done, the exact form factor can be computed using ray tracing to test for visibility. Since the factor for all interactions has approximately the same magnitude, it is also reasonable to perform the same number of visibility tests per interaction. This means that the number of visibility probes varies as the number of interactions, which is linear. Each probe, however, could require n intersection tests against other patches, which increases the total running time of the algorithm. These results will be reported in a companion paper.

Acknowledgements

The authors wish to thank Andrew Appel, Toby Orloff and Jeffrey Posdamer.

References

[1] A.A. Appel. An efficient program for many-body simulation. *SIAM J. Sci. Stat. Computing*, 6(1):85–103, 1985.

[3] D. R. Baum, H. E. Rushmeier, and J. M. Winget. Improving radiosity solution through the use of analytically determined form-factors. *Computer Graphics*, 23(3):335–344, July 1989.

[4] S.E. Chen. Incremental radiosity: an extension of progressive radiosity to an interactive image synthesis system. *Computer Graphics*, 24(3), 1990.

[5] M. Cohen and D. Greenberg. The hemi-cube, a radiosity solution for complex environments. *Computer graphics*, 19(3):31–40, 1985.

[6] M.F. Cohen, D.P. Greenberg, D.S. Immel, and P.J. Brock. An efficient radiosity approach for complex environments. *IEEE Computer Graphics and Applications*, 6(2):26–30, 1986.

[7] Michael F. Cohen, Shenchang E. Chen, John R. Wallace, and Donald P. Greenberg. A progessive refinement approach to fast radiosity image generation. *Computer Graphics*, 22(4):75–84, 1988.

[8] E. Esselink. Computing science Note KE5-1, University of Groningen, 1989.

[9] D.K. Faddeev and V.N. Faddeeva. *Computational methods of linear algebra.* W.H. Freeman and Co., San Francisco, 1963.

[10] C. M. Goral, D. P. Greenberg K. E. Torrance, and B. Battaile. Modeling the interaction of light between diffuse surfaces. *Computer Graphics*, 18(3):213–222, 1984.

[11] D.P. Greenberg. Introduction to radiosity. SIGGRAPH'90 Course Notes, 1989.

[12] L. Greengard. *The rapid evaluation of potential fields in particle systems.* MIT Press, Cambridge, MA, 1988.

[13] H.C. Hottel and A.F. Sarofim. *Radiative transfer.* McGraw-Hill, New York, 1967.

[14] J.T. Kajiya. The rendering equation. *Computer Graphics*, 143–150, 1987.

[15] G. Maxwell, M.J. Bailey, and V.W. Goldschmidt. Calculation of radiation configuration factor using ray tracing. *Computer Aided Design*, 18(7):371–379, 1986.

[16] R. Siegel and J. R. Howell. *Thermal Radiation Heat Transfer.* Hemisphere Publishing Corporation, New York, 1981.

[17] F. Sillion and C. Puech. A general two-pass method integrating specular and diffuse reflection. *Computer Graphics*, 23(3):335–344, July 1989.

[18] E.M Sparrow and R.D. Cess. *Radiation heat transfer.* Hemisphere Publishing Co., Washington, DC, 1978.

[19] J. R. Wallace, K. A. Elmquist, and E. A. Haines. A ray tracing algorithm for progressive radiosity. *Computer Graphics*, 23(3):315–324, 1989.

[20] G. J. Ward, F. M. Rubinstein, and R. D. Clear. A ray tracing solution for diffuse interreflection. *Computer Graphics*, 22(3):85–92, 1988.

Fast Radiosity by Parallelization

Werner Purgathofer, Michael Zeiller

Abstract

A parallel solution of the radiosity approach for realistic image rendering is presented. The tremendous costs of computation power and memory of radiosity implementations are met by parallelization on a computer architecture based on transputers. Form-factors are computed in parallel and independently on several processors, thus giving a high acceleration of this most computationally intensive task. Parallel solutions for equation solving and rendering are also introduced. These parallelizations of the radiosity approach leed to an extraordinary speed-up in image generation and can be adapted for different kinds of parallel computer architectures.

1 Introduction

Algorithms for realistic image rendering, like ray-tracing [13][10] and radiosity [6][2][3], are known for their high costs in memory and computation power. Radiosity, for example, is affected by the quadratic order of the form-factor computation which makes the image generation of complex scenes very expensive. Several variations of the radiosity algorithm have been developed to achieve an algorithmic improvment [4][12]. Another way of accelerating radiosity is by using parallel processors for the radiosity computation [1][9]. Ideally the speed-up on image generation would be linear to the number of processors. However, by using parallel processors a much higher speed-up can be achieved than by new algorithms. Nevertheless, parallel computer architectures will gain more and more influence when supercomputer power is required, since they offer enormous, scaleable amounts of computing resources. Radiosity, like ray tracing [8], fits perfectly for implementation on a parallel computer architecture. Form-factor computation, the computationally most intensive task of quadratic order, can be split into independent jobs that can be computed in parallel.

This paper presents a parallel implementation of the conventional non-progressive radiosity approach on a transputer architecture that supports parallel computation. No extensions to the theoretical background of the radiosity formula are made. This project concentrates on the efficient utilization of a multiprocessor system for the radiosity computation.

2 Parallel Architecture

The computer architecture which was used for this project is based on transputers. Transputers are a highly flexible solution for assembling parallel computers whose performance figures can be easily increased by simply adding new processors without changing the software. Since there are many different types of parallel computers, the architecture has great influence on the development of parallel algorithms.

We are using a system of 29 INMOS T800 transputers (10 MIPS, 1.5 MFlops) [11] with 2MB RAM each, arranged on 5 motherboards. The T800 has an on-chip Floating Point Unit which leads to further acceleration of the radiosity evaluation because many floating point operations have to be performed. Transputers can communicate with other transputers via 4 links, but there is no common bus and therefore the transputers have to be arranged in a way which meets the communication requirements of the application. One of the transputers is connected to the host (in our configuration an IBM-PC) and therefore serves for input/output of the transputer network.

Most important for parallel algorithms is the fact that transputers do not have shared memory, but only local memory assigned to each processing unit. Thus the 2MB memory of each transputer module has to contain the program and all data. Adding more transputers to the network not only increases the performance, but also the memory capacity. The best utilization of transputer power can be achieved by programming in OCCAM [7], a language for parallel programming which was developed for transputers.

3 Radiosity

3.1 Radiosity Algorithm

The radiosity algorithm calculates the radiated light intensity of polygonal surfaces, i.e. patches, in a closed environment. Given a number of n patches with their emission and reflectivity in the basic colors red, green and blue, the radiosity of each patch can be evaluated if the radiated intensity is considered to be constant for the whole area of the patch. Thus the relationship between the radiosities of all patches in the closed environment can be expressed as a set of equations:

$$B_i = E_i + \rho_i \sum_{j=1}^{n} F_{ij} B_j$$

B_i ... radiosity of patch i, total intensity of radiated light, sum of emitted and reflected light energy
E_i ... emitted light energy of patch i
ρ_i ... reflectivity of patch i
F_{ij} ... form-factor, fraction of radiated light energy of patch j, that reaches patch i

These n equations make up a linear equation system that can be expressed in matrix form:

$$\begin{pmatrix} 1-\rho_1F_{11} & -\rho_1F_{12} & \cdots & -\rho_1F_{1n} \\ -\rho_2F_{21} & 1-\rho_2F_{22} & \cdots & -\rho_2F_{2n} \\ \vdots & \vdots & & \vdots \\ -\rho_nF_{n1} & -\rho_nF_{n2} & \cdots & 1-\rho_nF_{nn} \end{pmatrix} * \begin{pmatrix} B_1 \\ B_2 \\ \vdots \\ B_n \end{pmatrix} = \begin{pmatrix} E_1 \\ E_2 \\ \vdots \\ E_n \end{pmatrix}$$

Form-factors F_{ij} can be computed using hemi-cubes or other techniques, which represents the main part of the radiosity computation.

The linear equation system can be solved by Gauss-Seidel iteration. Changes in light emission or reflectivity of some patches do not affect the form-factor computation, but only cause another run of equation solving.

The computed radiosity values can be visualized by a z-buffer or other technique for hidden-surface removal. Other rendering techniques interpolate the radiosity values which are computed in the middle of the patches to the vertices and use various shading methods for the generation of high quality, smooth shaded images.

3.2 Form-Factor Computation

3.2.1 Overview

The form-factors F_{ij} are evaluated using hemi-cubes [2]. A z-buffer is applied for visibility detection by placing a hemi-cube above each receiving patch i and projecting all other patches j onto its faces. The high costs of the form-factor computation are caused by this $O(n^2)$ projections of patches and are also influenced by the discretization of the hemi-cube.

Each patch j passes through a pipeline where simple tests are applied, checking whether further computations are necessary. After a patch j has run through this pipeline, the form-factor F_{ij} can be calculated as a weighted sum of all pixels of the hemi-cube on which patch j is seen. The weight factors are the delta form-factors as introduced in [2].

3.2.2 Hemi-Cube

The base of the hemi-cube of height 1 and length 2 is placed in the plane of the patch with its center in the center of the patch (Fig. 1). This point is also the origin of a local coordinate system made up of the vectors X_i, Y_i, and Z_i, with Z_i the normal vector of the patch plane, X_i an arbitrary vector in the patch plane and Y_i a vector orthogonal to X_i and Z_i.

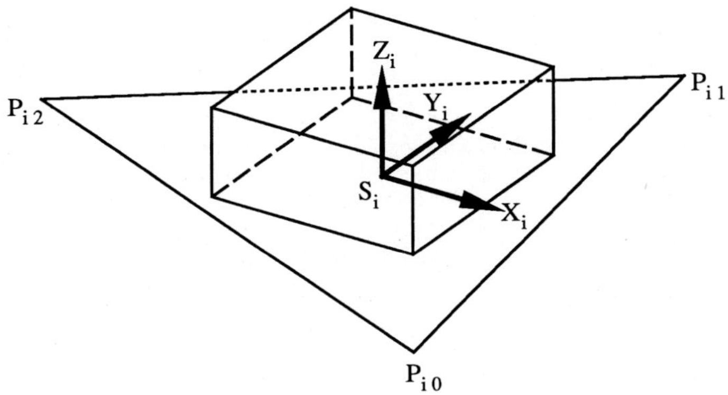

Fig. 1: Hemi-cube on patch

The upper face of the hemi-cube is divided into 2Rx2R grid cells and the lateral faces are divided into 2RxR grid cells. Therefore $12R^2$ pixel values have to be stored for each hemi-cube consisting of a Z-value and a patch number. The delta form-factors have to be calculated and kept in local memory, too.

3.2.3 Projection Pipeline

The patches j which are projected onto the hemi-cube of patch i have to pass a pipeline. Each step of this pipeline applies various tests to decide whether further computations have to be done or the projection of this patch can be terminated.

First of all it has to be checked whether the patch is potentially visible, i.e. patch i and patch j are facing against each other, by evaluating the formula $N_j.(S_j-S_i) < 0$ (N_j .. normal vector of patch j; S_i, S_j .. centers of patch i, j).

If this check is true, the patch can be visible and then the visibility of the patch vertices is examined. Since we are using hemi-cubes a vertex is visible if it is situated above the patch plane and therefore each vertex P_{jk} is tested against the patch plane: $N_i.(P_{jk}-S_i) > 0$. If no vertex is visible the processing of this patch can be terminated.

Otherwise the vertices of patch j are transformed into hemi-cube coordinates:

$$Q_{jk}^{x} = X_i \bullet (P_{jk} - S_i)$$
$$Q_{jk}^{y} = Y_i \bullet (P_{jk} - S_i)$$
$$Q_{jk}^{z} = Z_i \bullet (P_{jk} - S_i)$$

P_{jk} ... vertex k of patch j in global coordinates
Q_{jk} ... vertex k of patch j in hemi-cube coordinates

Now patch j has to be projected onto the five hemi-cube faces. The clipping planes Z=X, Z=-X, Z=Y and Z=-Y devide the hemi-cube world into five projection spaces, each of them belonging to a hemi-cube face. At first the patch is projected onto the hemi-cube face which corresponds to the space the patch center is placed in. For each projection the patch is clipped at its bounding planes [5] and the vertices of the resulting polygons are projected onto the hemi-cube faces. By remembering on which planes the polygon has been clipped, the number of projections can be reduced.

The patch, now available in 2D coordinates of the hemi-cube faces, has to be written into the corresponding z-buffers using a filling algorithm for convex polygons [5]. Z-values are computed incrementally based on the formula

$$z = \frac{(S_j - S_i) \cdot N_j}{V_{xy} \cdot N_j}$$

where V_{xy} is the vector from the hemi-cube origin to the center of the pixel.

After all patches have been projected on the hemi-cube of patch i, the form-factors F_{ij} are determined by summing the delta form-factors of all pixels which are covered by patch j.

3.3 Equation Solving

The linear equation system is solved with the Gauss-Seidel method. The iteration starts with using the emission of the patches as initial radiosities. New radiosities are computed until Gauss-Seidel converges and the radiosities do not change during two successive iterations.

The Gauss-Seidel method has to be applied to each of the colors red, green and blue since the emission and the reflectivity of the patches vary for these basic colors, thus giving the radiosities in red, green and blue.

3.4 Rendering

The actual implementation is using a simple z-buffer algorithm for visualization. The same method as used for form-factor computation is applied, now projecting onto a single hemi-cube whose center is the eye-point. The resolution of the image determines the length and width of the hemi-cube whereas the distance of the eye-point to the image plane corresponds to its height. After applying transformations to a height of 1 and a length and width of 2 and a transformation of the camera coordinate system into the origin of the coordinate system, the rendering can be done in the same way as demonstrated for the form-factor computation.

4 Parallel Radiosity

4.1 Transputer Network

Based on the transputer hardware and the interconnection capabilites of transputers a relatively simple arrangement of the transputers has been chosen that meets the requirements of all three steps of the radiosity computation: a ring.

The first transputer in the network - let's call it the 'Manager' - is connected to the host. It is used for input/output and controls the radiosity computation. The other transputers perform the evaluation of the radiosity approach and therefore they are called 'Workers'. This results in the arrangement of transputers as shown in Fig. 2.

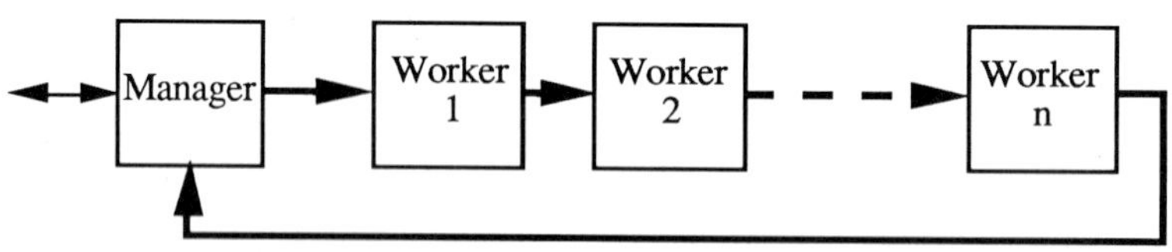

Fig. 2: Transputer network

Each of the Workers has to do the same job which can be separated into communication and calculation tasks. These tasks are performed by two processes running in pseudo-parallel - the 'Communicator' and the 'Calculator' (Fig. 3). The Calculator, which is performing the radiosity computation, communicates with other transputers only via the Communicator. The Communicator transfers only data - between neighbouring transputers or between its neighbours and the Calculator.

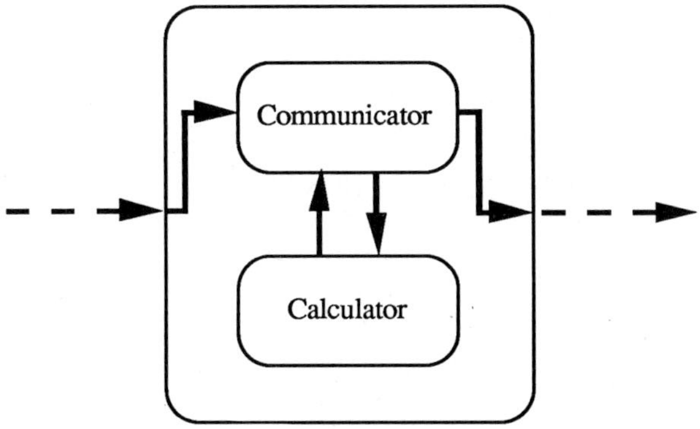

Fig. 3: Parallel processes of Worker

The following presentation of the parallel evaluation of radiosity values is separated into the description of the three parallel processes:

- Manager
- Calculator
- Communicator

4.2 Parallel Form-factor Computation

4.2.1 Overview

Form-factors are computed by projecting all patches onto the faces of a hemi-cube placed over each receiving patch. The description of the scene is not kept in local memory of the Workers because this would require high amounts of memory. Therefore all patches of the scenen have to be transmitted to the Workers by the Manager which has direct access to the scene data, where they are projected onto the hemi-cubes. This has to be performed several times since in each pass only a certain number of hemi-cubes, i.e. rows of the form-factor matrix, can be evaluated by each Worker due to restrictions in memory.

4.2.2 Manager

The Manager starts the form-factor computation by transmitting the hemi-cube half width resolution to the Workers which then compute the delta form-factors. Depending on the number of patches of the scene and the number of Workers in the transputer network the number of hemi-cubes (number of equations) for each Worker is determined by equally distributing the hemi-cubes to all Workers. The allocation of the patches to the Workers is done at the beginning of the computation because it has to be fixed for the equation solving. To ensure an almost equal utilization of all transputers the patches are assigned randomly to the Workers. Therefore no real load balancing is performed since the allocation remains unchanged throughout the computation.

After these initializations the first run of form-factor computation begins. Each Worker sends a message to the Manager telling it how many hemi-cubes (patches) it can process because the amount of free memory for hemi-cube data varies during the radiosity computation (see also 4.2.3). Depending on this number the Manager sends several patch descriptions to each Worker. Afterwards all patches are transmitted through the ring. Thereby several patches are combined to a block, a block of size 0 indicating the end of patch transmission. Then the

Manager has to wait until the Workers return the number of patches they can process in the next run.

This run is repeated several times until all patches have been processed and all form-factors have been computed. During each run a certain amount of patches can be processed in parallel, thus computing several rows of the form-factor matix at the same time. The results are kept in the local memories of the transputers which have calculated them.

The task of the Manger can be expressed in pseudo-code:

```
WHILE some patches unprocessed
  send 'Next Round Flag'
  receive 'Hemi-cube free'-messages from all Workers
  send description of receiving patches to Workers
  FOR all patches DO
    send block of patches to Workers
  END
  send empty block
END
send 'Stop Flag'
```

4.2.3 Calculator

After the Calculator receives the hemi-cube resolution, the delta form-factors are computed and the arrays for the hemi-cube data are initialized.

Now the hemi-cube loop begins. A message, how many patches, i.e. hemi-cubes, can be evaluated in the next run, is sent to the Manager via the Communicator. The patch descriptions are received and the hemi-cubes for each patch are initialized. Then all patches of the scene are read in block by block. For each hemi-cube which is evaluated in this run the patches of each block are projected onto all hemi-cube surfaces as described in section 3.2. After all patches of the complete scene have been processed, the corresponding form-factors are computed.

The hemi-cube loop is performed until no more patches are left whose form-factors need to be computed.

Transputers only have access to their local memory (2MB in our configuration). Therefore the complete program code and all data have to be kept in this local memory. Since the program code has fixed length there is a certain amount of memory left for data. Besides some local data like delta form-factors, there is some memory free for both hemi-cube data and form-factors.

The form-factors, which are computed in a single run of the hemi-cube loop, have to be stored in the local memory of the transputer on which they have been computed, because they are needed as input for the parallel equation solving. However, the matrix is very sparse and the form-factors can be stored in a compressed format. After evaluating the form-factors for a receiving patch those fom-factors which are non-zero are stored consecutively by identifying the number of the sending patch (INT16) and the form-factor value (REAL32). Therefore each form-factor entry requires 6 bytes of memory.

On the other hand the amount of memory for a single hemi-cube depends on the half width resolution R of the hemi-cube faces. One hemi-cube consits of $12R^2$ grid cells, each containing a Z-value (REAL32) and a patch number (INT16), thus requiring 6 bytes of memory for a single grid cell.

Since a single form-factor and a single grid-cell require the same amount of data, a large data array can be shared between form-factors and hemi-cubes. At the beginning of the form-factor computation no form-factors have to be stored and all free memory can be dedicated to hemi-cubes. Depending on the number of entries in the data array E and the hemi-cube resolution R, the number of hemi-cubes H which can be processed in one pass can be determined as $H = \mathrm{trunc}(E / (12R^2))$. In the first hemi-cube loop some form-factors are computed which have to be compressed and written into the data arry shared between form-factors and hemi-cubes. Therefore at the beginning of the next hemi-cube loop there is less memory left for hemi-cubes. Depending on the number of remaining entries E' the number of hemi-cubes for the next run can be determined by evaluting the above formula again. That is why Workers have to inform the Manager before each run how many hemi-cubes and consequently patches they can process. The more runs are performed, the more form-factors have been computed and the fewer patches can be processed in the next run.

The amount of local memory restricts the complexity of the scene and the hemi-cube resolution. Adding further transputers to the network results in more complex scenes that can be rendered by parallel radiosity. The hemi-cube size determines the number of hemi-cubes which can be processed in one pass because less hemi-cubes can processed in one pass if the resolution is increased since they need more memory. The number of passes for computing the form-factors for all patches is also increased which furthermore leads to a higher computing time.

4.2.4 Communicator

The Communicator represents an interface between the Manager and the Calculator. After forwarding the hemi-cube resolution to the Calculator and the next Worker in the ring the hemi-cube loop, which will be expressed in pseudo-code, starts.

```
receive 'Next Round Flag' and forward it to the successor
WHILE some patches unprocessed
  receive 'Hemi-cube free'-messages from predecessor and forward it to the successor
  receive 'Hemi-cube free'-message from Calculator and forward it to the successor
  receive descriptions of receiving patches and send it to the Calculator
  receive patch descriptions for successive Workers and forward them to the successor
  receive block of patches
  WHILE not empty block
    send patch block to successor
    send patch block to Calculator
    receive next block of patches
  END
  send empty block to successor
END
send 'Stop Flag' to Calculator
```

4.3 Parallel Equation Solving

4.3.1 Overview

The linear equations are solved by the Gauss-Seidel method which is modified for running on parallel processors. It has to be applied for each of the basic colors red, green, and blue, thus giving three runs of equation solving.

The equation system consists of as many equations as there are patches in the scene to be rendered by the radiosity algorithm. These equations are distributed over all processors. After the form-factor computation each Worker has stored some rows of the form-factor matrix, each row belonging to a certain equation. Therefore each Worker has to solve those equations corresponding to its local form-factors.

4.3.2 Manager

The Manager initiates the equation solving on transmitting the patch emissions and reflectivities to the Workers which start solving the equations. After the first iteration the results are exchanged between the Workers by simply transmitting their own results and forwarding the other results to their successors. The Manager receives the results from the last Worker, stores them in a local buffer and transmits them to the first Worker. After all results have passed the Manager, the next iteration begins.

After each iteration the new results are compared with the previous results thus determining whether the Gauss-Seidel method has converged or another iteration has to be performed.

4.3.3 Calculator

Each Calculator stores some rows of the form-factor matrix. For each of these rows the corresponding radiosity equation

$$B_i = E_i + \rho_i \sum_{j=1}^{n} F_{ij} B_j$$

can be evaluated.

Therefore one iteration consists of computing the radiosities B_i of each equation whose form-factors F_{ij} are stored in the local memory of the Calculator.

After the computation of all local radiosities these B_i are passed to the Communicator and the current radiosities of all other Workers are received. Now the Calculator has a new set of updated B_i and the iteration starts again until the Manager determines that the changes of the radiosity values between two consecutive iterations are beyond a given accuracy.

4.3.4 Communicator

The Communicator only has to forward radiosity values from the predecessor to the Calculator and the successor and from the Calculator to the successor.

4.4 Parallel Rendering

4.4.1 Overview

The image is divided into horizontal sectors depending on the number of Workers (Fig. 4). These sectors can be rendered in parallel on different transputers. Each Worker is responsible for rendering one image sector.

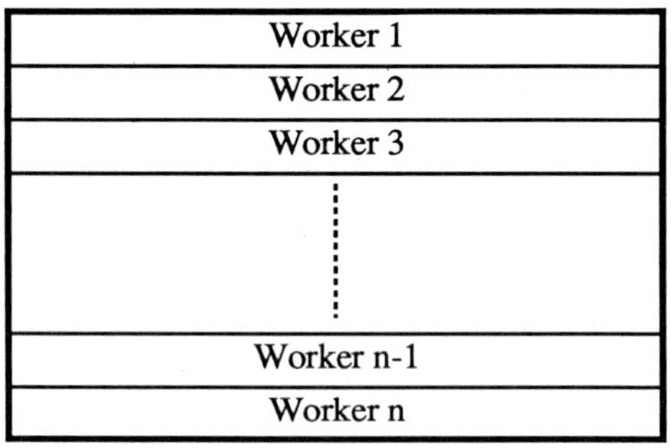

Fig. 4: Image sectors related to Workers

As described in section 3.4 the rendering based on a z-buffer algorithm is similar to the form-factor computation. However, the renderer uses four special clipping planes that are bounding the image sector.

In our implementation only a z-buffer is used for rendering. Therefore the radiosity value of a patch is applied to the whole patch area and no interpolation of radiosities is performed.

4.4.2 Manager

The Manager computes the transformation matrix for transforming the camera coordinate system for rendering a certain sector of the image into the z-buffer coordinate system and transmits the results to the Workers. Then all patches of the scene are sent in blocks to the

Workers. Afterwards the Manager has to collect the z-buffer values, i.e. patch numbers, of all Workers which make up the generated image and output them on a display device or image file.

4.4.3 Calculator

The Calculator first receives the specification of the geometric transformation. Based on this data the following patches are projected onto the upper face of the camera hemi-cube which has been divided into pixels depending on the image resolution. After all patches have been processed the z-buffer values are sent to the Manager via the Communicator.

4.4.4 Communicator

The Communicator only has to pass incoming data to its destination. At first init values for the transformation are received from the predecessor and then forwarded to the corresponding Calculator or the successor. The incoming patches are sent to the Calculator and to the next Worker as well. At the end of the computation it has to receive the z-buffer values from the predecessor and forward them to the next successor.

5 Results

Table 1 shows computation times for various numbers of transputers in the network. The scene which was used for testing consists of 1463 patches. All results were computed with hemi-cube half width resolution 50, thus making up 100x100 grid cells of the upper face and 100x50 grid cells on the lateral faces, blocksize 100 for transmitting the scene data and an image resolution 800x520.

Table 1: Computing times for various numbers of transputers

transputers	form-factor computation	equation solving	rendering	total time	efficiency
1	1243.6 sec	29.5 sec	19.8 sec	1292.9 sec	100.0 %
2	656.4 sec	17.0 sec	18.4 sec	691.8 sec	93.4 %
4	349.7 sec	9.6 sec	17.6 sec	376.9 sec	85.7 %
8	185.8 sec	5.7 sec	17.2 sec	208.7 sec	77.4 %
16	106.0 sec	4.0 sec	17.2 sec	127.2 sec	63.5 %
24	80.1 sec	3.6 sec	18.0 sec	101,7 sec	52.9 %
28	76.7 sec	3.5 sec	18.4 sec	98.6 sec	46.8 %

The best improvements in computation times can be achieved for the form-factor computation. This is the computationally most intensive task where the processing time for evaluating the form-factors highly exceeds the communication time. The equation solving makes up only a small fraction of the total computation time and since it consits of a high amount of data tranfer more processors only lead to a smaller speed-up. As the results of Table 1 demonstrate, the implemented parallel rendering is very inefficient because more transputers even lead to larger rendering times. This is caused by the huge amont of data which has to be transfered to gather the computed pixels. Therefore the communication time, which rises as more transputers are added to the network, is much higher than the computation time for evaluating the z-buffer. However, using a more sophisticated rendering technique instead of a simple z-buffer algorithm will increase calculation with respect to communication and thus a better speed-up due to parallelization will result.

The parallel radiosity solution was implemented on a network of transputers where each processing element only has access to its local memory. Therefore the parallelization has to cope with this restriction in memory. The 2MB RAM of each transputer module has to include the program and all data as well. As mentioned in section 4 a common data array is shared between the hemi-cubes and the form-factor array. The maximum data array is made up of 315.000 entries of 6 bytes each. Form-factor computation using hemi-cubes half width resolution 50 starts with 10 hemi-cubes on each Worker, using hemi-cube resolution 75 reduces the number of hemi-cubes to 4 and resolution 100 even leads to 2 hemi-cubes per Worker. Therefore hemi-cube resolution 100 is the maximum value which can be performed with this implementation unless the amount of local memory is not increased. Table 2 gives some computing times for different hemi-cube resolutions R for the above test scene.

Table 2: Form-factor computation for different hemi-cube resolutions

transputers	R = 50	R = 75	R = 100
2	656.4 sec	1184.5 sec	1968.7 sec
4	349.7 sec	622.1 sec	991.1 sec
8	185.8 sec	325.0 sec	540.0 sec
16	106.0 sec	183.0 sec	306.9 sec
24	80.1 sec	136.0 sec	232.1 sec
28	76.7 sec	124.4 sec	213.2 sec

6 Conclusion

A parallel solution to the radiosity algorithm for realistic image generation based upon light radiation in closed environments has been presented. The tremendous costs of evaluating the radiosity equations are met by distributing the processing power over several parallel processors. Methods for form-factor computation, equation solving and rendering on a parallel computer architecture based on transputers are given.

Several aspects of generating images of high quality using radiosity have not been considered yet, like interpolation of radiosities on the patch area or adaptive refinement of patches. In future work we will also implement a parallel shooting approach, for which a first concept already exists.

However, test results show that parallel processing is obviously a very promising approach to radiosity evaluation since this parallel radiosity solution leads to remarkable results in computation times.

Acknowledgements

The transputer equipment which was used for this project was sponsored by the Fonds zur Förderung der wissenschaftlichen Forschung under project number P6594 - Optimization of Ray-Tracing. Thanks to Robert Tobler and Andreas Muster for their work on implementing the parallel radiosity solution.

References

1. Baum, Daniel R., James M. Winget, "Real Time Radiosity Through Parallel Processing and Hardware Acceleration", Computer Graphics (Proceedings 1990 Symposium on Interactive 3D Graphics), Vol. 24, No. 3, March 1990, pp. 67-75.

2. Cohen, Michael F., Donald P. Greenberg, "The Hemi-Cube: A Radiosity Solution for Complex Environments", Computer Graphics (Proceedings SIGGRAPH'85), Vol. 19, No. 3, July 1985, pp. 31-40.

3. Cohen, Michael F., Donald P.Greenberg, David S. Immel, Philip J. Brock, "An Efficient Radiosity Approach for Realistic Image Synthesis", IEEE Computer Graphics and Applications, Vol. 6, No. 2, March 1986, pp. 26-35.

4. Cohen, Michael F., Shenchang Eric Chen, John R. Wallace, Donald P. Greenberg, "A Progressive Refinement Approach to Fast Radiosity Image Generation", Computer Graphics (Proceedings SIGGRAPH'88), Vol. 22, No. 4, August 1988, pp. 75-84.

5. Foley, James D., Andries Van Dam, Fundamentals of Interactive Computer Graphics, Addison-Wesley Publishing Co., 1982.

6. Goral, Cindy M., Kenneth E. Torrance, Donald P. Greenberg, Bennett Battaile, "Modeling the Interaction of Light Between Diffuse Surfaces", Computer Graphics (Proceedings SIGGRAPH'84), Vol. 18, No. 3, July 1984, pp. 213-222.

7. Occam 2 Refernece Manual, Prentice Hall Internationsal Series in Computer Science, INMOS Limited, 1988.

8. Purgathofer, Werner, Michael Zeiller, "Configuring Transputers for Ray-tracing", Applications of Transputers 1 (Proceedings First International Conference on Applications of Transputers 1989), IOS Press, 1990, pp. 276-283.

9. Recker, Rodney J., David W. George, Donald P. Greenberg, "Acceleration Techniques for Progressive Refinement Radiosity", Computer Graphics (Proceedings 1990 Symposium on Interactive 3D Graphics), Vol. 24, No. 2, March 1990, pp. 59-66.

10. Roth, S.D., "Ray Casting for Modeling Solids", Computer Graphics and Image Processing, Vol. 18, 1982, pp. 109-144.

11. IMS T800 transputer, IMS T800 Data Sheet, INMOS Limited, 1987.

12. Wallace, John R., Kells A. Elmquist, Eric A. Haines, "A Ray Tracing Algorithm for Progressive Radiosity", Computer Graphics (Proceedings SIGGRAPH'89), Vol. 23, No. 3, July 1989, pp. 315-324.

13. Whitted, Turner, "An Improved Illumination Model for Shaded Display", Communications of the ACM, Vol. 23, No. 6, June 1980, pp. 343-349.

Chapter 5

Physics Based Methods

Newton's Colors: Simulating Interference Phenomena in Realistic Image Synthesis

Brian E. Smits and Gary W. Meyer*

Abstract

The laws of physics that govern thin film interference are reviewed and the colors in nature that are produced by this mechanism are simulated. An efficient technique for adjusting out of gamut colors is developed and is applied to the problem of synthesizing the highly saturated interference colors. Common examples of thin film interference are reproduced, including the iridescent colors created by multiple film layers.

1 Introduction

In order to determine the color of an object in a synthetic scene, the spectral composition of the light reaching the observer from that object must be calculated. In nature there are a variety of mechanisms by which a spectral energy distribution can be produced and altered. Simulation of these mechanisms in computer graphics is an example of a physically based approach to realistic image synthesis. In this paper we explore the types of colors that are produced by the modelling of one specific phenomena: interference.

Light striking the surface of a material must be either reflected, transmitted, scattered, or absorbed. In addition, the material itself may emit some light. The reflected light consists of a specular component that is sent off at an angle equal to the angle of incidence, and a diffuse component that goes off in many directions. The path of the transmitted light will be changed due to refraction of the light at the surface of the material. Some portion of the light will be absorbed by the material and turned into heat. Finally, scattering will cause some of the light to be released from the sides of the material.

Interference phenomena are the result of both the reflection and transmittance mechanisms mentioned above. Perhaps the most common example of interference is the colors produced on the surface of oil slicks and soap bubbles. These types of interference phenomena were first studied by Newton and the sequences of colors that are produced by them are called Newton's colors. Interference effects can also be seen on old vases, metal, and peacock feathers. Structural engineers analyze stress by viewing interference patterns in plastic models.

In most cases, these interference effects are caused by very thin films which determine the amount of light at each wavelength that is reflected back to the viewer. As the thickness of the film varies, the spectral composition of the light and therefore the color that gets reflected back to the viewer changes as well. Interference effects have not been modeled in computer graphics so this work enlarges the set of natural phenomena that have been simulated in computer graphics. They are another example of using the physical properties of light and the way it interacts with surfaces to more accurately model the natural world.

---

*Department of Computer and Information Science, University of Oregon, Eugene, OR 97403. Current address for Brian Smits: Program of Computer Graphics, Cornell University, Ithaca, NY 14953

2 The Physics of Interference Phenomena

Interference phenomena are the result of the wave-like properties of light. According to the superposition principle, when two waves meet the amplitude of the resultant wave is the sum of the amplitudes of the two component waves. Suppose two waves with the same wavelength and amplitude merge together. If the crest of both waves match up exactly, perfect constructive interference occurs and the resulting wave has twice the amplitude of the two original waves. These two waves are said to have a phase difference of zero. If the crest of one wave matches up with the trough of another, perfect destructive interference results and the waves cancel each other completely. The phase difference in this case is equal to π. Given the phase difference δ of two waves with amplitude A, the resulting amplitude A' is given by

$$A' = 2A\cos\left(\frac{\delta}{2}\right). \tag{1}$$

Because light has wave-like properties, it obeys this rule (Tipler, 1976). The amount of interference can be different for each wavelength producing a change in the color of the light we see.

Interference phenomena are affected by the speed of the light waves through the medium in which they are travelling. Each medium, such as water, air, glass, or oil, has what is called an index of refraction n given by

$$n = \frac{c}{v} \tag{2}$$

where c is the speed of light in a vacuum and v is the speed of light in the medium. A vacuum has an index of refraction $n = 1$ and air is assumed to have the same index for most calculations. Water, however, has an index of refraction $n = 1.33$ showing that light travels at only seventy-five percent of its usual speed through water. The relationship between the speed v, wavelength λ, and frequency f of a wave is given by

$$v = \frac{f}{\lambda}. \tag{3}$$

When a wave enters a new medium, its speed changes. This means that the wavelength must change because, for a given wave, the frequency is fixed. The new wavelength λ' in the new medium is given by

$$\lambda' = \frac{\lambda}{n}. \tag{4}$$

The index of refraction also determines how the wave is reflected back from the boundary. If, at the boundary of two different mediums, the new medium has a higher index of refraction than the old one, when the wave bounces off of the boundary it will be inverted ($\delta = \pi$) with every trough becoming a crest and every crest a trough. A wave will not be inverted if it reflects off a boundary with a medium having a lower index of refraction. This is important because it makes two different kinds of interference effects possible, one with a phase change, and one without.

When light with wavelength λ strikes a thin film, such as a soap bubble or an oil film on water, it is reflected back at both surfaces of the film. If the film has an index of refraction greater than the surrounding medium, the wave will be inverted when it is reflected off of the back face of the film. When the ray reflected from the top surface meets the ray reflected from the bottom surface, they interfere with one another (Figure 1). Assume, for the moment, that the light waves travel perpendicular to the surface and the inversion of the wave can be neglected. Then the extra distance or path difference that the light rays travel is equal to two times the thickness t of the film. There are $2t/\lambda'$ waves within the film where λ' is the wavelength of the light modified by the index of refraction of the surface. If the film has a thickness of $t = 0$, then there are no waves within the film and the phase difference is 0. If the film has a thickness of $t = \lambda'/4$ then there are

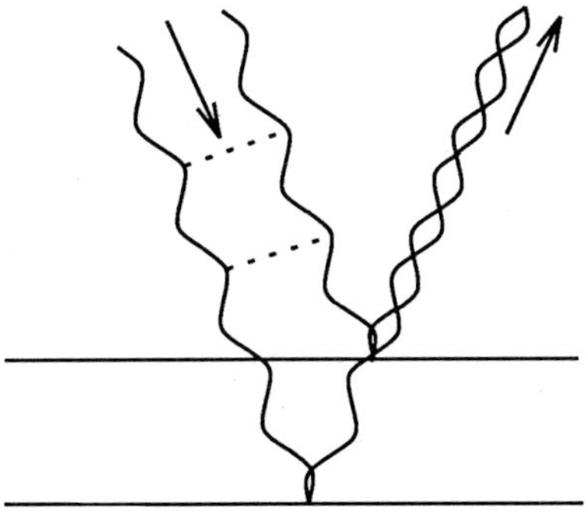

Fig. 1: Interference occurs between light wave that has reflected off the bottom of the film and light wave that has reflected off the top.

$(2 * \lambda'/4)/\lambda' = 1/2$ waves within the film and the phase difference is π. In addition to the phase difference that is a result of the thickness of the film, there is a one half cycle phase change that occurs when the light reflects off of the back boundary. To accomodate this phase change, a factor of π is added to the phase difference. Given these considerations, the phase difference of light reflecting perpendicularly off of a thin film is

$$\delta = 2\pi\left(\frac{2t}{\lambda'}\right) + \pi \tag{5}$$

and the amplitude $A_r(\lambda)$ of the resulting wave is

$$A_r(\lambda) = 2A_0(\lambda)\cos\left(\frac{\delta}{2}\right) = 2A_0(\lambda)\cos\left(\frac{2\pi tn}{\lambda} + \frac{\pi}{2}\right) \tag{6}$$

where $A_0(\lambda)$ is the amplitude of the light wave at wavelength λ striking the surface (Tipler, 1976). For a film with thickness t near zero, the resulting amplitude is close to zero for all wavelengths of light. This causes the top of a soap bubble to appear black, because this is where the bubble is thinnest. This shows that the waves are inverted when they reflect off of the back face and cancel out almost all of the light reflecting off of the front face.

Given this information we can calculate the spectral energy distribution of the light reflecting perpendicularly off of a thin film. The intensity $I(\lambda)$ of that reflected light for a film with thickness t and index of refraction n is

$$I(\lambda) = [A_0(\lambda)\cos\left(\frac{2\pi tn}{\lambda} + \frac{\pi}{2}\right)]^2 \tag{7}$$

where $A_0(\lambda)$ is the amplitude of the light striking the surface of the film. The expression in brackets is squared because the intensity of a wave is equal to the square of its amplitude.

Some interference phenomena are caused by a film with air on one side and some other medium with a higher index of refraction than the film on the other side. In this case, the light waves are not inverted when they reflect off of either the back boundary or the front boundary. The constant π that was added to the previous equation for a film with mediums of lower refractive index on each side should not be used for this case. For this type of interference phenomena, the intensity $I(\lambda)$ of the reflected light for a film with thickness t is defined to be

$$I(\lambda) = [A_0(\lambda)\cos\left(\frac{2\pi tn}{\lambda}\right)]^2. \tag{8}$$

In both of these types of interference phenomena, the path difference is affected by the angle at which the viewer is looking at the film. When light strikes a film at an angle,

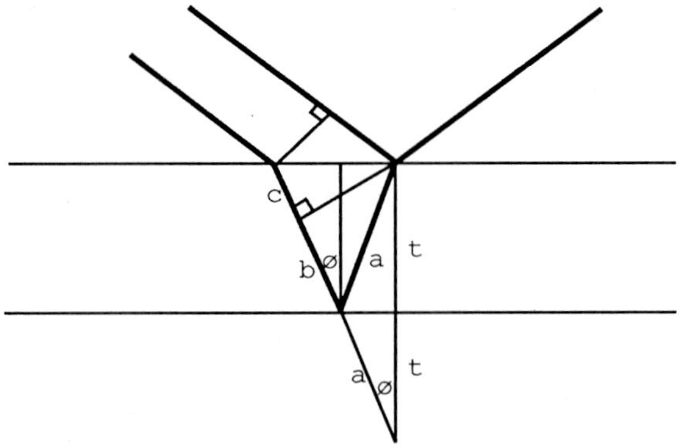

Fig. 2: Angle of view contributes to a difference $a + b$ in path length that is equal to $2t\cos\theta$.

the exit point of the wave is different from the entrance point. At the exit point, the wave interferes with a wave that has just reflected after making its initial contact with the film surface. The light travels farther through the film than before, but the path difference ends up being less. This is because the light wave that the exiting ray interferes with has also traveled farther. The light wave that enters the film travels a distance of c before the corresponding point on the other wave reaches the film. The path difference between the two waves is $a + b$ which is equal to $2t\cos\theta$ (Figure 2). For a perpendicular wave, θ is zero and the path difference is twice the thickness. Therefore, to accomodate the angle of view θ, we replace t in Equation 8 with the expression $t\cos\theta$.

Another interference phenomenon occurs when light strikes a surface that is composed of multiple uniform layers of a transparent substance. This multiple film interference produces iridescence which is seen as the bright colors on the feathers of birds (such as peacocks), some insect wings, and opals. Each film of the surface tends to reinforce certain ranges of wavelengths. The more films that are present, the narrower and brighter the range of reflected light. This repeated reinforcement of limited ranges of wavelengths causes the very bright and almost spectral colors that are found in multiple film interference phenomena. The intensity $I(\lambda)$ is

$$I(\lambda) = \frac{1}{2}A_0(\lambda)\left(\frac{\sin 2\pi(l+1)t/\lambda}{\sin 2\pi t/\lambda}\right)^2 \tag{9}$$

where $A_0(\lambda)$ is the amplitude of the light striking the film, l is the number of layers, and t is the thickness of a layer (Anderson and Richards, 1942). One of the properties of iridescence is that the colors change as the angle of incidence changes. The path difference between light reflecting off the surface and light reflecting off an internal layer is a function of the angle of incidence θ and the index of refraction n. The derivation of the change with angle is much more complicated for multiple film interference than for single film interference because of the interaction between films. To accomodate the angle of incidence θ, t in Equation 9 must be replaced by (Anderson and Richards, 1942)

$$t(n^2 - sin\theta)^2. \tag{10}$$

Often in nature the results do not follow these formulae exactly because the films may not be uniform or the films are composed of interlaced layers of different materials.

2.1 Calculating Newton's Colors

In order for interference effects to be used in computer graphics, it is necessary to determine the spectral energy distribution of the light reflected from the film and to convert this spectral energy distribution to the proper point in the *RGB* color space of a color television monitor. (A previous attempt to model interference phenomena (Watt, 1989) incorrectly performed the calculations directly in terms of the *RGB* monitor primaries.) Given the amplitude $A_0(\lambda)$ of the light striking the film, the spectral energy distribution $I(\lambda)$ of the reflected light can be found from the thickness t and index of refraction n by employing Equation 8. Using the matching functions $\overline{x}(\lambda)$, $\overline{y}(\lambda)$, and $\overline{z}(\lambda)$ for CIE XYZ space, we can convert this spectral energy distribution into CIE XYZ tristimulus values and then into into the *RGB* space of the monitor (Meyer and Greenberg, 1987).

For some ranges of interference colors, the *RGB* tristimulus values become negative. This occurs where the film is relatively thin, because in some cases only very narrow bands of wavelengths have a high intensity. These ranges are closer to monochromatic colors and cannot be displayed on a monitor. The process of deciding what color to display for these out of gamut colors will be covered in Section 3.

A table of *RGB* values for interference effects with a phase change and one for effects without the phase change is precomputed and is indexed based upon the thickness of the film and the index of refraction. This is done so that the expensive processes of calculating the color need only be done once for each thickness. Note from Equation 7 that the table can be precomputed for an index of refraction of 1 (Nassau, 1980). When a single thin film with thickness t and index of refraction n is seen at an angle θ, the product t' of the thickness and the index of refraction becomes

$$t' = tn \cos\theta \tag{11}$$

Once the product t' is determined, the color for that thickness is looked up in the table. This makes the rendering much more efficient. A similar approach is taken in the case of multiple thin films.

3 Out of Gamut Colors

The gamut of a color device is the set of colors that it can produce. The primaries used in the device determine its gamut, and when the primaries of two devices differ, the gamuts do not match up exactly. This gamut mismatch problem causes ranges of color on one device that cannot be reproduced on the other. These colors are called out of gamut colors.

Gamut mismatch occurs in several different circumstances. One of the situations in which gamut mismatch is a major problem is between color monitors and color printers. The vivid, highly saturated colors that a monitor can display are impossible to reproduce using a color printer because color printers use different primaries and a different process for creating color. This problem makes the final printed results look much different than the display on the monitor. Gamut mismatch also occurs between monitors, causing dissimilarity between the same picture seen on different monitors. This is because the red, green, and blue phosphors vary slightly between monitors. The gamut mismatch that happened while modeling interference phenomena was a third mismatch, that between nature and the monitor. Interference effects produce colors that are almost spectral and that lie outside of the gamut of almost all reproduction devices.

3.1 A Solution to Out of Gamut Colors

In all of these gamut mismatches, adjustments need to be made to the colors that are out of the destination gamut. The color that is chosen as a replacement for the out of gamut color must be in the destination gamut and should be as close as possible to the original color. One potential solution is to clip the colors outside the destination gamut to the boundary of the gamut. This involves finding a color on the boundary of the gamut that is close to the original out of gamut color. Another idea is to compress the input gamut and all colors in the image down to fit within the destination gamut. This involves scaling the colors down by some amount that is determined by the input gamut.

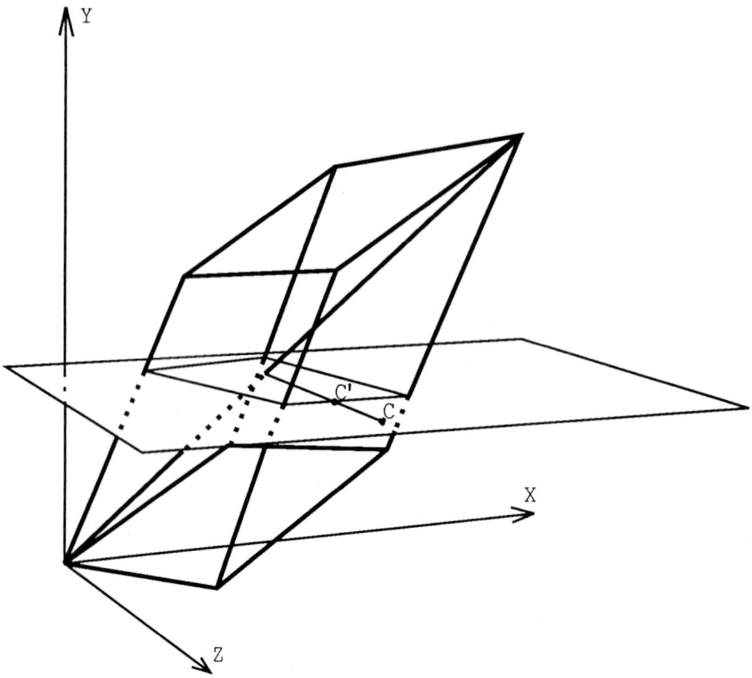

Fig. 3: Out of gamut color is approximated by following a line of constant hue and lightness in towards the neutral diagonal.

In a recent paper (Gentile and Allebach, 1989) thirteen different techniques for dealing with out of gamut colors were compared. All but one of these techniques (the control) were performed in the perceptually uniform $L^*u^*v^*$ space. The control was done in RGB space and used the Euclidean distance formula to select the closest color to the out of gamut color. Both clipping and compression techniques were tested, keeping various subsets of lightness, saturation, and hue constant while performing the color adjustment. Considering only techniques which did no analysis on the picture prior to clipping or compression, the best techniques were clipping with a constant lightness, or clipping with constant lightness and hue. For this work, we have chosen to use the clipping with constant lightness and hue approach.

The problem with all of the techniques investigated in Gentile and Allebach (1989) is that they operate in $L^*u^*v^*$ space. $L^*u^*v^*$ space is not computationally efficient for large pictures because of the non-linear transformation that is required for every color in the image. What is needed is an algorithm which will work in CIE XYZ space and have similar properties to the constant lightness and hue $L^*u^*v^*$ space algorithms. By holding lightness and hue constant, only the saturation of the color changes. The color is being pulled in towards the achromatic colors that lie on the diagonal line between black and white in the color space. In this paper, we will refer to this line as the neutral diagonal. In CIE XYZ space lightness is a function of Y alone, so we could pull back in towards the neutral diagonal while keeping Y constant (Figure 3). This will desaturate the color and bring it within the gamut of the output device. In CIE XYZ space, colors with constant hue do not lie on a straight line from the neutral diagonal to the edge of the gamut, but are curved somewhat (Meyer and Greenberg, 1987). No linear transform will make the lines of constant hue straight. Because the constant hue lines are curved, the hue will not remain constant as the out of gamut color is brought back in towards the neutral diagonal. The change in hue, however, should not be significant enough to cause problems.

The gamut that will be used in this case as the destination gamut is the RGB space of a color television monitor. The input gamut is the calculated interference colors, but it could just as easily be an input device such as a scanner, or the RGB space of a different monitor. Some ranges of the interference colors and the entire spectrum are the worst case for an input gamut because they are spectral colors. The techniques used here to deal with out of gamut colors should be applicable to any type of gamut mismatch. The following algorithm is designed to work on a gamut that has the shape of a parallelpiped such as an RGB monitor gamut in CIE XYZ space.

3.2 The Clipping Algorithm

The clipping algorithm is composed of three steps. Given a color to be reproduced, it first checks to see if the color needs to be clipped. Next it determines the direction of the neutral color with the same lightness as the color. Then the intersection with the monitor parallelpiped must be found for a ray from the color to the neutral diagonal. Most of the work in this algorithm is done in finding the direction to bring the ray into the gamut and in doing the intersections with the gamut boundaries. If the color already exists in the RGB space of the destination instead of CIE XYZ space, a very similar but faster algorithm with identical properties will work. Both of these algorithms are variations on the Cohen-Sutherland clipping algorithm for line segments.

The first step involves checking to see if the color lies within the output gamut. The monitor parallelpiped is defined by six planes, three of which pass through the origin, and three of which are parallel to the first three. For each pair of planes, the point can either be above both of them, between them, or below both of them. If the point is between them, it could lie in the gamut. If the point lies outside of the planes, it is outside the gamut and it can only intersect the plane that lies between it and the gamut. If for each pair of planes the point lies between the planes, the point must be within the gamut and the color does not need to be clipped.

The out of gamut color must be pulled back towards the center of the gamut defined by the neutral diagonal running from black through grey to white. The grey point lies on the line from white to black and has the same lightness as the point being clipped. In CIE XYZ space, keeping lightness constant is easy because lightness is just a function of Y. The neutral diagonal, however, is not the line defined by $x = y = z$ since this is not always white in the output gamut. The white point is the location in CIE XYZ space produced when R, G, and B are at maximum intensity. Given the white point of the output gamut, the intersection of the neutral diagonal with the plane $Y = y_p$ is found, where y_p is the luminance Y of the color being clipped. The vector from the input color to this grey point is used to find the point on the edge of the gamut that is closest to the input color.

Once the direction along which to bring the out of gamut color back into the gamut is found, it is necessary to find where on the edge of the gamut the point of intersection lies. In the process of checking whether or not the input point was within the gamut, the results told which planes the point could intersect as it is pulled back into the gamut. There is a possibility of up to three intersections that need to be done. The intersections are computed and the one furthest from the input point is the output color. The furthest point is used because otherwise the point will still be outside at least one pair of planes.

The clipping algorithm was tested on the spectral colors. This is the worst case since every color in the spectrum is monochromatic and as far out of the gamut of the monitor as possible. Numerically, the lightness remains fixed for all colors that get clipped. In general, the saturation of the clipped colors goes down, and the hue changes only a little. For some ranges of colors, however, the hue changes are more severe. These ranges correspond to regions where the plane defining a gamut edge is closer to parallel with the plane of constant lightness. This fact makes sense because in these regions, the color will travel farther towards the grey line before it intersects the gamut. In most practical situations, however, the input colors will not be monochromatic to the extent that the spectrum is. Visually, the spectrum looks best when clipped so that lightness remains constant and hue changes as little as possible (Figure 4).

4 Examples

The physical theory and color correction techniques discussed in the preceeding sections were applied to the synthesis of pictures showing interference phenomena. The first example is of the colors produced by a drop of oil on wet asphalt pavement. The colors seen on the surface of a soap bubble provides the second example. The final example is of the iridescent colors exhibited by the wings of the *Morpho* butterfly. In all three cases the nearly spectral colors that were produced by the interference effects provided an opportunity to evaluate the effectiveness of the color correction techniques.

4.1 Oil Film on Water

When a drop of oil falls onto a surface it often forms a pattern of concentric circles. On a completely smooth and level surface the oil would spread slowly, staying thicker in the middle and becoming very thin at the edges. It forms a mound on the surface with the thickness of the oil being a function of distance from the center. Based on these observations and an illustration from Minnaert (1954), the thickness was modeled as an exponential function of the square of the distance from the center point. For an oil spill centered at the origin, this normal distribution is

$$t = e^{-k_1(x^2+y^2)}, \tag{12}$$

where k_1 is a constant that determines how quickly the oil diminishes to a negligeable thickness.

This method is a good approximation to an oil slick on a perfectly smooth surface. Oil, however, is most commonly seen on pavement and does not spread out evenly due to the roughness and slope of this surface. Using a turbulence function from Perlin (1985), the distance from the center can be randomly perturbed at each point in a way that keeps the oil slick roughly concentric. The resulting formula is as follows

$$t = e^{-k_1(x^2+y^2+k_2\mathrm{turb}[x,y])} \tag{13}$$

where k_2 is a constant that affects how irregular the spreading of the oil is. The turbulence function returns a self-similar pattern of perturbation which gives a good visual impression of a turbulent flow (Perlin, 1985). This formula approximates how each area of the oil slick spreads out at different rate. Further distortions could be done to t to model the effects of a sloped surface or other irregularities, but this formula serves as a good representation for a basic oil slick (Figure 5). For a point on the surface, the thickness t is computed based on the distance from the center and the value of the turbulence function at that point. The thickness t is then changed based on the angle between the viewer and the surface. The resulting t is used as an index into a precomputed table of colors and the color in RGB space is finally determined for that point.

In order to get a good picture, the slick needs to lie on an appropriate surface. The most familiar surface for an oil slick is pavement, but pavement is a very complex surface because of all of its irregularities. To get a realistic effect, a surface that had an irregular scale of bumps and an irregular amount of roughness to it had to be approximated. This was done by using two separate calls to a noise function to determine the scale and the roughness of the final texture. After doing this distortion, very fine bumps were mapped over the result to make the surface appear even rougher.

4.2 Soap Films

A soap film is another example of interference phenomena. The bright colors that reflect off of a soap bubble are caused by the very thin film of the bubble. As with the oil slick, the light changes phase when it strikes the back face of the film. The proof of the phase change can be seen near the tops of bubbles and soap films. Just before they pop, the tops of the bubbles look black because this is where they are the thinnest. The blackness is caused by almost complete destructive interference resulting from a phase difference of π due to almost identical path lengths.

Soap films are affected by gravity. The water in the film is being pulled down by gravity and up by the surface tension in the film. In still air the film is thicker near the bottom than the top, and therefore the color at each point on the film is a function of its height. This relationship causes bands of color to appear on a soap film after it has stabilized. In modeling soap bubbles, height was normalized to a zero to one range, the result from a call to the turbulence function was added to the height, and the thickness was taken as being directly proportional to the height. The turbulence approximates the effects of air currents and other irregularities that influence the thickness of the film. Using a simple linear function for the thickness is probably incorrect, but because of the large amounts of turbulence that are added, the inaccuracy is not noticeable (Figure 6).

4.3 Iridescence

Iridescence effects are found on the wings of *Morpho* butterflies. The vanes of this butterfly's wings have twelve horizontal mullions with the spacing and thickness necessary to create a multiple film interference effect (Anderson and Richards, 1942). The surface reflectance that results has a peak at about 400nm. Because of the thickness of the mullions, the path difference between light reflecting off the surface and light reflecting off an internal layer is a function of the angle θ between the incident ray and the surface normal, of the spacing between the mullions d_1, of the thickness of the mullions d_2, and of the refractive index of the mullions n which is 1.53 for *Morpho* butterflies (Anderson and Richards, 1942). To accomodate the thickness and spacing of the mullions as well as the angle of view, t in Equation 9 must be replaced by

$$d_1 \cos\theta + d_2(n^2 - \sin^2\theta)^{\frac{1}{2}}. \tag{14}$$

An iridescent surface was modeled based on the colors of the butterfly wings. A table referenced by angle was generated for $d_1 = 150$ nm and $d_2 = 50$ nm and used to determine the color at each point. The surface was made to look wavey to show the colors that occur with varying angle (Figure 7). The mullions vary in thickness between 50 nm and 150 nm, so the actual colors reflected from the wings of the butterfly are a blend of multiple film interference colors resulting from the variations in the thicknesses of the mullions (Anderson and Richards, 1942).

5 Conclusion

Modelling interference phenomena is another example of applying the laws of physics to the synthesis of realistic images. Interference effects have not been accurately simulated in computer graphics, and by doing so we have enlarged the set of available techniques for synthesizing color and for modelling the natural world. Three specific examples of naturally occuring interference effects were simulated and images depicting these phenomena were produced. Because very pure colors are created by the interference of light waves, an efficient color correction technique for out of gamut colors was also devised. This technique is applicable to other situations such as color printing where there is a need to adjust colors.

6 Acknowledgments

Mark VandeWettering developed some of the ray tracing software employed in this research.

References

Anderson, Thomas F. and Richards, A. Glenn, Jr. (1942) An Electron Microscope Study of Some Structural Colors of Insects. *Journal of Applied Physics, 13,* 748-758.

Gentile, Ronald S. and Allebach, Jan P. (1989) A Comparison of Techniques for Color Gamut Mismatch Compensation. in *Human Vision, Visual Processing, and Digital Display (SPIE Proceedings Series), 1077,* 342-354.

Meyer, Gary W. and Greenberg, Donald P. (1987) Perceptual Color Spaces for Computer Graphics. In *Color and the Computer* edited by H. John Durrett. Academic Press, Boston.

Minnaert, M. (1954) *The Nature of Light and Color in the Open Air.* Dover Publications, New York.

Nassau, Kurt (1983) *The Physics and Chemistry of Color: The Fifteen Causes of Color.* John Wiley and Sons, New York.

Perlin, Ken (1985) An Image Synthesizer. *Computer Graphics, 19.* 287-296.

Tipler, Paul A. (1976) *Physics.* Worth Publishers, New York.

Watt, Alan (1989) *Fundamentals of Three-Dimensional Computer Graphics.* Addison-Wesley, Wokingham.

Light Sources in a Ray Tracing Environment

Marc Roelens, Gilles Fertey, Bernard Peroche*

Abstract

Desk lamps, automobile headlights, streets lamps,..., usually illuminate by light cones. This article describes two methods adapted to simulate those typical light sources, using a CSG model, in a Ray Tracing environment. These methods allow to visualize illuminated objects but also the light beams. The first one is completely empirical ; the second one is an improvement of the previous one, physically-based, with spherical particles inside the light beam.

1 Introduction

One of the aims of computer graphics is to produce more and more realistic images. Thus, numerous works have been done these last years on lighting models, shadows, refractions, reflections, transparencies, textures, antialiasing ... ([21]). In this paper, we are concerned with the problem of light sources. This problem is important when the aim is to perform realistic simulations of scenes in which colored spotlights, desk lamps, car headlamps, street lamps must appear ... Our goal is threefold : first, define directional sources that illuminate an area of the space corresponding to the type of the source (cone, cylinder or prism) ; secondly, make the beam of the source both visible and transparent, as in real space ; finally render some natural phenomena such as smoke or dust in the air inside the light beam.

A computer graphics system, called ILLUMINES ([3]) has been developed these last years at l'Ecole des Mines de Saint-Etienne. Since the kernel of this system is a CSG based modeler, we chose to define light sources as special primitives of a CSG tree : cones, cylinders or prisms. In order to visualize pictures containing light sources, we use a ray tracing algorithm.

Our paper is organized as follows : in section 2, we describe the main physical characteristics of light sources : the geometry, the emitted spectral distribution and the luminous intensity distribution. In section 3, we survey previous works on simulation of light sources in computer graphics. In section 4, we present the work developed at Saint-Etienne. In a first part, we present an early work ([11]), which is completely empirical. In a second part, we describe an improvement of the first model, using a physically-based model, with spherical particles inside the light beam. In section 5, some considerations about the current implementation are given and we prospect some future works that could be done.

2 Light Sources

In order to correctly describe the physical characteristics of light sources, three attributes have to be modeled : light source geometry, emitted spectral distribution and luminous intensity distribution.

2.1 Light Source Geometry

According to Verbeck and Greenberg ([25]), there are five kinds of emissive geometries :

- **directional sources** : in this case, a light source is defined by a direction and an intensity value. This kind of source, which has been the first one used in computer graphics, allows to simulate the sun ;

* Authors Address : Ecole Nationale Supérieure des Mines de Saint-Etienne, Département Informatique Appliquée, 158, Cours Fauriel, 42023 SAINT-ETIENNE CEDEX 2.

- **point light sources** : here, a light source is specified by the location of a point in the world space ; it is supposed to emit light equally in all directions. This kind of light source simulates a bare light bulb ;

- **linear light sources** : such sources are described in [14, 19]. The shape of a linear light source is assumed to be a line segment. These light sources are intended to simulate fluorescent tubes ;

- **area sources :** such sources can be found in [14], where the geometry is defined as a surface of revolution, or in [5], where the shape of a light source is modeled as a polyhedral surface. In the latter case, the effect of the distributed light source is simulated by a set of point sources that lie on the polyhedral surface. Points can be generated either randomly or by superimposing a lattice of points with some resolution. A uniform random generation of points appears to be better than using of a lattice, since evenly spaced points may cause visual banding effects. A sufficient number of points should be generated so that the addition of one more point to the set of point sources will not visibly affect the illumination.

- **volume sources :** described in [5, 14], these sources are defined by polyhedrons, some faces of which are assumed to be area light sources ; these area sources are then modeled as described above.

2.2 Luminous Intensity Distribution

In usual models, light sources are supposed to emit light isotropically. However, these models do not accurately simulate real scenes, since light can be emitted as cylindric beams by means of reflectors, or emitted only over a sector of the surrounding sphere, by means of diffusers.

In order to obtain a much better realism, it is necessary to describe the directional intensity variation over the surface of the light source. This distribution can be thought of as a vector field : the intensity of the light emitted in any direction is the magnitude of the vector in that direction.

Since it is difficult to represent such a vector field, the lighting industry uses goniometric diagrams. These diagrams represent a planar slice through the vector field and thus plot the intensity as a function of angular direction (see figure1). When the geometry of the source and the intensity distribution have rotationally symmetries, one goniometric diagram is sufficient. For light sources with less symmetric luminance functions, such as linear sources, multiple polar curves are used. Two polar curves are used to represent the luminance across the major and minor axes of the source. The intensity in a point which does not belong to one of the two planesis obtained by interpolation.

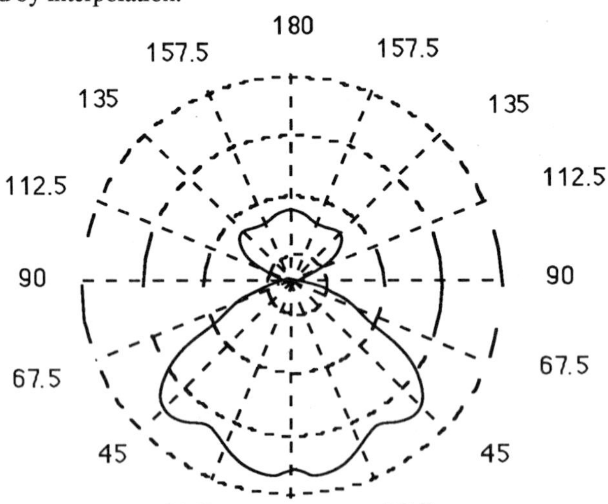

Fig. 1 Goniometric diagram

2.3 The Emitted Spectral Distribution

2.3.1 Definitions

Light is an electromagnetic energy, characterized by a spectral distribution.

The *light power* $\varnothing_e(\lambda)$ is the energy leaving a surface or arriving at a surface per unit time. With this light power is associated the *light flow* $\varnothing$, which takes into account the visual spectral sensitivity $V(\lambda)$ of the human eye :

$$\varnothing = 680 \int_0^{\infty} V(\lambda)\, \varnothing_e(\lambda)\, d\lambda$$

Several radiometric quantities can be derived from the light flow :

- *Intensity* I, the light flow per unit solid angle ;

- *Irradiance* E, the light flow, per unit area, arriving at a surface, defined as

$$E = I \frac{\cos \theta}{r^2}$$

where θ is the angle between the normal to the surface element and the line defined by the source and the center of the surface element and r the distance between the source and the center of the surface element ;

- *Radiance*, the energy leaving a surface per unit area and per unit projected solid angle. This quantity is then dependent on both view direction and normal direction to the surface ;

- *Radiosity*, the energy emitted by unit area ;

- *Reflectance* the ratio of the reflective power to the incident power for a small surface element ;

- *Transmission* the ratio of the transmitted power to the incident power for a small surface element.

2.3.2 Spectral Sampling for Color Computations

Illumination reflection and transmission characteristics of light sources and surfaces are wavelength dependent functions (the human eye has three color receptors, which can be quantified by tristimulus matching functions : the response received by the brain is a result of multiplying the stimulus distribution by these tristimulus matching functions to obtain the trivariant response functions).

Historically, computer graphics has relied on the principles of tristimulus colorimetry, but has performed calculations only on the red, green and blue components. Since all the concerned curves are continuous functions, this approach consists of point sampling in the intensity domain. It can lead to color aliasing artifacts.

The aim would be to perform the color calculations for several wavelengths, to compute the spectral distribution on a continuous wavelength basis.

For this purpose, Hall and Greenberg ([14]) made experiments by generating comparison images. They produced a control image using spectral description maintained at one-nanometer increments from 360 nm to 830 nm. They generated additional images, one using the CIE-XYZ color space, another one the RGB color space and a last one produced with nine spectral sample values. They found that the nine spectral samples closely approximate the correct intensity function. Furthermore, the total computation time for the nine-sample-point approach was less than two percent greater than the tristimulus approach. However, no selection criteria for the nine sample points was given in the paper.

Meyer proposed in [17] a method to select the correct number and values of wavelengths over the visible spectrum. For this purpose, he used a color space whose axes are aligned with the most significant axes of the tristimulus values. To find a transform of the CIE coordinate system giving the axes defined above, Meyer used the discrete Karhunen-Loeve expansion. He obtained new coordinates called A, C_1 and C_2. These tristimulus values can simply be evaluated through calculations of sums, thanks to the gaussian quadrature method.

In conclusion, to produce realistic computer generated images, it seems to be necessary to supply the spectral distribution of the light sources, and not only the three spectral samples in the RGB color space. Figure 2 shows two spectral distributions of common light sources (from [25]).

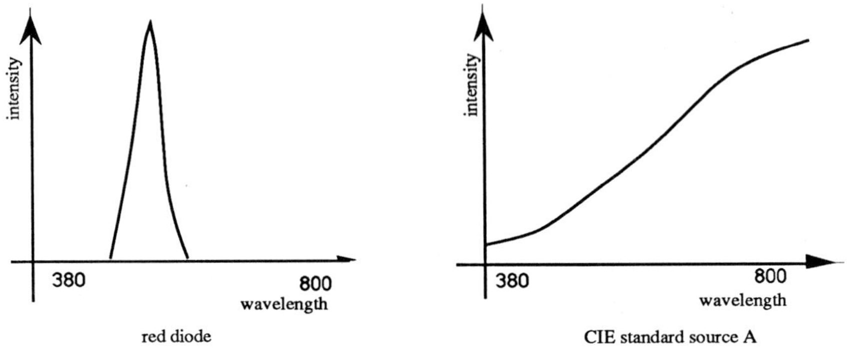

Fig 2 Examples of spectral distributions

3 Previous Works on Light Sources

3.1 Lighting Models

Due to the importance of a correct simulation of light sources to obtain realistic computer generated images, numerous works have been concerned with this problem. We present the most important ones below, specifying the geometric model used to describe the physical environment, the lighting model and the visible surface algorithm used to compute the final image.

In early approaches to realistic image synthesis, only directional light sources were used. So, first works deal with lighting models, allowing to compute the color of visible objects. The first model is the so-called Lambert model, which describes diffuse reflection for polygonal surfaces. Gouraud [13] proposed a method of color interpolation across polygonal approximations that would simulate smoothly curved surfaces. Phong proposed [22] an empirical reflection model, which includes a diffuse term that provides surface color and shading, and a specular term that provides realistic highlights from direct light source reflections. Furthermore, Phong proposed an alternate method in order to interpolate surface normals across each polygon.

Based upon the Torrance-Sparrow [24] reflection model, Blinn [4] proposed a less empirical improvement of the Phong reflection model.

Cook and Torrance [9] proposed a reflection model that describes the behavior of light in terms of energy equilibrium and electromagnetic wave theory. This model is based both upon the Torrance-Sparrow reflection model and the Beckmann scattering model.

Ray tracing is a more global approach for lighting models. Suggested by Appel [1] to solve the hidden surface problem, the methodology was extended by Whitted [28] to solve the global illumination problem.

Goral et al. [12] adapted radiosity techniques used in thermal engineering to model the movement of light energy through an environment. This technique assumes rough surfaces and opaque materials. The radiosity method describes the creation and solution of the equation set that describes the energy interrelationships of all the polygons in the scene. So the ambiant illumination is explicitly evaluated by this method and no empirical terms appear in the illumination model.

Extensions of this method were proposed by [8, 19, 26, 7, 23, 6] ..., either to improve methods for building the radiosity equation set or to allow non diffuse surfaces.

3.2 Light Sources

One of the first who attempted to model sophisticated light sources is Warm ([27]). Its model is a part of GMR AUTOCOLOR, a system developed at the General Motors Research Laboratories for generation of synthetic images, and used for cars CAD. The system uses polygonal representation for objects, a Watkins based scan line algorithm for hidden surface removal and the Phong lighting model. Warm's paper describes controls and adjustments on individual lights. The two most basic lighting controls are direction and concentration ; additional light controls, flaps and variable sized cone surrounding the light direction, allow to generate special effects by limiting the illuminated area. In fact, the light controls proposed by Warm are intended to simulate lighting used by photographers in a studio.

Hall and Greenberg [14] described a testbed system for the generation and display of realistic images developed at Cornell University. The system implements a light source primitive with the three characteristics defind in section 2. The geometry of the light sources is defined as either a point, a surface of revolution or a line segment. The system has an environment modeling module, which can create planar polyhedra, objects of revolution, parametric surfaces and quadric surfaces. A ray tracer is used to perform the visualization process. Finally, the lighting model is an improvement of the Whitted model.

Cook, in his paper on shade trees [10], proposed five parameters to define a light source in the form of a light tree. These are :

- location ;
- intensity ;
- a parameter which is the distance from which the intensity begins to decrease ;
- a parameter which is the distance from which the intensity is zero ;
- the kind of intensity decreasing (linear, exponential ...) between the two previous parameters.

We must notice that none of these three models can visualize the beam of the light source.

Nishita and Nakamae ([19, 20] proposed a light scattering model that allow to simulate fog illuminated by automobile headlights or light beams of studio spotlights. Light sources can be defined as point sources with variable angular intensity distributions or as parallel sources. They use a polyhedral modelization. For visualization, they proceed in two steps. In a first one, they make a pre-calculation to compute shadow and illumination volumes, by casting rays from light sources. In a second step, they produce the image with a scan line algorithm. We must notice that in [20], they introduced a particle model for the atmosphere, with density distribution of particles.

Inakage [15] proposed an illumination model in the presence of atmosphere. The model allows to produce images such as : blue sky, sunset or sunrise effects, hazy sky at night scattering the city lights, effect of dispersive refraction by water droplets in the atmosphere shaft of light beam pouring over a suspended sphere, ... The model is based upon three concepts :

- the atmospheric cube, which is a finite volume that encloses the three dimensional scene to be displayed ;

- the atmospheric equation, which is a combination of modeling techniques covering the four cases of interaction of light with the atmosphere : absorption, Rayleigh scattering, Mie scattering and geometric optics ;

- a volume sampling strategy : as the entire space is filled with atmospheric particles or objects, all the points in space contribute to the illumination model. To calculate the total intensity, a sampling process is performed in three dimensions : a regular sampling based on the screen and a depth direction sampling. Then the atmospheric equation is applied to each sampled point in order to compute the total intensity by summation.

4 Our Light Source Model

We now present the work made at Saint-Etienne. This work can be divided into two parts. In the first one, we used a completely empirical model ; in the second one, we improve first results by using a physically-based model, with spherical particles inside the beam light.

4.1 The Empirical Model ([11])

The purpose of this work was to give a model of light sources allowing not only to visualize the illumination of objects by the light source but also the light beam.

Our computer graphic system, is based on a CSG modeler ; we therefore define light sources by the way of primitives of the CSG modeler (cone, cylinder or prism). A point source located at the vertex of the cone is associated with the cone primitive. Cylinder and prism are associated with area sources (the base) emitting light beams parallely to the axis of the cylinder. In particular, we must notice that illumination due to a primitive is visible only inside the geometry of the primitive (the sources are directional). As these light sources are primitives for the modeler, affine transformations and boolean operations can be applied : this increases the range of available light sources.

In the model, a light source is able to illuminate the scene in two distinct ways :

- **directly**, when the light beam hits an object ;
- **indirectly**, when either the light beam is in front of an object or the light beam is the only primitive seen in a particular direction.

As mentioned above, the model is empirical ; its purpose is to take into account the thickness of the dust crossed by the light ray .

For direct illumination, we need two parameters : first, the distance between the vertex of the cone (resp. the base of the cylinder) and the projection on the cone axis of the point of intersection between the ray and the cone (resp. the point of intersection between the ray and the cylinder) ; secondly, the distance between the entering point in the primitive and the point of intersection between the ray and the object. For indirect illumination, parameters are similar ; we just replace the point of intersection by the exit point of the ray out of the primitive.

Since light primitives are primitives for the CSG modeler, intersection calculations are standard for ray tracing and CSG modeling. Light primitives are flagged as being transparent (among other properties). To compute an image, we have to manage three lists of records. The first one corresponds to light primitives illuminating the studied point of intersection. The second list contains light primitives located before the studied point of intersection (they will be called primitives_before). The last list represents light primitives hit by the studied ray (this list is necessary because of the boolean, intersection and difference operators).

The ideas developed above are exposed (in the case of a cone) in the next algorithm, with the following notations (see figure 3) : the cone is defined in a local coordinates system ; it has vertex Ω, Ωz as axis and is a unit one. We will call I the entering point of the ray in the cone, O the exit point, A the projection of I on the axis, K (resp. L) the diametrally opposite point to I (resp. O). We will denote I_x, I_y, I_z the coordinates of point I, d the distance between Ω and A, *int* the maximum intensity of the source and *d_max* the greatest of the lengths of segments IK and OL.

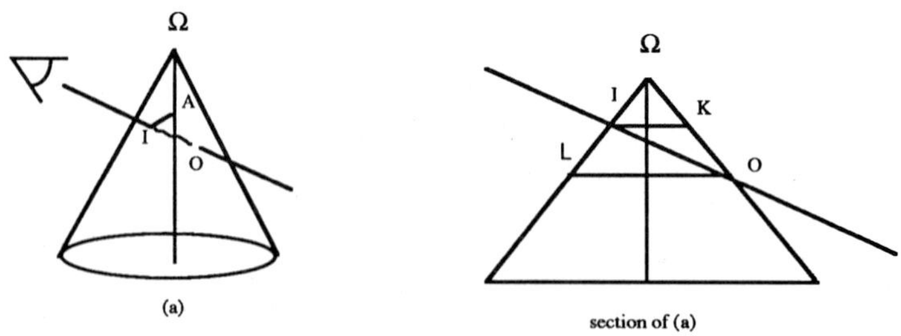

Fig 3 Geometry for a cone

```
{
    if (Iz = 0 and the eye is in the half-plane z<0) then
        /* the base of the cone is seen */
        i := int * (1- √(Ix² + Iy²) ) * (-cos(cone_axis, view_axis)) ;
    else
    {
        d1:= d(Ω,A) ;
        i_indirect := 0 ;
        i_direct := 0 ;
        if the cone is a before one  then
        {
            if d1 = 0 then i_indirect := 0 ;
            else
            {   if the eye is inside the cone then
                        dust_thickness := min(d(eye,inter_point), d(eye,O)) ;
                else
                dust_thickness := min(d(I,inter_point), d(I,O)) ;
                i_indirect := int * (1-d1) * dust_thickness ;
            }
        };
        if the cone is a light cone then
        {
            if d1 = 0 then i_direct := int ;
            else
            {   if the eye is inside the cone then
                        dust_thickness: = d(eye,O) ;
                else
                dust_thickness := d(I,O) ;
                d_max := max(d(I,K), d(L,O)) ;
                i_direct := int * (1-d1) * dust_thickness / d_max ;
            }
        };
        i := i_direct + i_indirect ;
    };
}
```

4.2 The Physically-based Model

The beam will be associated with a primitive of the modeler which has two attributes : a geometry and lighting characteristics.

The geometry of the primitive can be a cone, with a circular or elliptic base, a cylinder, with a circular or elliptic base or a prism (cylinder with a polygonal base). This attribute is similar to that described for the empirical model.

Space inside light primitive is partly filled by spherical particles with radius ρ. The model assumes that the distribution of particles is uniform in the primitive. We will denote by μ the density of these particles, i.e. the ratio of the global volume filled by particles to the volume of the primitive.

4.2.1 Description of the Model

We will give some details about the following points :
- description of light sources ;
- light reflection on a particle ;
- light ray scattering.

4.2.1.1 Description of Light Sources

4.2.1.1.1 Cone

We deal here with a point source O. Spatial and spectral distributions of the source are assumed to be known. Let $d\omega$ be an elementary solid angle with vertex O and direction (θ, φ) (see figure 4). Energy emitted by the source in the solid angle $d\omega$ for wavelengths between λ and $\lambda + d\lambda$ is :

$d^2E = I(\theta, \varphi)\, g(\lambda)\, d\lambda\, d\theta$ where

• $g(\lambda)$ is the spectral density function ; $g(\lambda)\, d\lambda$ is the ratio of energy emitted between wavelengths λ and $\lambda + d\lambda$. We have :

$$\int_{\lambda_{min}}^{\lambda_{max}} g(\lambda)d\lambda = 1$$

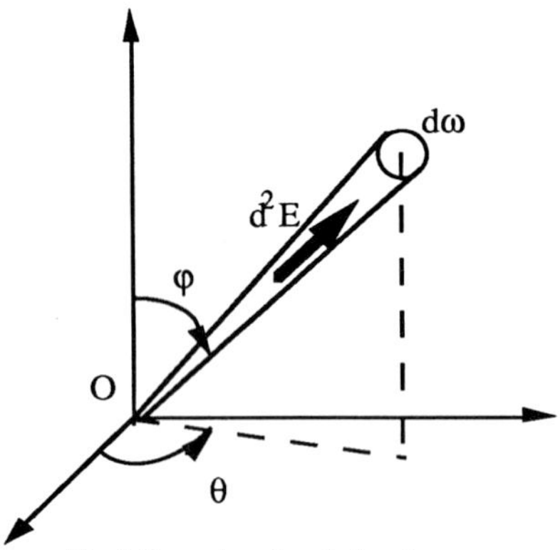

Fig 4 Geometry of emission for a cone

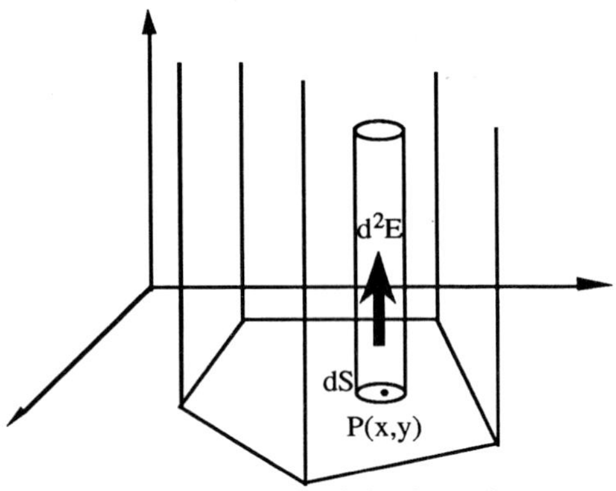

Fig 5 Geometry of emission for a prism

• $I(\theta, \varphi)$ is the source intensity in the direction (θ, φ), i.e. the energy emitted by a solid angle unit.

4.2.1.1.2 Area Sources (cylinder or prism)

The light source is now an area source ; energy is assumed to be emitted perpendicularly to the surface. Let P be a point with coordinates (x,y) belonging to this surface, and dS a surface element centered at P. Energy emitted by the source in the cylinder with base dS, with wavelengths between λ and $\lambda + d\lambda$ is (see figure 5)

$d^2 E = B(x,y)\, g(\lambda)\, d\lambda\, dS$ where

• $g(\lambda)$ is the spectral density function

• $B(x,y)$ is the radiosity of the surface at point (x,y)

4.2.1.2 Light Reflection on a Particle

In our model, we assume particles small enough to let the scattering effect be preponderant. We now give some more information about the scattering process. Let P_o be a particle receiving energy E_{in} and let $d\omega$ be an elementary solid angle with vertex P_0 and direction (θ',φ') (see figure 6).

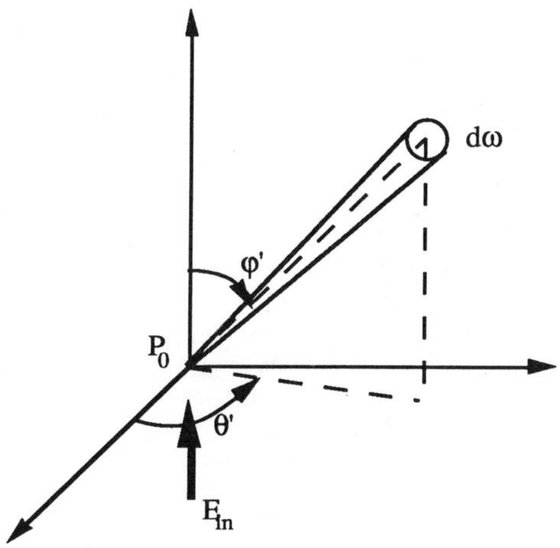

Fig 6 Geometry of light reflection on a particle

The elementary energy scattered in the solid angle $d\omega$ due to E_{in} is given by :

$$dE = E_{in}\, f(\varphi')\, d\omega$$

where $f(\varphi')$ is the phase function.

Remark 1 : Due to the symmetry around the incidence axis, dE is not θ dependent.

Remark 2 : $\frac{dE}{d\omega}$ can be thought as the intensity of a point source located in P_o. The intensity is therefore $E_{in}\, f(\varphi')$: it is θ' independent, and it is proportional to the incident energy, the ratio being the phase function.

Remark 3 : As the whole incident energy is supposed to be scattered, conservation of energy gives :

$$\int dE = E_{in}$$

which is equivalent to

$$\int_o^{\Pi} f(\varphi')\, \sin\varphi'\, d\varphi' = \frac{1}{2\Pi}$$

Remark 4 : In the previous formula, we don't take into account the spectral composition of the energy. In fact, the previous calculation must be done for each wavelength, as the phase function may be wavelength dependent.

4.2.1.3 Light Ray Scattering

When light energy goes through a light primitive, it interacts with particles located in the primitive. We now explicit this interaction. Let $d\omega$ be an elementary solid angle with vertex P, and dE_0 the elementary energy emitted in $d\omega$. Let M be a point located inside the solid angle $d\omega$. We denote dS the cross section to the solid angle $d\omega$ coming through point M, l the distance ||PM|| and d^2V the volume element included in the solid angle $d\omega$ between the distances l and l+dl. We denote dE (l) the energy going through the surface element dS and dE (l+dl) the energy going through dS' (see figure 7).

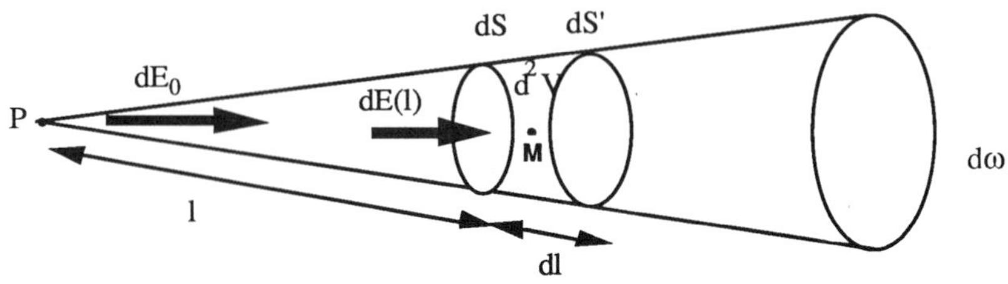

Fig 7 Geometry for scattering

Remark : The model takes into account only "direct" energy, not the energy which has been shut off by particles and then rediffused.

We have dE (l+dl) = dE (l) (1 - dK), where dK is the proportion of energy blocked by particles between dS and dS'. dK can be represented by the portion of surface dS which is covered by projections onto dS of particles being inside volume d^2V.

We have :

$$dK = \frac{d^2S_i}{dS}$$

If we denote d^2n the number of particles present in volume element d^2V, we have, as the distribution is assumed to be uniform :

$$\mu = \frac{d^2n \text{ x volume of a particle}}{d^2V}$$

and then :

$$d^2n = \frac{\mu d^2V}{\frac{4}{3}\Pi\rho^3}$$

The projection of a particle onto surface dS is $\Pi\rho^2$. If we assume the density small enough ($\mu \ll 1$), recovering phenomena of projections of particles onto dS can be neglected ; and therefore :

$$\begin{aligned} d^2S_i &= d^2n \times (\text{area projection of a particle}) \\ &= d^2n\, \Pi\rho^2 \\ &= \frac{\mu\, \Pi\rho^2}{\frac{4}{3}\Pi\rho^3} d^2V = \frac{3\mu}{4\rho} d^2V \end{aligned}$$

then

$$dK = \frac{3\mu}{4\rho}\frac{d^2V}{dS} = \frac{3\mu}{4\rho} dl$$

and we obtain

$$dE(l+dl) = dE(l)\,(1 - \frac{3\mu}{4\rho}\,dl)$$

So

$$dE(l) = dE_0\, e^{-\frac{3\mu}{4\rho} l}$$

Remark : As before, previous calculations must be done for each wavelength, but attenuation effect is wavelength independent.

4.2.2 Calculation for Light Scattering

We now detail the illumination calculation in the presence of a light primitive ; this calculation is made with the ray tracing method. Assume that a ray goes through a light primitive and then hits an object (which can be the background). Two phenomena will contribute to the energy received by the eye :

- energy emitted by the object in the eye direction and attenuated by the passage through the light primitive ;
- energy emitted by particles inside the light primitive illuminated by the light source.

We now give more details about these two effects.

4.2.2.1 Calculation for a Cone

Let $d\omega$ be an elementary solid angle with the eye as vertex leaning on a surface d^2S of the light cone (see figure 8). Ray tracing allows to find the entering point I and the exit point O in the light primitive and the object which is seen behind the cone. Let us denote d^3E_{in} the elementary energy coming from the intersected object which enters the cone at O and $d^3E'_{in}$ the elementary energy leaving the cone at I and due to d^3E_{in}. The attenuation laws seen in section 4.1 give :

$$d^3E'_{in} = d^3E_{in}\, e^{-\frac{3\mu}{4\rho} d}, \text{ with } d = \left\|\overrightarrow{OI}\right\|$$

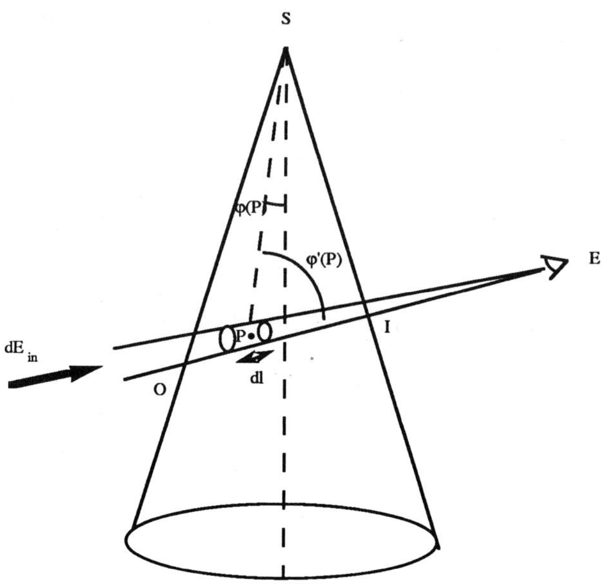

Fig 8 Calcutation for a cone

Let P be a point from $d\omega$ and d^3V be a volume element of the solid angle $d\omega$ centered at P. Particles contained in d^3V and illuminated by the point source will contribute to the energy coming to d^2S. Let us denote $\varphi'(P)$ the angle $\widehat{SPE}$; then, the point P is located in the cone at $\varphi(P)$, $\theta(P)$, $l(P)$, where $l(P) = \|\overrightarrow{SP}\|$.

If we denote d^3E_D the elementary energy coming from the point source and scattered in the volume d^3V, we have :

$$d^3E_D = d^2E_0\,(\varphi(P), \theta(P))\,\frac{3\mu}{4\rho}\,e^{-\frac{3\mu}{4\rho}l}\,dl$$

Part of this energy will be scattered toward d^2S following the law :

$$d^4E_O = d^3E_D\, f(\varphi'(P))\, d\omega\, e^{-\frac{3\mu}{4\rho}d'}$$

with

$$d' = \|\overrightarrow{PI}\|$$

The expression $e^{-\frac{3\mu}{4\rho}d'}$ takes into account the attenuation from P to I. Furthermore, the spatial distribution law of the source is given by :

$$d^2E_0\,(\varphi(P), \theta(P)) = I\,(\varphi(P), \theta(P))\, d^2\omega'$$

where $d^2\omega'$, is the elementary solid angle from which d^3V is seen . We have :

$$d^2\omega' = \frac{dl \times dl}{l^2}$$

and

$$d^4E_O = I(\varphi(P), \theta(P))\,\frac{(dl)^2}{l^2}\, f(\varphi'(P))\,\frac{3\mu}{4P}\,e^{-\frac{3\mu}{4P}(l+d')}dl\, d\omega$$

As $dl^2 = d^2S$, we determine the global contribution of particles by integrating over $\overrightarrow{IO}$:

$$d^3E_O = \frac{3\mu}{4\rho}\int_{\overrightarrow{IO}} \frac{I(\varphi(P), \theta(P))\, f(\varphi'(P))e^{-\frac{3\mu}{4\rho}(l+d')}dl}{l^2}\; d^2S\, d\omega$$

Then luminance comes :

$$L = \frac{d^3E_O}{d^2S\, d\omega} = \frac{3\mu}{4\rho}\int_{\overrightarrow{IO}} \frac{I(\varphi(P), \theta(P))\, f(\varphi'(P))e^{-\frac{3\mu}{4\rho}(l+d')}dl}{l^2(P)}$$

Remark : the term $\frac{1}{l^2(P)}$ incites to believe that luminance becomes infinite when the ray comes close to the point source. In fact, the term $d^2\omega'$ can be approximated by $\frac{d\,l^2}{l^2}$ only if dl is very small compared to l ; of course, this cannot be done when l tends to zero. The correct value for $d^2\omega'$ is :

$$d^2\omega' = 2\Pi - 8\,\mathrm{Arcsin}\frac{1}{\sqrt{2(1 + \frac{d\,l^2}{4\,l^2})}}$$

4.2.2.2 Calculation for a Cylinder (see figure 9)

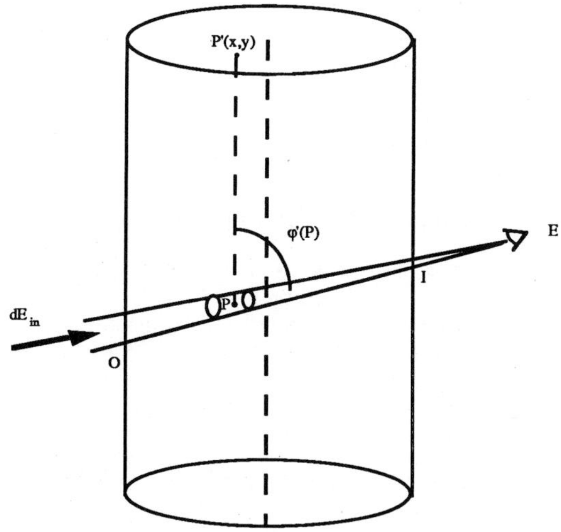

Fig 9 Calculation for a cylinder

Calculation is similar to the previous one :

$$d^3E'_{in} = d^3E_{in}\, e^{-\frac{3\mu}{4\rho}d} \qquad \text{where } d = \left\|\overrightarrow{OI}\right\|$$

Let P be a point belonging to d^3V ; its projection onto the base of the cylinder is P'. P is located in the cylinder at:

$$x(P'),\ y(P'),\ l(P) = \left\|\overrightarrow{PP'}\right\|$$

Here, the angle $\varphi'(P) = \widehat{P'PE}$ is constant. We obtain a similar expression :

$$d^4E_O = B(x(P'),\ y(P'))\ d^2S\ f(\varphi'(P))\ \frac{3\mu}{4\rho}\, e^{-\frac{3\mu}{4\rho}(l(P)+d'(P))} dl\ d\omega$$

Then

$$d^3E_O = \frac{3\mu}{4\rho}\int_{\overrightarrow{IO}} B(x(P'),\ y(P'))\ d^2S\ f(\varphi'(P))\ e^{-\frac{3\mu}{4\rho}(l(P)+d'(P))} dl\ d\omega$$

and

$$L = \frac{d^3E_O}{d^2S\ d\omega} = \frac{3\mu}{4\rho}\, f(\varphi'(P))\int_{\overrightarrow{IO}} B(x(P'),\ y(P'))\ e^{-\frac{3\mu}{4\rho}(l(P)+d'(P))} dl$$

5 Implementation And Future Works

The first (empirical) model has been implemented in a ray-tracer written in our team [2]. This ray-tracer performs some improvements for faster intersection calculations, and basically uses a Whitted lighting model. It also uses an original method for solving the aliasing problem. Few extensions have been made in order to fully integrate the light primitives.

Now, the ray-tracer is about to be fully rewritten. The main goal of this new ray-tracer is to separate as far as possible the geometric calculations and the photometric calculations. This will give new advantages :

- easy modifications of the geometry without changing the photometry.
- conversely, easy modifications of the photometry without changing the geometry (this is useful when changing the lighting model).
- easy use of parallelism between intersection calculations and rendering calculations.

In order to integrate light primitives in this new ray-tracer, we defined two kinds of objects :

- transparent objects : objects which transmit light without changing the direction when light enters or exits the object.
- non-transparent objects, which either do not transmit light, or transmit light with changing the direction when entering or exiting the object.

For example, a thin window can be considered as a transparent object, since the effects of refraction can be neglected, but a glass sphere should be considered as a non-transparent object.

Light primitives are also considered as transparent objects.

We will also be able to perform boolean operations on both kinds of objects. The main law used to perform these operations is as follow : a point in space can be either inside one (and only one) non-transparent object, or in one (or several) transparent object. Space not explicitly occupied by objects of the scene can be considered as a special transparent object, which enclose the whole scene.

Eventually, we must define the geometry and the photometry of the light primitives. The geometry can be any object modelled by a CSG tree (a primitive or a more complex object).The photometry is fully defined by the following parameters :

- the average radius of the particles inside the primitive
- the ratio of space occupied by these particles
- the light distribution of the source associated with the primitive
- the phase function of the particles.

The light distribution can be analytically known, or tabulated using the goniometric diagramms and interpolated.

The phase function can be choosen to represent several kinds of particles :

- isotropic particles (phase function is constant)
- Rayleigh particles or approximated Mie particles (for further details, see [15]).

Future works could be done on the followings points :

- the model actually used is a once-scattering model. It will improve realism if we consider a light density distribution inside the light primitive, perhaps using methods based upon volume rendering or participating medias.
- the distribution of particles inside the primitive is supposed uniform. It can be interesting to use no uniform distributions in order to simulate clouds or fogs, in which the density varies with height, as well as smokes.

References

[1] APPEL A., Some techniques for shading machine renderings of solids, SJCC, 1968, 37-45.

[2] ARGENCE J., Antialiasing for ray tracing using CSG modelling, New trends in Computer Graphics (Proceedings of CGI 88), 199-208.

[3] BEIGBEDER M. et PEROCHE B., Un système de synthèse d'images 3D : ILLUMINES, Actes des journées UNIX de Grenoble, 1989, 265-276.

[4] BLINN J.F., Models of light reflection for computer synthesised pictures, Computer Or, Vol. 11, n° 2, 1977, 192-198.

[5] BROTMAN L.S. and NORMAN J.B., Generating soft shadows with a depth buffer algorithm, IEEE CG&A, 1984, 5-12.

[6] BOUVILLE C. and BOUATOUCH K., A unified approach to global illumination models, Actes de PIXIM'89, Hermes, Paris, 249-263.

[7] COHEN M. F.and GREENBERG D. P., The hemi-cube, a radiosity solution for complex environments, Computer Graphics, Vol. 19, n° 3, 1985, 31-40.

[8] COHEN M.F., CHEN S.E., WALLACE J.R. and GREENBERG D.P., A progressive refinement approach to fast radiosity image generation, Computer Graphics, Vol. 22, n° 4, 1985, 75-84.

[9] COOK R.L. and TORRANCE K., A reflectance model for computer graphics, ACM Transactions on Graphics, Vol. 1, n°1, 1982, 7-24.

[10] COOK R.L., Shade tree, Computer Graphics, Vol. 18, n° 3, 1984, 223-231.

[11] G. FERTEY et B. PEROCHE, Sources directionnelles en tracé de rayons, Actes de PIXIM'89, Hermes, Paris, 219-232.

[12] GORAL C. M., TORRANCE K.E. and BENNETT D.P., Modeling the interaction of light between diffuse surfaces, Computer Graphics, Vol. 18, n° 3, 1984, 213-222.

[13] GOURAUD H., Continuous shading of curved surfaces, IEEE Trans. Comput., Vol. 20, n° 6, 1971, 623-628.

[14] HALL R.A. and GREENBERG D.P., A testbed for realistic image synthesis, IEEE CG&A, 1983, 10-20.

[15] INAKAGE M., An illumination model for atmospheric environments, News advances in Computer Graphics, R.A. Earnshaw and B. Wyvill Eds., Springer Verlag, 1989, 533-547.

[16] KAJIYA J. T., Ray tracing volumes densities, Computer Graphics, Vol. 18, n° 3, July 1984.

[17] MEYER G., Wavelength selection for synthesis image generation, Computer Vision, Graphics, and Image Processing, Vol. 41, n° 1, 1988, 57-79.

[18] NELSON M.,Atmospheric illumination and shadows, Computer Graphics, Vol 20, n° 4, August 86, 117-124.

[19] NISHITA T. and NAKAMAE E., Shading models for points and linear sources, ACM Trans. on Graphics, Vol. 4, n° 2, 1985, 124-146.

[20] NISHITA T. and NAKAMAE E., A shading model for atmospheric scattering considering luminous intensity distribution of light sources, Computer Graphics, Vol. 21, n° 4, 1987, 303-310.

[21] PEROCHE B., ARGENCE J., GHAZANFARPOUR D. et MICHELUCCI D., La synthèse d'images, Editions Hermès, 1988.

[22] PHONG B.T., Illumination for computer generated pictures, Comminication of the ACM, Vol. 18, n° 6, 1975, 311-317.

[23] SILLION F. and PUECH C., A general two-pass method integrating specular and diffuse reflection, Computer Graphics, Vol. 23, n° 3, 1989, 335-344.

[24] TORRANCE K. and SPARROW E., Theory for off-specular reflection from roughened surfaces, J. Opt. Soc. Am., Vol. 57, n° 9, 1967, 1105-1114.

[25] VERBECK C.P. and GREENBERG D.P., A comprehensive light source description for computer graphics, IEEE CG&A, 1984, 66-75.

[26] WALLACE J.R., COHEN M.F. and GREENBERG D.P., A two-pass solution to the rendering equation : a synthesis of ray tracing and radiosity methods, Computer Graphics, Vol. 21, n° 4, 1987, 311-320.

[27] WARM D. R., Lighthing controls for synthetic images, Computer Graphics, Vol. 17, n° 3, 1983, 13-21.

[28] WHITTED T., An improved illumination model for shaded display, Communications of the ACM, Vol. 23 (6), 1980, 343-349.

Methods for Efficient Sampling of Arbitrarily Distributed Volume Densities

Stefan Haas [1], Georgios Sakas [2]

Abstract

In recent years, a number of techniques have been developed for rendering volume effects (haze, fog, smoke, clouds, etc.). Such techniques have been implemented for projective scanline renderers, ray-tracers and for radiosity. Roughly speaking, such a method depends on an illumination model which accounts for the light-material interaction, together with a sampling strategy for reading the data of the density field. The illumination models proposed in the literature are quite complicated and require several time-consuming operations, such as exponential functions, roots and trigonometrical functions. Ray-tracing and radiosity evaluate the illumination model at every voxel of the density field. Since several hundred complicated calculations are necessary for each ray, such a rigorous evaluation is very time-consuming. On the other hand, methods proposed for scanline renderers solve the equations describing scattering and reflection of light analytically along each ray within a volume; thus, such methods do not account for arbitrary density distributions.

The purpose of this paper is not to propose a new illumination model, but to compare several methods for efficiently sampling arbitrary distributed data, i.e., efficiently distribute the samples within the sampling volume. We propose that several sampling strategies can be used to reduce the number of evaluations of the illumination calculations along a ray and, thus, reduce the rendering time needed. Such methods are well suited for scanline renderers but can be used with ray-tracers. We compare a Monte-Carlo approach and an approximative method with user-adjustable accuracy to sample the volume data.

Key Words and Phrases: rendering, volume densities, solid texturing, sampling, Monte-Carlo techniques.

1 Motivation

For quite some time, rendering techniques have not considered effects caused by participating media. Natural effects, like "depth of field", "fog", "mist" etc., play a very important role in the realistic appearance of a scene. They are caused by "volume objects", which differ substantially from the well-known polygonal objects. Volume objects have neither a well-defined surface, nor a surface normal and they cause effects on the light traveling *through* them, not reflected *on* them. Also, the physics describing the absorption and scattering of light are far more complicated than those describing reflection. As a result, volume effects caused by natural "objects", such as those above, have not been widely concerned.

[1] Fraunhofer Arbeitsgruppe für Graphische Datenverarbeitung, Wilhelminenstr. 7, D-6100 Darmstadt, Telefax: +49 6151 155 199, e-mail: haas@fhg.agd.de

[2] Technische Hochschule Darmstadt, Fachgebiet Graphisch-Interaktive Systeme (GRIS), Wilhelminenstr. 7, D-6100 Darmstadt, e-mail: gsakas@agd.fhg.de

When studying the literature dealing with rendering of such volume objects, one can observe that each of the proposed rendering methods for volume densities consists of two parts: an illumination model capable of calculating the light-material-interaction (and thus the light intensity and colour) at a specific location within the volume, and a sampling technique for traversing the volume. The illumination model defines which calculations have to be carried out at a specific point, while the sampling method determines how often and at which locations those calculations have to be evaluated. A brief review of the most important published methods will now be given.

The demand for volume rendering first appeared in the field of scientific visualization. Blinn ([Blin82]) proposed a method for rendering such volumes in order to visualize the rings of the planet Saturn. He thus proposed his well-known physics-based illumination model applied on an algorithmically defined (and thus non-arbitrary) density distribution. In this way he was able to solve the illumination equations analytically for each ray, thereby simplifying the sampling problem of the volume data. Similar methods have been used by Max and Willis ([Max86], [Will87]) for visualizing haze, mist, atmospheric effects, etc. Both authors consider the density to remain constant or to change continuously with altitude, thus solving the integral equations analytically, too. The most sophisticated approach suitable for polygonal projective renderers has been presented by Nishita et.al. ([NiMN87]). Density distribution is defined by means of areas or layers of constant density bounded by polygonal surfaces. Because of the homogeneity of the participating medium within each layer, the sampling problem is trivially solved. All authors used projective renderers and a single-scattering approximation as an illumination technique which is similar to that used by Blinn.

Different approaches for handling arbitrary density distributions have been proposed by Kajia/Herzen, Inakage and Rushmeier/Torrance. Kajia/Herzen ([KaHe84]) and Inakage ([Inak89]) used ray-tracing to trace volumes and introduced a new illumination model, which accounts for both the single and the multiple-scattering case. Rushmeier and Torrance ([RuTo87]) presented the "zonal method" as an extension of the known radiosity approach. All authors were able to present highly realistic images. In the above approaches, the volume has been rigorously sampled, i.e., the illumination calculations have been evaluated at each voxel of the field. Since such an evaluation is very slow, both approaches require a large computing time (e.g., 6 cpu-hours on VAX 8700 for the zonal method).

Because of the complicated nature of the physics describing volume effects, the resulting illumination models contain a number of time-consuming functions such as exponentials, roots and trigonometrical functions. The analytical solution of the resulting integrals is only possible in limited cases: One has to make several simplifying assumptions regarding the distribution and the properties of the volume, e.g., constant layers, linear density distribution, etc. Such simplifications have been used in combination with scanline renderers (Blinn, Max, Wills) and do not account for arbitrary distributed densities. On the other hand, the rigorous evaluation of the illumination calculations at every point within the volume, as performed by ray-tracing and radiosity (Kajia/Herzen, Inakage, Rushmeier/Torrance), can handle any particular distribution, thereby producing images of very good quality, but it requires extremely large computation times. Thus, a large performance gap exists between both approaches with respect to image quality, computing time, and versatility.

The aim of this paper is to provide a method for rendering arbitrary distributed densities using fast scanline renderers and thereby obtaining good visual results. From this point of view, such an approach is a reasonable compromise between the extremes mentioned above. Since we use an illumination model similar to those of Blinn and Kajia/Herzen, time can only be saved by reducing the number of evaluations of the illumination model along a ray. Since in any point-sampling technique a reduction of the number of sampling points results into an increase of aliasing, it is necessary to find ways for keeping aliasing as small as possible. Several sampling techniques are presented and tested, and the ratio computing time vs. image quality is examined. As an alternative to the analytical solution, a Monte-Carlo method for stochastic sampling of arbitrary distributions, as well as an extension of the well-known DDA incremental traversing technique to trace the density field are examined.

Our aim is to visualize natural, stochastically-distributed "objects" such as fog, mist, smoke, clouds, etc.; thus the proposed method is not necessarily appropriate for "medical imaging" or other scientific visualization applications (such an extension will be published soon in a different paper). The proposed method works particularly well with "classical" scanline renderers with 3D-texture capabilities. The rendering of arbitrary volumes requires approximately the same time as needed for polygonal objects and only a fraction of the time needed with ray-tracing or radiocity . All figures presented in this paper have been made using such a scanline renderer.

2 Background

2.1 Underlying Physics

The physics of illumination and the related illumination models have been published in several books and papers ([Ishi78], [Blin82], [SiHo81], [SpCe78] etc.). The illumination model used in this publication and the corresponding rendering technique for the figures can be found in [Saka90]. Thus, only the outlines and some important equations describing the phenomena taking place in participating media are summarized herein.

Volume density ρ is defined to be the mass m per unit volume (kg/m^3). *Radiation intensity* I_λ is defined as the energy of a given wavelength λ leaving a surface per unit time per unit area normal to the pencil of rays and per unit solid angle ($W \times m^{-2} \times srad^{-2}$) ([SpCe78]).

Absorption is called the transformation of radiant energy from the visible spectrum to another, invisible energy form, e.g., thermal energy. *Scattering* is defined as any change in the direction of the propagation of the light beam without losing its complete energy. Together, both phenomena are termed *volume attenuation* and are described by Bougner's law, which gives the intensity of a light beam at location s in the material as a function of the traversed distance:

$$I_\lambda(s) = I_\lambda(0) \times e^{-\int_{\dot{s}=0}^{\dot{s}=s} \kappa_\lambda(\dot{s}) \times d\dot{s}} \tag{1}$$

k_λ (units: m^{-1}) is a wavelength-dependent material property called the *extinction coefficient* which can be expressed as the sum of the *absorption coefficient* α_λ *(λ) and the scattering coefficient* σ_λ *(λ):*

$$\kappa_\lambda = \alpha_\lambda + \sigma_\lambda$$

The above linear or volumetric coefficients can also be expressed as mass coefficients by dividing them by the material density ρ:

$$\frac{\kappa_\lambda}{\rho} = \kappa_{\lambda,m} = \alpha_{\lambda,m} + \sigma_{\lambda,m} = \frac{\alpha_\lambda}{\rho} + \frac{\sigma_\lambda}{\rho}$$

The ratio $\frac{\sigma_\lambda}{\kappa_\lambda}$ is also called the *albedo* or *reflectivity* of the participating medium. The spatial distribution of the scattered energy is given by the *phase function* Φ (ψ). The value of the phase function depends only on the angle ψ.

The integral $\tau(s) = \int_{\dot{s}=0}^{\dot{s}=s} \kappa_\lambda(\dot{s}) \times d\dot{s}$ in equation (1) is also called the *optical depth* $\tau(s)$ of the point s; equation (1) can then be expressed as:

$$I_\lambda(s) = I_\lambda(0) \times e^{-\tau(s)} \qquad (2)$$

2.2 The Illumination Model

As illumination model we consider the calculations describing the phenomena taking place at a specific location within the illuminated volume, i.e., only the light-material interaction for a given constellation. Thus, sampling of the density, calculation of light sources intensity, and the like, are not considered to be a part of the illumination model; such values have to be calculated separately before evaluating the illumination. For the purposes of this paper, from all light-material interaction phenomena within a volume object we consider only absorption and scattering, since they are the most important phenomena involved. Further, we use the single-scattering approximation. Accordingly, volume densities are illuminated only directly by the light sources; "internal illumination" as a result of multiple internal scattering is not considered. All used approximations are reasonable for low density and low albedo volumes such as mist, fog or smoke. Dense "cumulus" clouds cannot be handled correctly. The total intensity I_v reaching the viewer is calculated as the integral over all $dI_{2,i}$ along $x_0 x_1$ and over all light sources, plus the background intensity I_b attenuated along the same distance, see Figure 1.

According to the above approximations, the integral describing the light propagation is as follows (see [Saka90] for a detailed derivation and a more detailed discussion):

$$I_v = \sum_{i=1}^{i=L} \int_{\ddot{x}=x_0}^{\ddot{x}=x_1} I_{l,i} \times e^{-\int_{\dot{x}=\ddot{x}}^{\dot{x}=x_3} \kappa_{\lambda,m} \times \rho(\dot{x}) \times d\dot{x}} \times \sigma_{\lambda,m} \times \rho(\ddot{x}) \times \Phi(\psi)$$
$$\times e^{-\int_{\dot{x}=\ddot{x}}^{\dot{x}=x_0} \kappa_{\lambda,m} \times \rho(\dot{x}) \times d\dot{x}} \times d\ddot{x} + I_b \times e^{-\int_{\bar{x}=x_0}^{\bar{x}=x_1} \kappa_{\lambda,m} \times \rho(\bar{x}) \times d\bar{x}} \qquad (3)$$

whereby L is the number of all light sources illuminating the point s, $I_{l,i}$ is the intensity contributed by the i-th light source, $d\ddot{x}$ is a differential way-piece along the path $x_0 x_1$, ρ ($\ddot{x}$) the density at location $\ddot{x}$, and Φ (ψ) the phase function.

This integral formula cannot be solved analytically for arbitrary density distributions ρ (x). On the other hand, large summing operations, increasing with the third exponent of the resolution of the texture field, as well as many exponential functions, make an exact (or numerical) evaluation extremely time-consuming and are therefore in general unsuitable for computer graphics.

A very useful simplification of the above formula when applied with voxel fields is given in [Saka90]. In the case the attenuation of the light sources through the volume can neglected (first exponential in eq. 3), the above integral can be expressed in a simplified form:

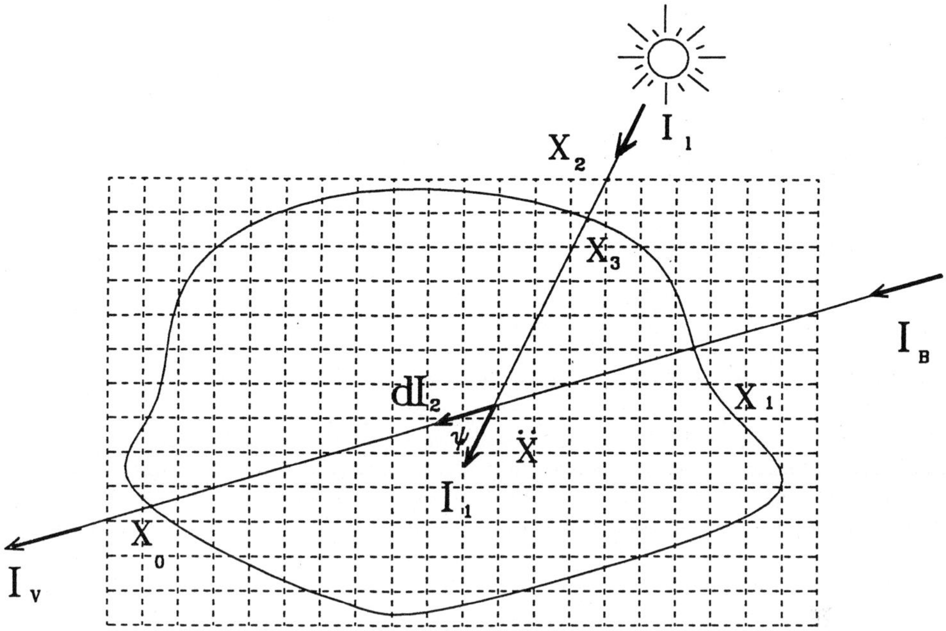

Figure 1: Geometry of light propagation through a medium

$$I_v = I_{l,i} \times w_{\lambda,m} \times \Phi(\psi) \times (1 - e^{-\kappa_{\lambda,m} \times l\tau}) + I_b \times e^{-\kappa_{\lambda,m} \times l\tau} \quad (4)$$

whereby $w_{\lambda,m}$ the albedo and $l\tau$ the optical depth along the ray x:

$$l\tau = \sum \rho_i \times l_i \quad (5)$$

Note that in this case only a weighted sum over all densities along a ray-path has to be calculated. The evaluation of the formula requires only one exponential function per ray.

2.3 Modeling the Cloud Texture

The modeling of arbitrary or stochastic volume densities using algorithms, such as particle systems or fractals, has been proposed by several authors in recent years. Blinn uses an analytical formula which varies the optical depth, albedo and size distribution of the scattering particles as a function of distance. A similar approach is used by Rushmeier and Torrance for their room interior. Willis and Max use either constant densities, or express density as a function of altitude. Nishita et. al. also use either uniform densities or layers bounded by curved surfaces. Finally, Kajia and Herzen use a 3-D 1/f fractal-noise-FFT algorithm proposed by Voss to generate a fractally distributed density field.

We also use a stochastic fractal algorithm to generate volume data. Stochastic fractals are a well known method for generating clouds, terrain, waves, and other natural "objects" like those we want to simulate. A modified 3-D version of the "diamond/square" midpoint subdivision algorithm ([PeSa88]) generates a 3-D density matrix (voxel field). We found that 256 density values are sufficient, so that only one character (1 byte) is used for each matrix element. The bounding geometry of the body is defined using a closed polygonal bounding volume (e.g., cube, ellipsoid, etc., see also [Gard85]). The density field is attached to the bounding volume as a "solid texture" ([Perl85], [Peac85]); the cloud is thereby "carved" out from the field. The actual density can be calculated by dividing the total mass m by the bounding volume. In this way the density can easily be altered without changing the relative distribution and/or recalculating the distribution matrix. By setting an upper and lower threshold and scaling the values from the matrix midpoint to the edges, an undesirable voxel-like appearance of the cloud can be reduced.

3 The Algorithm

The effect of light scattering and absorption in clouds has been briefly introduced using a physical model. The next modeling step has to be performed to transform the physical model into a suitable rendering model. We used the rendering system DESIRe ([Haas89]), which was designed to be extended easily. DESIRe splits rendering into separate parts for *Geometry Conversion, Texture Mapping, Texture Sampling, Illumination, Interpolation,* etc. For each part, several techniques have already been available. Although DESIRe supports projective techniques as well as ray-tracing even in the same image, only the scanline part of the renderer has been used.

In this Chapter we will present the basic illumination algorithm as the implementation of the physical model discussed in Chapter 2. As already mentioned, single-scattering and a isotropic phase function $\Phi(\psi) = \text{const.}$ are assumed (see equation (3)). The ray from x_0 towards x_1 (see Figure 1) will be traversed between the front and the back face of the volume (*MicroFace*). As an extension, if a face of another object lies between front- and backface of the volume, this "foreign" face is handled as volume backface. If the "foreign" face is transparent, or does not cover the pixel totally, then the evaluation of the volume continues behind this face until the pixel is totally covered. By means of this technique, one can handle volume objects and usual polygonal objects in the same scene and by the same scanline renderer. Objects, viewer, and light-sources can be placed around or inside a volume object; multiple volumes can be used in the scene, even within each other (inclusion).

Each traversed distance ("eye-ray") will be divided into *step* sections (*steps* can also be equal to one; this is indeed the case when *distance sampling* and the illumination model of eq. (4) is employed, see Chapter 4.3). Within each section, averages for all values affecting the volume illumination are calculated, e.g., mean section density, value of Φ, attenuation of the source light I_l, etc.; these values are then assumed to remain constant within each section. After calculation of these values the illumination model is evaluated; in this paper we use either the "complete" model of eq. (3) or the approximation of eq. (4). The color and transparency of the complete volume is calculated by the accumulation of all *steps* partial results for all sections along a ray. It is obvious that for any point-sampling technique an increase in the number of *steps* will produce a more accurate calculation of the illumination, as well as an increase in the computation time for the image. Thus, one has to find the lower number of steps to meet the runtime and quality requirements.

The algorithm is given in Table 1 as pseudo-code. The instruction *evaluate* computes a value for the related optical attribute; such an attribute may be a singular value as well as a texture. The *determine* instruction computes values in parenthesis for the given *MicroFaces*. The boldfaced parameters and their computation are most interesting and will be discussed in detail in Chapter 4.

This basic algorithm can easily be extended for non-isotropic phase functions and for transparent or non-transparent objects inside the volume. Effects, such as multi-scattering and illumination of inside objects by the volume, e.g. as a locally-dependent ambient term,

Table 1: The algorithm in pseudocode

```
for each pixel    /* for each position of the scanline */
{  /*      initialize accumulation variables */
   attenuation = 1.0;
   colour = (0, 0, 0);
   /* evaluate section-independent values, determine pixel colour */
   evaluate object.colour, σ, α, steps;

   for each step
   { /* section computation, find geometrical and texture coordinates */
     /* for the section limits*/
     determine start, end (position, txc) ;
     length = | end.position - start.position |;
     /*  evaluate section-dependent values, calculate section mean density*/
     evaluate ρ  (start.position, end.position);
     /*  compute transparency and scattering in this section */
     transparency = exp (- ρ * α * length);
     scatter = σ/α * ρ;
     /* accumulate contribution of each light source */
     for each light
     { /* find ray toward the light */
        determine light_position (position, txc) ;
        light_length = | (end.position + start.position)/2 - light.position |;
        evaluate ρl ((start + end)/2, light.position);
        light_attn = exp (-ρl * α * light_length);
        colour += light.colour * light_attn * attenuation * scatter * (1 - transparency);
     }
     /* accumulate attenuation along the ray */
     attenuation *= transparency;
   }
   /* accumulate results along the ray */
   colour += background.colour * attenuation;
}
```

are still under research.

4 Implementation

In this chapter we will introduce the techniques needed to render volume data. In addition to the already existing ones, we will test new sampling techniques and compare them. This comparison, which investigates the special demands for 3-D texture sampling, will be discussed afterwards.

For the rendering of volume data, the following steps have to be performed:

- Volume Data Generation

  The data describing a density distribution, as computed from a fractal synthesis program, form a 3-D equidistant raster texture. A file will be used to store the data between generation and rendering. Please note that even 128^3 voxels require 2 MBytes of memory.

- Geometry Conversion

  An arbitrary shaped polygonal object will be used to cut an appropriate section out of the 3-D texture (solid texturing). Such a shape can be rigid, since no surface illumination will be performed on its polygons. The *Geometry Conversion* part of the rendering process will generate *MicroFaces*, i.e., the pixelwise planar approximation of arbitrary surfaces, which are to be used from *Illumination* after a pixelwise depth buffering. If no backface culling is made, there will be a front and back face for every "cloud" object at each pixel covered by this object. Since every volume object has to be a closed body (no holes), the pixel coverages of the front and back faces for any ray will always be identical to each other.

- Illumination

  Between the front and the back MicroFace of each volume object *Density Illumination* will be performed. According to equation (3), light scattering and attenuation will be accumulated along the ray between these two faces. The density data will be derived from the volume texture by means of *Texture Sampling*. Therefore, texture coordinates have to be determined via *Texture Mapping*.

- Texture Mapping

  In DESIRe, the assignment of texture coordinates to some point in space is called *Texture Mapping*. This assignment can be done using different techniques. In this paper we use a reprojection between the global coordinate system and the (locally attached) texture coordinate system of the volume object. The texture coordinates will be stored together with the other *MicroFace* data. If "foreign" faces are included within a volume object, these faces have to be mapped to the texture coordinate system of the volume object.

- Texture Sampling

  Texture coordinates will be used to address points in the texture data field. The coordinates will be normalized to a range between 0 and 1. The sampling routine will scale these coordinates according to the resolution of the density texture in order to cover the whole texture raster. Coordinates outside the normalized range will be handled according to a flag, which defines out-of-limit action.

- Interpolation

  The interpolation technique is used by *Illumination* for the sectioning of the ray through the cloud.

As a result from the above discussion, we consider the following three user-controllable parameters (see Figure 2):

The first parameter is the *Texture Sampling* method. *Point Sampling* (nearest raster element) and *Dot Sampling* (average between surrounding raster elements) are usually available. *Distance Sampling* (sampling along a ray by summing the corresponding values) was implemented especially for this research. In addition, we will discuss *Volume Sampling* as an extension of the previous techniques.

The second parameter is the *number of sampling sections* to be made along a ray through a cloud object. *Constant* user-supplied sectioning counts, *stochastic* and *adaptive* variations of user-supplied sectioning counts should be tested. The basic value is supplied by the user as a scalar attribute of the object. Since *Point Sampling* and *Dot Sampling* may produce gaps between successive samples, the sections count has to be a compromise between speed and sampling accuracy. The other two sampling techniques always cover the complete path/volume, using sectioning to control the accuracy of the illumination calculation.

The third parameter is the *distribution of sampling sections* along the ray. Here we propose *equidistant, stochastically varying*, and *adaptive* distributions. This parameter is controlled through the object's *Interpolation* strategy.

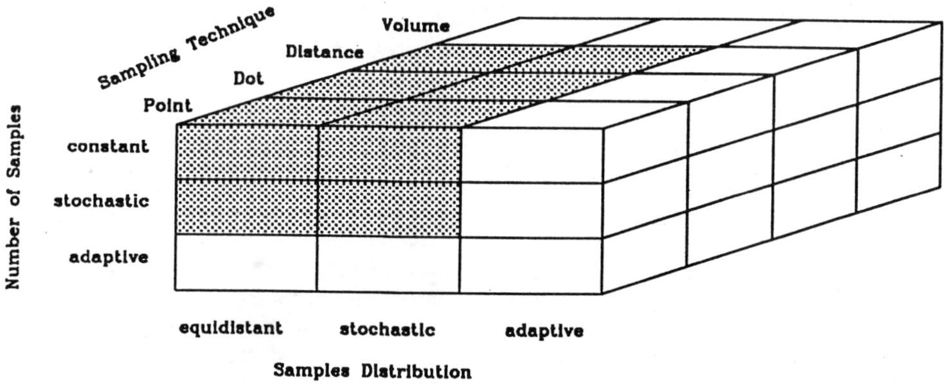

Figure 2: The parameter space

Each of these three parameters is practically independent of the other two, so that a 3-D parameter space has to be investigated (see Figure 2). For each of the first three sampling techniques, we compare the visual and runtime results. Since each of these techniques may be parameterized in different ways, we will select certain parameter ranges which we expect to be characteristic for a given combination. The following sub-chapters are devoted to the discussion of these combinations. Many of these have been used previously for 2D textures, thereby guiding the analysis by experience. Temporal analysis, necessary in conjunction with animated sequences, is not considered in this paper.

4.1 Point Sampling

This texture sampling technique provides a direct, and thus the fastest, access to texture data. The texture coordinate *txc* will be projected to the nearest fitting index in the raster *texture* and its *value* will be returned. In the 2-D case, this straight-forward technique works well for applications which sample almost every pixel:

$$value \;=\; texture\,[\,\mathrm{round}\,(\,txc_u\,)\,]\,[\,\mathrm{round}\,(\,txc_v\,)\,]\,[\,\mathrm{round}\,(\,txc_w\,)\,] \qquad (6)$$

This technique may be useful in our case, since it provides the fastest possible texture access for one sampling call. After segmenting the complete ray into a number of *steps* sections, the texture value of one point for each section is accessed and evaluated during the illumination. When equidistant distribution is employed the midpoint of the section is used, while when using stochastic distribution the point is selected at random within each section. From our experience with 2-D textures, we expect this technique to work well with low-frequency data and sectioning rates of at least one-half to one-fourth of the texture resolution. Unfortunately, due to the fractal nature of the used texture, the texture data itself will contain many high-frequency parts, which could cause aliasing. Accordingly, the test strategy will be:

- Test *equidistant* and *stochastic distributions of sampling sections*,
- Test *number of sampling sections* with $\frac{1}{2}$, $\frac{1}{4}$ and much lower than texture resolution,
- Test with different texture resolutions.

4.2 Dot Sampling

This texture sampling technique was developed from the above one by averaging the values of the eight neighboring voxels for each sample. This has been done by adding a distance-weighting function, whereby the distance d between the texture coordinate (txc) and the next index (u,v,w) in the texture raster ($texture$) will be used for an interpolation between the nearest eight texture values. This smoothing effect reduces the frequency bandwidth of the texture, and reduces aliasing when the texture sampling is performed at a rate of nearly 1/4 of the texture resolution. Our experience with 2-D textures has shown that *Dot Sampling* requires about 10 % more computation time as compared to plain *Point Sampling*. The texture value is calculated as

$$value = \sum_{i,j,k} d_{u_i} * d_{v_j} * d_{w_k} * texture\,[u_i\,][v_j\,][w_k\,] \tag{7}$$

with i,j,k to be the next smaller and next bigger texture index and d_{u_i}, d_{v_j}, d_{w_k} the distance between coordinate and raster $|\ 1.0 - (txc_{u,v,w} - (u_i,v_j,w_k)\ |$, where $\sum d_{u_i} * d_{v_j} * d_{w_k} = 1.0$.

In the comparison below we use this technique to test whether the results from *Point Sampling* could be improved by anti-aliasing in texture space. We expect a lower sampling rate (than with *Point Sampling*), due to a higher coverage of texture space (more raster elements used), and less aliasing, due to the interpolation. Our test strategy will thus be:

- Test *equidistant* and *stochastic distributions of sampling sections*,
- Test *number of sampling sections* with $\frac{1}{4}$, $\frac{1}{10}$ and much lower than texture resolution,
- Test with different texture resolutions.

4.3 Distance Sampling

This technique was developed to deal with the *traversal* of a 3-D texture by a light ray ([Saka90]). The texture value to be returned is the average of all texture elements passed by the ray from txc_{start} towards txc_{end}. In our implementation we used a 3-D DDA to generate the indices for the ray. As compared to the Bresenham algorithm, a DDA will generate a few more steps selecting a larger number of voxels. Thus, DDA will cover more texture space producing more "muddy" values reducing thereby aliasing by averaging

$$value = \frac{1}{\sum_{txc_{\text{start}}}^{txc_{\text{end}}} c_{u,v,w}} * \sum_{txc_{\text{start}}}^{txc_{\text{end}}} c_{u,v,w} * texture\,[u\,][v\,][w\,] \tag{8}$$

with $c_{u,v,w}$ length of ray in raster element $texture\,[u\,][v\,][w\,]$.

When used with the illumination model of eq. (4), Distance Sampling will cover the entire path of the ray addressing all voxels lying between the start and the end point using only one section, and thus, requiring only one evaluation of the illumination model. If a sectioning is used, this has an effect only on the calculation of the attenuation of the light coming from the light source within the volume (I_l along $\overline{xx_3}$ in Figure 1), i.e., the intensity of the light source at different locations within the volume, but *will not* affect the density sampling along the eye-ray $\overline{x_0x_1}$. Experience has shown, that our vision is far more sensitive to "structural" aliasing due to inaccurate sampling along the eye-ray, than to crude volume illumination. As a result, a rather small number of sections is able to provide visually appealing images. The advantage of this method is a strong reduction in the computation time needed for illumination and texture coordinates interpolation. Due to the complete coverage of the sampling ray, non-equidistant sampling techniques are less interesting with this sampling technique. With an increasing sampling rate, the difference in the length $c_{u,v,w}$ of the sections within each voxel becomes practically negligible in comparison to the total ray length. In this case, non-equidistant sectioning will not further improve the image quality. The test strategy will therefore be:

- Test *equidistant* and *stochastic distributions of sampling sections*,
- Test with *number of sampling sections* significantly lower than texture resolution,
- Test with different texture resolutions.

4.4 Volume Sampling

With this technique, density is sampled within the complete volume of the viewing pyramid between the front and back faces (MicroFace). Texture sampling would then imply the approximation of the average density within such a volume of a (truncated) pyramid. This approach is similar to 2-D area sampling methods ([Will83], [Crow84]). On the other hand, it requires the calculation of eight instead of two texture coordinates. The question of under-averaging and over-averaging, respectively, will arise here, too. If pyramids are approximated by cubes in discrete texture space, pre-filtering level-of-detail methods could be used to preclude the inverse relationship between the number of texture elements to be sampled, and the detail represented at a certain image pixel. The sampling along an eye-ray requires additional knowledge about the "size" of the sampled region d_u, d_v, d_w around a sampling point u, v, w:

$$value = \sum_{txc_{start}}^{txc_{end}} \left(\sum_{d_u} \sum_{d_v} \sum_{d_w} texture\,[u + d_u\,][\,v + d_v\,][\,w + d_w\,] \right) \tag{9}$$

Since this technique requires an administration scheme for *MicroFaces* not yet implemented in DESIRe, we are not yet able to implement this technique. Based on our previous experience with area sampling techniques ([Haas87]), we expect very low aliasing (high over-averaging) and fast evaluation of texture values for cubic sub-volumes (pre-filtered texture data). Otherwise, additional time and coding will be needed for *MicroFace* administration, and the storage requirements for texture data will increase (summed-area-like strategies)[1].

5 Results

In the previous chapters we proposed a 3-D parameters space to be investigated for sampling arbitrarily distributed scalar volume densities. With our renderer, we verified these proposals, yielding different test patterns to be presented in this Chapter. In the following section we present the runtime measurements and computation costs of the different cases.

---

[1]Although not presented at that time, this *Pyramidal Volume Sampling* technique has been investigated during the months following the workshop and the results have been published in [SaGe91]. Volume Sampling has been proven to be the best from all sampling methods proposed above.

On Figures 3 and 4 the influence of different sampling rates (horizontal) and constant or stochastic distribution of the samples (vertical) for Point Sampling and Dot Sampling is demonstrated. For each sampling method, 5, 10 and 15 samples have been tested for constant (upper row) and stochastic (lower row) distributions. The texture resolution for all figures is 64^3 voxels, while all frames have been rendered by 300 × 300 pixels (1000 x 700 for each figure). Table 2 shows the computation times for our tests on a SUN 4/330 in CPU-seconds for the rendering itself (disregarding system access times).

Table 3 shows the results of varying the number of steps along a ray. For all images isotropic scattering and Distance Sampling have been used, the resulting images are shown in Figure 5. The upper raw has a texture of 64^3 voxels and has been sampled with 1, 7 (= 10%) and 13 (= 20%) steps. The lower raw has a texture of 128^3 voxels and has been sampled by 1, 13 (= 10%) and 26 (= 20%) steps. The remaining Figures demonstrate the application of the above techniques, especially of Distance Sampling, in generating images.

Table 2: Runtimes (in CPU-seconds for SUN 4) for Point and Dot Sampling

	Sampling Rate and Distribution							
	Constant				Stochastic			
nr. points	5	10	15	30	5	10	15	30
Point	36	50	72	118	41	64	87	155
Dot	43	65	90	152	56	85	110	208

Table 3: Runtimes (in CPU-seconds for SUN 4) for Distance Sampling and various number of steps

resolution	32^3	64^3	128^3
single_scatter	24	29	48
1	37	48	81
10%	65	158	545
20%	110	318	1035
100%	508	1450	4925

6 Comparison of the Approaches

A comparison of the above runtimes reveals, that rendering time increases almost linearly with the number of samples used. Although *Point Sampling* is somewhat faster than *Dot Sampling*, there is no significant difference in the runtime. This relatively small runtime difference shows that the number of texture accesses (one vs. eight) and the additional smoothing calculations does not greatly change the rendering performance; due to the complicated illumination model, the illumination calculations (and not the access and sampling of the texture) dominate the total rendering time. Accordingly, the method providing the best visual results by a low sectioning rate will be preferred, even if more texture accesses are needed.

In accordance with our expectations, the images yielded by *Point Sampling* give only a crude and aliased idea of the volume data, even with relatively high sampling rates.

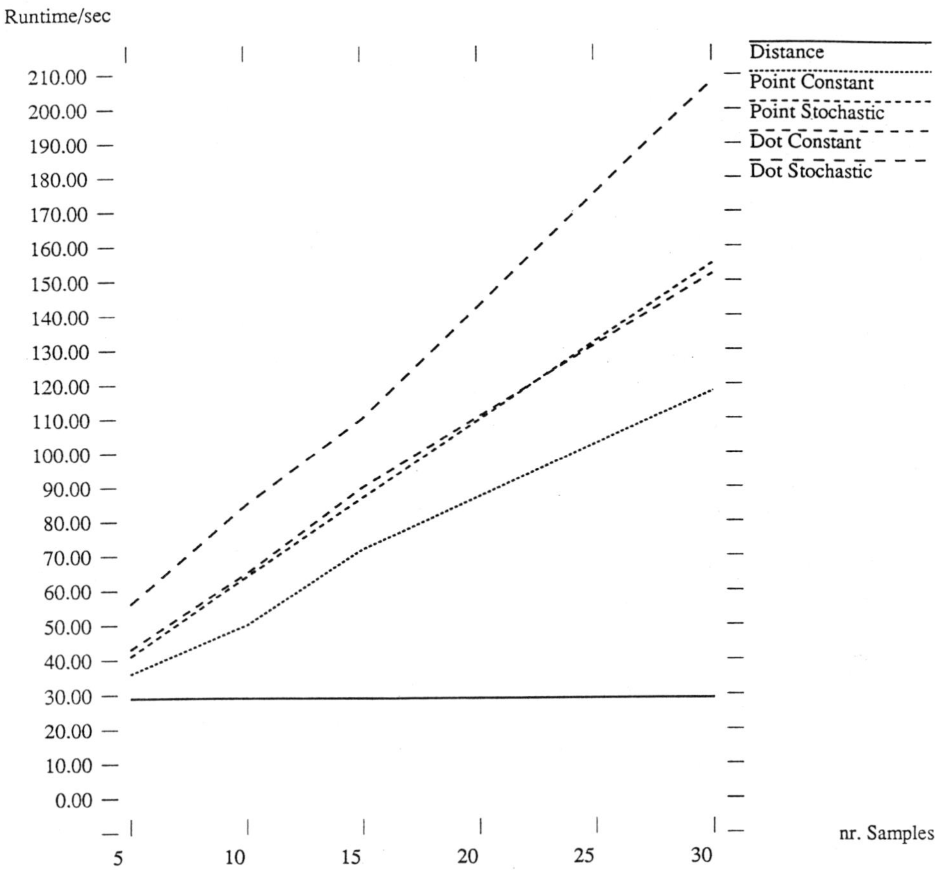

Figure 6: Graphical representation of the runtimes for the various sampling strategies (Table 2)

Stochastic distribution of the sampling locations did not improve the results: aliasing can only be decreased by *significantly increasing* the sampling rate. Thus, *Point Sampling* is regarded here merely as a previewing technique.

We achieved similar results with *Dot Sampling*. Due to the still low coverage of texture space, low sampling rates can cause *Point Sampling*-like errors (gaps) in the sampled density values, especially at high frequency locations. As a result, Dot Sampling can reduce aliasing when used with renderers which support only Point Sampling.

The images produced by *Distance Sampling* meet our expectation of low aliasing due to high texture space coverage as well as small runtimes due to the low number of illumination model evaluations. The runtimes for a "typical" scene lay between 5 and 15 minutes, depending on the scene complexity, the texture resolution and the number of sections. Although every texture point on the ray has been considered, the run-time required was significantly less than that for Point Sampling and Dot Sampling. Therefore we propose Distance Sampling as the most powerful technique for rendering volume data.

Interesting results have been noted by the variation of the number of sections. As one can see on Figures 5 and 9, the differences between one sample on Figure 5 and 128

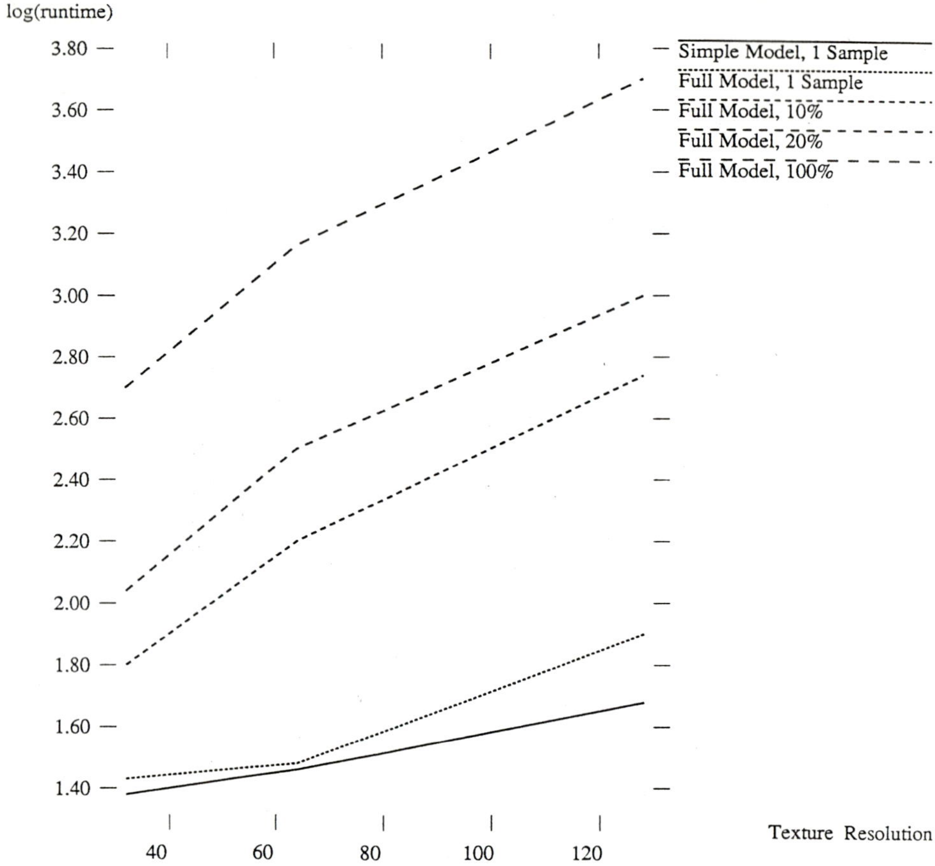

Figure 7: Graphical representation of the influence of the number of steps (Table 3)

samples on Figure 9 are very small. In fact, in most cases one can hardly see any differences caused by a crude illumination approximation when watching still frames of volume densities; such differences can only be seen on animated sequences, or on the high-resolution monitor by a direct comparison of the two figures. As mentioned above, the human eye seems to be far more sensitive for "structural" aliasing along the eye-ray, than for aliasing caused by a crude illumination approximation. A further explanation lies in the fact that the sections positioned far from the viewer are covered by the previous ones, so that their colour is partially "filtered". When using Distance Sampling, the attenuation of the background is always calculated correctly; thus an increasing in the sectioning number results in a more accurate illumination of the volume, and does not affect the visibility of the background. In any case, a sectioning rate of ca. 10% of the texture resolution seems to be sufficient for the most practical requirements. This means considerable time saving, especially when used for generating animated sequences.

As a result of the above tests, we found that Point Sampling techniques are not appropriate solutions for the volume sampling problem. Even a Monte-Carlo stochastic distribution of the samples could not improve the results. At the present time, only *Distance Sampling* unifies the effects of high-speed and low aliasing. This can be more important when Volume Sampling techniques are used, due to the significant part of pre-filtering supported by these methods. We are currently implementing such an extension of 'MipMap' for 3D-data.

Acknowledgements

The authors wish to express their thanks to Professor J. Encarnacao and all their colleagues and students for valuable discussions and support and C. Distasio and S. Wurster for proof reading. This research has been carried out within the "Textur-Editor" project sponsored by the "Deutsche Forschungsgemeinschaft" (DFG; German Research Foundation), grant number ENC 123/10-1.

References

[Blin82] Blinn, J. F.: *Light Reflection Functions for Simulation of Clouds and Dusty Surfaces*, ACM Computer Graphics, SIGGRAPH-84, Vol. 16, No. 3, pp. 21-29, 1982

[Crow84] Crow, F. C.: *Summed-Area Tables for Texture Mapping*, ACM Computer Graphics, SIGGRAPH-84, Vol. 18, No. 3, pp. 207-212, July 1984

[Gard85] Gardner, G. Y.: *Visual Simulation of Clouds*, ACM Computer Graphics, SIGGRAPH-85, Vol. 19, No. 3, pp. 297-303, 1985

[Haas87] Haas, S.: *Echtzeitorientierte Bildgenerierung auf der Basis gespeicherter Bilder*, Studienarbeit, Technische Hochschule Darmstadt, Fachbereich 20 (Informatik), Fachgebiet Graphisch-Interaktive Systeme, 1987 (in German)

[Haas89] Haas, S.: *Entwicklung eines Rahmensystems für Renderer*, Diplomarbeit, Technische Hochschule Darmstadt, Fachbereich 20 (Informatik), Fachgebiet Graphisch-Interaktive Systeme, 1989 (in German)

[Inak89] Inakage, M.: *An Illumination Model for Atmospheric Environments*, R.A. Earnshaw, B. Wyvill (Eds), New Advances in Computer Graphics, Proceedings of Computer Graphics International, Springer-Verlag Tokyo, pp. 533-547, 1989

[Ishi78] Ishimaru, A.: *Wave Propagation and Scattering in Random Media*, Vol. 1 (Singe Scattering and Transport Theory) & Vol. 2 (Multiple Scattering) Academic Press, 1987

[KaHe84] Kajiya, J. T., von Herzen, B.: *Ray Tracing Volume Densities*, ACM Computer Graphics, SIGGRAPH-84, Vol. 18, No. 3, pp. 165-174, July 1984

[Max86] Max, N. L.: *Atmospheric Illumination and Shadows*, ACM Computer Graphics, SIGGRAPH-86, Vol. 20, No. 4, pp. 117-124, August 1986

[NiMN87] Nishita, T., Miyawaki, Y., Nakamae, E.: *A Shading Model for Atmospheric Scattering Considering Luminous Intensity Distribution of Light Sources*, ACM Computer Graphics, SIGGRAPH-87, Vol. 21, No. 4, pp. 303-310, July 1987

[PeSa88] Peitgen, H. O., Saupe, D.: *The Science of Fractal Images*, Springer Verlag, 1988

[Peac85] Peachy, D. R.: *Solid Texturing of Complex Surfaces*, ACM Computer Graphics, SIGGRAPH-85, Vol. 19, No. 3, pp. 279-286, 1985

[Perl85] Perlin, K.: *An Image Synthesizer*, ACM Computer Graphics, SIGGRAPH-85, Vol. 19, No. 3, pp. 287-296, July 1985

[RuTo87] Rushmeier, H., Torrance, K.: *The Zonal Method for Calculating Light Intensities in the Presence of a Participating Medium*, ACM Computer Graphics, SIGGRAPH-87, Vol. 21, No. 4, pp. 293-302, July 1987

[SaGe91] Sakas, G., Gerth, M.: *Sampling and Anti-Aliasing Discrete 3-D Volume Density Textures*, Proceedings EUROGRAPHICS'91, Vienna-Austria, North-Holland Publishers, September 1991

[Saka90] Sakas, G.: *Fast Rendering of Arbitrarily Distributed Volume Densities*, Proceedings EUROGRAPHICS' 90, Montreux-Switzerland, pp. 519-530, North-Holland Publishers, September 1990

[SiHo81] Siegel, R., Howell, J.: *Thermal Radiation Heat Transfer*, 2. Edition, pp. 1-163 and 412-447, McGraw-Hill, N.Y., 1981

[SpCe78] Sparrow, E.M., Cess, R.D.: *Radiation Heat Transfer*, McGraw-Hill, N.Y. 1978

[Will83] Williams, L.: *Pyramidal Parametrics*, ACM Computer Graphics, SIGGRAPH-83, Vol. 17, No. 3, pp. 1-11, July 1983

[Will87] Willis, P.: *Visual Simulation of Atmospheric Haze*, Computer Graphics Forum, No. 6, pp. 35-42, 1987

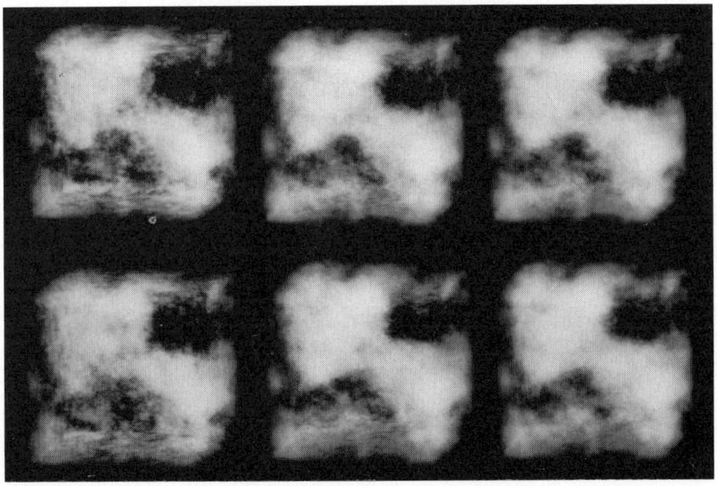

Figure 3: Results with sampling rates of 5, 10 and 15 points for Point Sampling, 64^3 voxels, constant (upper) and stochastic (lower) distributions

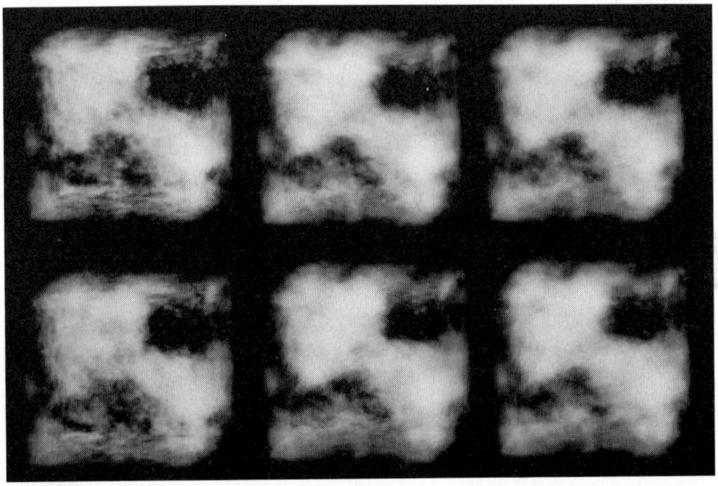

Figure 4: Results with sampling rates of 5, 10 and 15 points for Dot Sampling, 64^3 voxels, constant (upper) and stochastic (lower) distributions

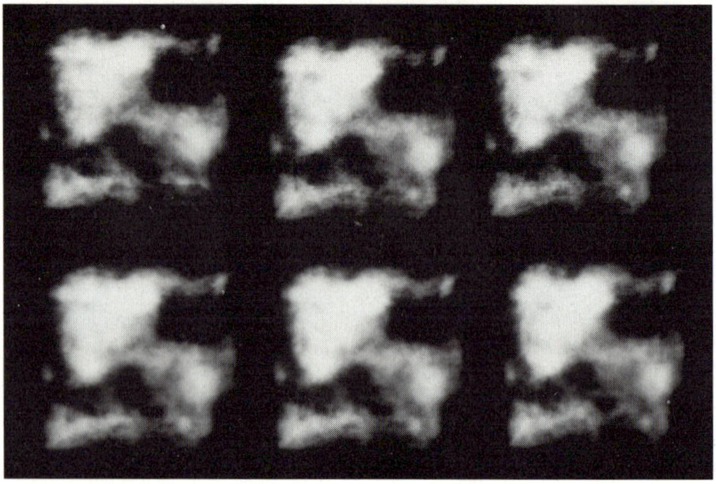

Figure 5: Results with sampling rates of 1, 10% and 20% points for Distance Sampling and 64^3 (upper) and 128^3 (lower) voxels

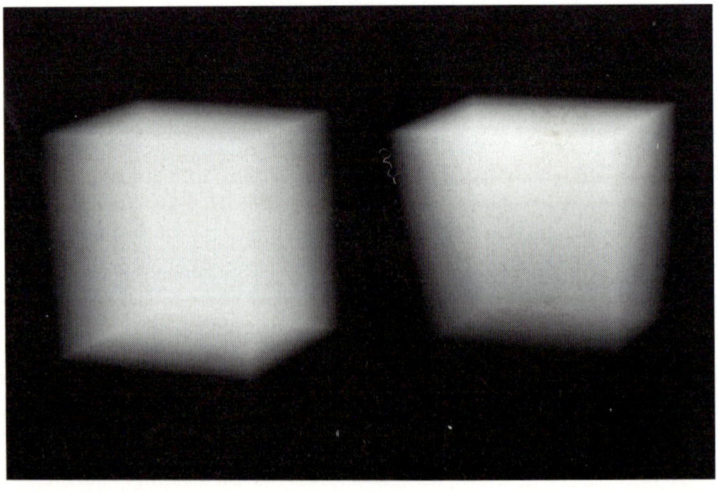

Figure 8: Two homogeneous volumina illuminated from the top. For the left volume the attenuation of the light source has been neglected (see also /Saka90/)

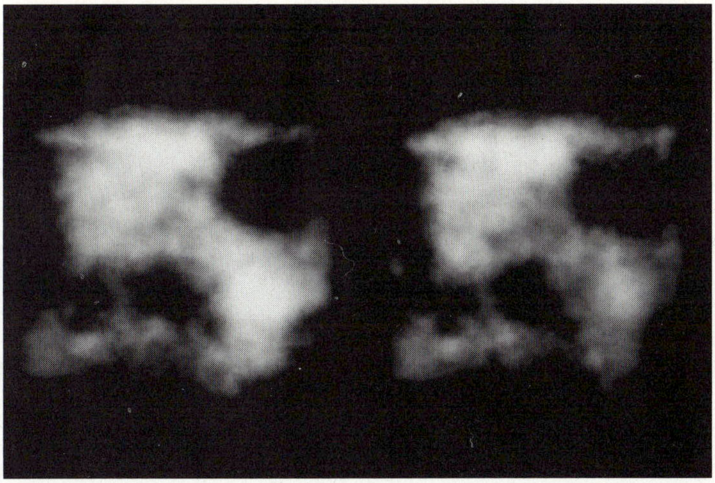

Figure 9: The same volumina with a 3D-texture. The texture resolution is 128^3, and 128 steps have been used

Figure 10: Clouds around the top of fractal mountains

Figure 11: Stills from an animated sequence demonstrating the mouvement of objects through the volume

EurographicSeminars

Tutorials and Perspectives in Computer Graphics

Eurographics Tutorials '83. Edited by P. J. W. ten Hagen.
XI, 425 pages, 164 figs., 1984

User Interface Management Systems. Edited by G. E. Pfaff.
XII, 224 pages, 65 figs., 1985

Methodology of Window Management. Edited by F. R. A. Hopgood, D. A. Duce, E. V. C. Fielding, K. Robinson, A. S. Williams.
XV, 250 pages, 41 figs., 1985

Data Structures for Raster Graphics. Edited by L. R. A. Kessener, F. J. Peters, M. L.P. van Lierop. VII, 201 pages, 80 figs., 1986

Advances in Computer Graphics I. Edited by G. Enderle, M. Grave, F. Lillehagen.
XII, 512 pages, 168 figs., 1986

Advances in Computer Graphics II. Edited by F. R. A. Hopgood, R. J. Hubbold, D. A. Duce. X, 186 pages, 96 figs., 1986

Advances in Computer Graphics Hardware I. Edited by W. Straßer.
X, 147 pages, 76 figs., 1987

GKS Theory and Practice. Edited by P. R. Bono, I. Herman.
X, 316 pages, 92 figs., 1987

Intelligent CAD Systems I. Theoretical and Methodological Aspects.
Edited by P. J. W. ten Hagen, T. Tomiyama. XIV, 360 pages, 119 figs., 1987

Advances in Computer Graphics III. Edited by M. M. de Ruiter.
IX, 323 pages, 247 figs., 1988

Advances in Computer Graphics Hardware II. Edited by A. A. M. Kuijk, W. Straßer.
VIII, 258 pages, 99 figs., 1988

CGM in the Real World. Edited by A. M. Mumford, M. W. Skall.
VIII, 288 pages, 23 figs., 1988

Intelligent CAD Systems II. Implementational Issues. Edited by V. Akman, P. J. W. ten Hagen, P. J. Veerkamp. X, 324 pages, 114 figs., 1989

Advances in Computer Graphics IV. Edited by W. T. Hewitt, M. Grave, M. Roch.
XVI, 248 pages, 138 figs., 1991

Advances in Computer Graphics V. Edited by W. Purgathofer, J. Schönhut.
VIII, 223 pages, 101 figs., 1989

User Interface Management and Design. Edited by D. A. Duce, M. R. Gomes, F. R. A. Hopgood, J. R. Lee. VIII, 324 pages, 117 figs., 1991

Advances in Computer Graphics Hardware III. Edited by A. A. M. Kuijk. VIII, 214 pages, 88 figs., 1991

Advances in Object-Oriented Graphics I. Edited by E. H. Blake, P. Wisskirchen. X, 218 pages, 74 figs., 1991

Advances in Computer Graphics Hardware IV. Edited by R. L. Grimsdale, W. Straßer. VIII, 276 pages, 124 figs., 1991

Advances in Computer Graphics VI. Synthesis, Analysis and Interaction. Edited by G. Garcia, I. Herman. IX, 449 pages, 186 figs., 1991

Intelligent CAD Systems III. Practical Experience and Evaluation. Edited by P. J. W. ten Hagen, P. J. Veerkamp. X, 270 pages, 116 figs., 1991

Graphics and Communications. Edited by D. B. Arnold et al. VIII, 274 pages, 84 figs., 1991

Photorealism in Computer Graphics. Edited by K. Bouatouch, C. Bouville. XVI, 230 pages, 118 figs., 1992

In preparation:

Advances in Computer Graphics Hardware V. Rendering, Ray Tracing and Visualization Systems. Edited by R. L. Grimsdale, A. Kaufman. Approx. 200 pages, 1992

Printing: Druckerei Zechner, Speyer
Binding: Buchbinderei Schäffer, Grünstadt